CSR for Purpose, Shared Value and Deep Transformation

Praise for *CSR for Purpose, Shared Value and Deep Transformation*

This book makes a significant contribution to the academic literature on Corporate Social Responsibility (CSR), and affiliated fields. It examines the development of CSR in response to successive waves of social and economic change and includes a number of case studies that illuminate the strengths and weakness of existing models of CSR which contribute not only to sustaining competitive advantage, but also social and environmental responsibility. The book also includes a comprehensive account of the literature on Creating Shared Value (CSV) and the United Nations Sustainable Development Goals (SDGs) complete with case studies to understand these concepts in practice. The book's greatest strength, however, is that it sets out an extended framework and new model (CSR 4.0), to accommodate the new challenges and systemic change posed for the Fourth Industrial Revolution. The book is a must reference read for economics, social science post-graduate students, and researchers interested in sustainability and corporate responsibility and for government, community and corporate leaders.

Colin Power AM, Ex Deputy Director-General UNESCO, Emeritus Professor, Flinders University of South Australia. and Adjunct Professor at University of New England (AU) and the University of Queensland.

This innovative book, by an accomplished expert in the field, provides a touchstone for the latest thinking and also provides a profound, evolutionary perspective that leads towards a deeper understanding of concepts, theory and practice. The book is suited for academics and practitioners alike and will serve to put a sharp edge on your knowledge and applications in the realm of CSR. Regardless of your generation or experience, I enthusiastically endorse and strongly recommend your acquisition and reading of this new book.

Archie B. Carroll, Chair of Management and Robert W. Scherer Professor Emeritus, Terry College of Business, University of Georgia, USA

This is a valuable and comprehensive book on Corporate Social Responsibility (CSR) from this author, which for the first time in the literature combines topics of Innovation, Entrepreneurship and Intrapreneurship plus value creation systems, such as Shared and Integrated Value in one book, under the theme of CSR. The book also provides important future perspectives on CSR and related fields and provides a much-needed fresh look on current issues in CSR. More importantly, this book covers the significance of the urgency toward the Sustainable Development Goals (SDG) within CSR strategy, while also providing material for future research opportunities in each topic area discussed. If you need to know everything there is about CSR and its proposed future, then you need to read this book to move forward in this field.

Dr Denni Arli, Assistant Professor, Labovitz School of Business and Economics, University of Minnesota Duluth, USA

CSR for Purpose, Shared Value and Deep Transformation: *The New Responsibility*

VIRGINIA MUNRO

Griffith University, Australia

emerald
PUBLISHING

United Kingdom – North America – Japan – India – Malaysia – China

Emerald Publishing Limited
Howard House, Wagon Lane, Bingley BD16 1WA, UK

First edition 2020

British Library Cataloguing in Publication Data
A catalogue record for this book is available from the British Library

ISBN: 978-1-80043-036-5 (Print)
ISBN: 978-1-80043-035-8 (Online)
ISBN: 978-1-80043-037-2 (Epub)

ISOQAR certified
Management System,
awarded to Emerald
for adherence to
Environmental
standard
ISO 14001:2004.

Certificate Number 1985
ISO 14001

INVESTOR IN PEOPLE

To anyone who is determined to make a *positive change* in this world, no matter how small.

If we begin with certainties, we shall end in doubts; but if we begin with doubts, and are patient in them, we shall end in certainties.
(Francis Bacon, English Philosopher and Lord Chancellor, Great Britain, 1561–1626)

Table of Contents

List of Figures

List of Tables

Chapter 4

Chapter 6

Foreword

Dr Virginia Munro's book is original, ground-breaking and thought provoking in how she is able to identify, isolate, and analyze relevant key concepts and present them in a coherent dialogue that is useful to newcomers to the field as well as seasoned veterans of theory, research and practice.

Beginning with an historical overview, the book moves through CSR as a research setting, accompanied by a relevant literature review and introduces an innovative Social Initiatives (SI) framework that builds upon and integrates CSR themes. These topics are explored with an emphasis on social 'purpose' and change, that is found throughout this book.

Taking a global perspective, the book addresses the universally proposed Sustainable Development Goals (SDGs) and discusses how these are integrated with the CSR trajectory of concepts and research. This is significant because the SDGs represent a universally accepted set of goals. In doing do, the book explores a serious problem: SDG-washing which should never be overlooked. The integration of SDGs and OECD methods is unique and appropriate. The future research focus is strong and effective. The discussions of creating shared value (CSV) and integrated value, with shared social 'purpose,' and impact are quite illuminating. These concepts are interrelated and though the nomenclature varies they significantly overlap in their essence.

Some of these topics have been discussed in other contexts, but I admire the fluidity of the integration of them found in this volume. It represents an excellent blending of theory, concepts, research and practice. The writing style is authoritative, coherent, and smooth and presents a comprehensive, integrative overview of concepts and themes within corporate social responsibility (CSR) and its' complementary and competitive concepts and frameworks.

The notion of linking innovation, entrepreneurship and solving wicked CSR problems and challenges are interesting, insightful and represents a strength of the volume. The relevance of social entrepreneurship and the importance of collaborative networks are appropriately aligned with the discussion of funding incubators for innovation and social entrepreneurship. These are often overlooked topics.

The book discusses and enlightens the future of CSR and new ecosystems while describing CSR 1.0, 2.0, 3.0 and transitioning to CSR 4.0. The idea of mapping CSR 4.0 onto Globalization 4.0 is useful, makes sense and is a clever and valuable contribution to the deep transformation required.

Finally, it must be stated that one of the strongest features of the book is the background, experience, and writing talent of its author. Dr Virginia Munro is remarkably qualified and well-connected with the leading organizations and associations in the field. The book obviously has been written by one who is profoundly knowledgeable about business practice, CSR and Social Issues in Management (SIM), plus Social Identity Theory (SIT) and literature. Whether you are an accomplished scholar or management practitioner, or a fledgling newcomer to the field, this book will bring you up to speed and place you on the cutting edge of knowledge and practice.

Professor Archie B. Carroll, Ph.D.
Chair of Management and Robert W. Scherer Professor *Emeritus,*
Terry College of Business
University of Georgia
Athens, Georgia, USA

Author of:
Business & Society: Ethics, Sustainability and Stakeholder Management, 10th edition, 2018.
Corporate Responsibility: The American Experience, Cambridge University Press, 2012.

Preface

2020 will be remembered for COVID-19, but it is also the year that leading companies will define their 'purpose' and reason for being. As we prepare ourselves for the 'new normal,' there is also new opportunities and a 'new type of responsibility' emerging. 'Purpose,' innovation, and transformation, have never been more important.

The 'purpose' of this book is therefore inseparable from the current and escalating need for renewed 'purpose', in both our business and personal lives, and our responsibility to act on the knowledge and situation that surrounds us. As we deal with the current context we also enter the Fourth Industrial Revolution and usher in the new era for Globalization 4.0. Committing to social and environmental change has never been greater nor more urgent, and corporate social responsibility (CSR) is evolving as a consequence.

Supporting this view is the often quoted, Larry Fink, CEO of BlackRock, who started 2019 with a strong message of 'purpose' to all companies. "Purpose is not the sole pursuit of profits but the animating force for achieving them. Profits are in no way inconsistent with purpose – in fact, profits and purpose are inextricably linked" (Fink, 2019). Harvard lecturer and consultant, Mark Kramer, responded to Fink's critics by providing examples of companies who understand that 'social impact' and 'purpose' is critical to their success, stating "business leaders must finally, once and for all, let go the outdated and erroneous notion that social factors are irrelevant to the economic success of our companies" (Kramer, 2019).

In 2020, Larry Fink once again started the year with a strong message, to major corporations, emphasizing the need for alignment with public awareness and mentioning the global climate action protests in September 2019. He stressed the need for "reallocation of capital," placing sustainability at the center of a corporate's investment approach (Fink, 2020). He also reconfirmed "the importance of serving *stakeholders*," not just *shareholders*. Matching this need is the 2020 theme of the World Economic Forum in Davos, focusing on *Stakeholders for a Cohesive and Sustainable World*. The forum's founder Professor Schwab emphasized that 2020 is the year "to reimagine the purpose and scorecards for companies" and "assist governments and international institutions in tracking progress toward the Paris Agreement and the Sustainable Development Goals" (Cann, 2019). With *stakeholder capitalism* a key theme for Davos 2020, the move away from *shareholder capitalism* focused on shareholder returns, now requires the consideration of *all stakeholders* in operations and performance. However, as Sundheim and Starr (2020) point out, the "narrative from shareholder to stakeholder won't happen overnight." A deep transformation is required for CSR and society, and this is a key theme of this book.

Reminding us that some of this transition is already commencing is the pre-2020 release of the new *Statement on the Purpose of a Corporation* by the Business Roundtable in August 2019. Signed by 181 CEOs of major corporations to make a commitment to lead their companies for the benefit of *all stakeholders*—customers, employees, suppliers, the environment and their communities— the new statement supersedes all previous statements and "outlines the (new) modern standard for corporate responsibility" (Business Roundtable, 2019).

Another prominent theme of this book is the sustainable development goals (SDGs), also referred to as the Global Goals. These goals are thought to provide history's "first universal matrix for achieving a flourishing future" (Gauri & Van Eerden, 2019). However, recent research from the UN Global Compact (UNGC)-Accenture Study (2019) notes a shift in CEO perspective, from one of opportunity in the earlier launch stages of the SDGs in 2015/2016, to a belief in 2019 that current business execution is not meeting the challenges of the Global Goals (UNGC- Accenture, 2019).

This book evolves current themes, explaining the movement toward a 'new responsibility' and a greater corporate 'social purpose' and responsibility toward *all stakeholders*. Backed by academic research throughout, this book places 'purpose' at the center of corporate and global responsibility, focusing on the development of CSR, for social innovation and 'change' alongside 'value' that is shared and integrated into a new systems approach.

To tell this story, this book commences with a historical and contemporary overview of CSR to determine the context from which 'change' and deep transformation can occur. Millennials and Generation Z, born between 1981–1996 and 1997–2012 respectively (Mental Floss, 2018), need to understand these topics as part of their drive for 'purpose' and *change.* They are opinionated about social responsibility and CSR activities (Reavis, Tucci & Pierre, 2017) and they desire to *'see change'* and *'be the change'* (Case Foundation, 2017; Millennial Impact Report, 2017). Millennials and Generation Z also want corporations, more than ever, to have a social conscience (Sharp, 2014) and they demand that organizations, both public and private, serve a *social* and *environmental* purpose and fix a broken system. At the time of writing this book, Greta Thunberg, the teenage activist, had just addressed another United Nations Summit and youth riots were escalating across major cities. Research reports were announcing the tipping point at the interface between business and society and the need for more rapid uptake of the SDGs before 2030, was becoming increasingly apparent.

As part of this demand, the 'purpose' and *'be the change'* movements are driving innovation faster than ever, and renewing corporate strategy and responsibility in the communities where organizations and global corporations operate. Academic teachers and research scholars need to follow this lead to evaluate the case for 'purpose' and go beyond this to integrate new areas of research into university curriculums. This book will allow them to dig deeper into these relevant and topical subjects by embracing the social side of CSR and its surrogate, alternative and overlapping terms alongside themes such as creating shared value (CSV) and integrated value creation (IVC), social entrepreneurialism and innovation for social impact and change. Aside from crowd funding across public and private networks, millennials (and Generation Z) will increasingly need the corporate dollar. In addition, corporates can provide a safe environment for entrepreneurs to set-up and incubate their social enterprise or innovative idea, within the CSR and R&D departments of the organization, allowing them to then unleash their concept to the world, only when it is ready. For this reason, millennials need to understand CSR and creating shared value (CSV) strategy alongside corporate innovation within R&D departments, which also include corporate entrepreneurialism and sources for public and corporate wealth, and private funding.

As business commentators focus on these areas and academics begin to teach and research these areas, university curriculums must follow suit, engaging communities and the general public in tackling systemic social problems (also referred to as complex 'wicked problems' or 'challenges'). These wicked challenges can be tackled at a local level and then 'go national' and global, in the attempt to scale up for greater coverage of each problem. At the very core of 'going global' is the multinational corporation. Their extensive global value chains will force them to become more accountable for their impacts in the communities where they operate. It is also an opportunity to localize the SDGs by turning internationally agreed goals into a local reality through developing more extensive Social Initiatives (SIs) and social projects as part of this mission. The introduction of the UN SDGs has helped escalate this movement, calling for corporations to collaborate with governments, civil servants, NGOs, and other partners, and to do this at scale in developing countries. As stated previously, recent research suggests these targets may not be met by 2030, with the SDGs requiring further: impact measurement; innovation; and an entire ecosystem *change*, requiring a new and evolving type of responsibility.

This book promises to cover these themes. Backed by academic literature and various discussions in the business community, this book also provides practical real-world case study examples throughout. A special focus of this book is the identification of emerging research opportunities for each topic discussed, in the hope that we march forward in this journey together, in both practice and research.

> *As we embark on this great collective journey, we pledge that no one will be left behind. Recognizing that the dignity of the human person is fundamental, we wish to see the goals and targets met for all nations and peoples and for all segments of society. And we will endeavour to reach the furthest behind first (UNDESA, 2018).*

Now more than ever, this journey will require a deeper transformation than we first thought, alongside a new and faster evolving responsibility, inseparable from our individual existence and inseparable from the need for each and every one of us to find a 'purpose' which is authentic and real, to strive for individual '*change*' and '*collective purpose*'.

References

Business Roundtable. (2019). *Business Roundtable Redefines the Purpose of a Corporation to Promote 'An Economy That Serves All Americans'*. Retrieved from https://www.businessroundtable.org/business-roundtable-redefines-the-purpose-of-a-corporation-to-promote-an-economy-that-serves-all-americans

Cann. (2019). *Davos 2020: World Economic Forum announces the theme*. Retrieved from https://www.weforum.org/agenda/2019/10/davos-2020-wef-world-economic-forum-theme/

Case Foundation. (2017). *Millennials: The rise of the everyday changemaker*. Retrieved from https://casefoundation.org/blog/millennials-the-rise-of-the-everyday-changemaker/

Fink, L. (2019). Larry Fink's 2019 Letter to CEO. *BlackRock*. Retrieved from https://www.blackrock.com/corporate/investor-relations/larry-fink-ceo-letter

Fink., L. (2020). *CEO Letter: A Fundamental Reshaping of Finance*. Retrieved from https://www.blackrock.com/corporate/investor-relations/larry-fink-ceo-letter

Gauri, P., & Van Eerden, J. (2019). What the fifth industrial Revolution is and why it matters. Retrieved from https://europeansting.com/2019/05/16/what-the-fifthindustrial-revolution-is-and-why-it-matters/

Kramer, M. R. (2019). *The backlash to Larry Fink's letter shows how far business has to go on social responsibility*. Harvard business review, January 1, 2019. Retrieved from https://hbr.org/2019/01/the-backlash-to-larry-finks-letter-shows-how-far-business-has-to-go-on-social-responsibility

Mental Floss. (2018). *New guidelines redefine birth years for Millennials, Gen-X, and 'Post-Millennials'*. Minute Media. USA. March 1, 2018. Retrieved from http://mentalfloss.com/article/533632/new-guidelines-redefine-birth-years-millennials-gen-x-and-post-millennials

The Millennial Impact Report. (2017). *10 years looking back*. Retrieved from http://www.themillennialimpact.com

Reavis, M. R., Tucci, J. E., & Pierre, G. S. (2017). Corporate social responsibility and millennials' stakeholder approach. *Journal of Leadership, Accountability and Ethics, 14*(4), 74-83.

Sharp, K. (2014). *Millennials' bold new business plan: Corporations with a conscience*. Salon, January. Retrieved from http://www.salon.com/2014/02/09millennials boldnewbusinessplancorporationswithaconscience/

Sundheim, D., & Starr, K. (2020). *Making stakeholder capitalism a reality*. Harvard Business Review. Retrieved from https://hbr.org/2020/01/making-stakeholder-capitalism-a-reality

UNDESA. (2018). *Leaving no one behind*. Retrieved from https://www.un.org/development/desa/en/news/sustainable/leaving-no-one-behind.html

UNGC-Accenture. (2019). *UN global compact-accenture strategy 2019 ceo study – The decade to deliver: A call to business action*. Retrieved from https://www.unglobalcompact.org/library/5715.

Acknowledgements

First, I would like to thank Cedwyn Fernandes, Associate Professor at Middlesex University and MBA program leader (now Pro-Vice Chancellor), who took an interest in my initial CSR research in the Middle East and Africa, while based in Dubai and London. The journey continued to the Asia Pacific region, where I was the recipient of a scholarship to further develop this concept.

I would like to take this opportunity therefore to thank the Australian Government and Griffith University who provided me with an APA scholarship to complete this research, which first commenced out of the UK and was finalised in Australia. Thank you also to Assistant Professor Denni Arli of the University of Minnesota and Professor Sharyn Rundle-Thiele of Griffith University, for taking an interest in this research and peer reviewing my earlier work in this topic area. I have since developed this body of work to embrace a number of fields including entra- and intrapreneurship, innovation, social impact assessment and investment, and of course co-creation and collaboration for a better world. All are vitally important as we work toward the UN sustainable development goals.

I am forever grateful for the positive peer review I receive for my work. In doing so, I would like to thank renowned CSR guru, Professor Archie Carroll for providing me with a supporting foreword to this book, and the ex Deputy Director-General of UNESCO Colin Power AM, for adding his endorsement of this book from a global United Nations and Educational perspective.

Thank you also for the kindness and gratitude I have experienced from students I have worked with and mentored on projects and in youth work, in particular Anthony (Minh Hoang) Vo (Griffith University, Brisbane), Phan Ngoc Huyen (Cheryl) (Toyo Univeristy, Tokyo) and Tran Bao Thanh (Foreign Trade University, Ha Noi).

Thanks must also go to family and friends (you know who you are), who allowed me to be absent during busy writing periods. Finally, I would like to thank the publisher – Emerald – for supporting this book. It has been a pleasure to work with you. Thank you.

Introduction

Many cast their eyes in despair at the current global economy, its reoccurring economic crises, its worsening environmental and ecological conditions, its health pandemics, gender and racial inequality and extraordinarily large streams of refugees forced from their homes, topped with increasing social deprivation to growing parts of the population. Many believe a zero-sum game can no longer work. As more academic, business, and science literature reveals, these existential challenges are interconnected, and the CEOs and managers pursuing a zero-sum management game (where one player gains and the other loses) will encounter growing difficulties (Advameg, 2018; George, 2014; Mühlbacher & Böbel, 2018). In many cases, a capitalist system has been blamed for creating these systemic problems. Corporate social responsibility (CSR) has been blamed as part of this system and many multinational corporations (MNCs) have been held accountable for not fixing these problems.

With the increasing reality of the complexity of these escalating economic, social, and environmental challenges and problems, a new business and management discourse is evolving to deal with climate change, poverty, food insecurity, resource depletion and inequality. Firstly, as part of this crisis-based discourse, this book will refer to all 'wicked problems' as 'challenges', and therefore "solvable" systemic issues. Secondly, the launch of the UN SDGs allows corporates to take on board these social issues both as business "opportunities" and as Social Initiatives (SIs), within CSR strategy. As we enter the Fourth Industrial Revolution and the era of Globalization 4.0, these challenges are increasingly highlighted:

> "... the challenges associated with the 'fourth industrial revolution' are coinciding with the rapid emergence of ecological constraints, the advent of an increasingly multipolar international order, and rising inequality. These integrated developments are ushering in a new era of globalisation. Whether it will improve the human condition will depend on whether corporate, local, national and international governance can adapt in time" (Schwab, 2018).

As we step forward into the future, we must examine the present – and therefore also the past. Arising from current circumstances is the notion upheld by some that CSR is outdated or in lay terms "has not worked." Furthermore, some

CSR for Purpose, Shared Value and Deep Transformation, 1–14
Copyright © 2020 Emerald Publishing Limited
All rights of reproduction in any form reserved
doi:10.1108/978-1-80043-035-820200003

commercial conferences, social media, and business conversations have referred to the notion that "CSR is decreasing or dying" or has been replaced by other themes such as sustainability, shared value, or the 'for purpose' or 'change the world' movements or something similar. While all are important movements, this book shows how these terms and themes co-exist and may also overlap and be complimentary to CSR development.

To further illustrate this point, a local conference held recently, titled by one word—'Purpose'—targeted a start-up social enterprise audience, with the theme 'CSR is dying' emerging from one of the panel discussions. However, the belief of this existed without knowing how to define CSR in its entirety or explain *all* its components. The belief is therefore easier to understand than the complexity and depth of the definition itself. For this reason, the evolution and social side of CSR and overlapping themes as part of this movement need to be embraced and understood by start-up audiences and millennials who wish to 'be the change' (Case Foundation, 2018; Millennial Impact Report, 2017) and wish to see corporations develop more of a social conscience (Sharp, 2014).

The academic literature often discusses CSR as being at a crossroads (Kim, An, Myung, & Bae, 2016; Munro, Arli, & Rundle-Thiele, 2016), rather than dead or dying. Kim (2018) also adequately explains some of the pressures on CSR in recent times:

> "These pressures include accusations of dressing up CSR as a business discipline (Rangan, Chase, & Karim, 2015), the challenge of effectively communicating CSR achievements without being accused of green-washing (Illia, Zyglidopoulos, Romenti, Rodríguez-Cánovas, & del Valle Brena, 2013), and the inability to turn the corporate landscape into a win–win wonderland (Marques & Mintzberg, 2015)" (Kim, 2018, p. 19).

The sentence – "… the inability to turn the corporate landscape into a win-win wonderland" – shows some introspective thought. The choice of the word "wonderland" resonates the thought that CSR is not to blame for the lack of ability to turn the world into a win-win Paradise or Neverland and makes it sound near impossible in the reality of the world's largest systemic problems. That is because there are many factors at play including the underlying system, economy, and ecosystem these problems exist within.

In this context, the landscape for CSR is in transition. CSR is no longer static, or just Philanthropic, as it was historically. It is evolving under a catastrophic blanket of 'need' and is turning into a more integrated concept. This journey is explained throughout this book and proposes CSR is evolving like many of its surrounding, surrogate, overlapping, and competing terms and themes. This book explains how this evolution began from the fourth and fifth century BC through to the information evolution of the Third Industrial Revolution and the current Fourth Industrial Revolution. As we embrace this new era, labeled Globalization 4.0, we see a revised sense of innovation and 'purpose,' and a new type of win-win strategy has evolved. CSR-related theory and research in the past has supported a win-win strategy through discussions of inclusive growth (George, McGahan, & Prabhu, 2012), social entrepreneurship (Besharov & Smith, 2014), corporate citizenship (Matten & Crane, 2005), and base of the pyramid (Hart & Prahalad, 2002), leading to creating shared value (CSV) (Porter & Kramer, 2011) and integrated value creation (IVC) (Visser, 2014). Included in these strategies is business organizations offering opportunities for co-creation, innovation, and shared collaboration (e.g., Korhonen, 2013). Increasingly, companies acknowledge they gain a sustainable and competitive advantage if they are able to implement social solutions to social problems while also creating business and social value (Michelini & Fiorentino, 2012; Mühlbacher & Böbel, 2018) and it is hoped the SDGs (and Global Goals) will assist this transition. This book covers these themes and attempts to dispel the myth of CSR extinction by embracing the social side of CSR, and integrating current research trends focused on inclusion, collaboration, evolution, co-creation, transformation, and innovation. This allows an update of academic research shaped alongside current business perspectives.

As part of writing this book and examining the academic literature related to these themes, it was noted that CSR research continues to proliferate (for example, Laudal, 2018). The research examined, however, calls for greater responsibility by firms and a request to use a broader range of novel concepts and models utilizing multilevel and multidisciplinary approaches (Aguinis & Glavas, 2012; Frynas & Yamahaki, 2016; Munro, 2017). With the current emphasis on measuring impact, there is also a call for the integration of different disciplines and topic areas such as performance measures for profit and not-for-profit organizations that reflect their diverse and complex *stakeholders* (Boateng, Akamavi, & Ndoro, 2016). Stifling some progress in this area is the perspective that academic research is often thought to have a narrow focus and therefore unable to cover every nuance or new 'fad' immediately or cross every overlapping boundary where it cannot be controlled, as academics needing to achieve tenure must often examine specific issues in greater depth rather than breadth. Academic research, however, can have ongoing impact and provide direction to entire disciplines of research. This research then trickles down to the business community through publishing in both academic and general publications while revising university curriculums and student training as a consequence.

Backed by theory and research, this book works toward this solution by integrating social innovation and bringing together contemporary themes to make them easily accessible to early researchers, students, their lecturers, and professional bloggers in the broader business community. CSR veteran and guru Archie Carroll provided one of the first accepted definitions of CSR in 1979 (Carroll, 1979) and corresponded with me recently to congratulate me on my early research papers in the area of CSR, relating to business and society. I took the opportunity to ask his perspective on CSR. His response is similar to mine and noted in Chapter 1 alongside other research perspectives on the transformation of CSR and its related and alternative themes including CSV, 'business-for-purpose,' social innovation, integrating social enterprise, corporate social entrepreneurship,

IVC, collaboration, co-creation, and implementation of the SDGs. These themes are all part of CSR strategy (Munro, 2018).

However, to create 'change' that is sustainable, the key ingredient is 'disruption' of current systems. A major stumbling block to disruption and global change, however, is regional differences. As early as 2008, Matten and Moon noted strong regional differences for CSR and its components. They argue that CSR is more "explicit" in the United States, describing it as voluntary, with self-interest-driven policies, programs, and strategies. In contrast, they argue that CSR is more "implicit" in the United Kingdom and Europe where CSR embraces the entirety of each country through the existence of formal and informal institutions that "assign corporations an agreed upon share of responsibility for society's concern" (Carroll & Brown, 2018, p. 47). However, in the United States (and Australia), CSR is considered to be more discretionary and often manifested in response to pressure from special interest groups or adopted because of a management philosophy, policy, or strategy. As a consequence, CSR is "a given" in the United Kingdom and Europe, with even small to medium enterprises (SMEs) prolific in their uptake of CSR. Australia in contrast has a tendency for only very large companies to practice CSR. The term CSR is then often diluted further by referring to it as 'sustainability' (as the larger component of CSR), and as the *replacement* term for CSR, in a country like Australia, with an economy driven predominately by natural resources and mining.

In different parts of the world, CSR is backed by strong associations. Research reveals that CSR in the United Kingdom and Europe (CSR Europe, 2018), for example, is strongly supported by associations such as *CSR Europe*, which support the 'new' European Commission's (EU's) definition of CSR. They have worked together to implement their *Enterprise 2020* initiative and to drive, innovate, and develop CSR strategy in these parts of the world (European Commission, 2011). This further supports the argument that CSR is evolving and refocusing and joining the 'business-for-purpose' movement and mission to solve social problems at scale.

Additional effort in social responsibility and sustainable development through the Global Goals is currently focused on developing countries. In developing Eastern countries, authors suggest that CSR has evolved from a 'collective' base (e.g. Ho, 1995; Matten & Moon, 2008; Triandis, Robert, Marcelo, Masaaki, & Lucca, 1988; Wei, Egri, & Yeh-Yun Lin, 2014). It is also noted that as a collective, employees and therefore citizens of these developing countries have a stronger identification and engagement with CSR activities – in relation to the significant *needs* of their country – in comparison to the 'individualistic' divide of Western developed countries (Munro, 2017). This stronger need and 'identification' of such has also been progressed by the 'identification' of the sustainable development goals (SDGs) in 2015. Since then, there has been a global gradual transition and worldwide movement of innovation, collaboration, and co-creation, with a further request from the United Nations to focus more SDG development in the developing countries.

Multinationals and corporations with large pockets can invest in these activities as part of their global 'CSR social and community projects' or SIs and their shared value mission toward 'social purpose'. As a result, they can also collaborate with social entrepreneurs, governments, and civil servants – to co-create and integrate – on wicked challenges as part of a strategy that incorporates the SDGs (and Global Goals). Several parts of this book (including Chapters 3 and 5, and a research paper example in Chapter 2) provide cases of this and explain how this can be researched in the business community and academically. An update of the current status of the SDGs is provided in Chapter 3, alongside an analysis of their ongoing impact and investment potential.

As many refer to the need for corporates to be made responsible for the wicked problems they have created as part of their global footprint, it is also suggested that these problems are part of a broken system. Research shows that wicked problems and challenges occur in a complex social context, where there are diverse views on who is responsible and what the original cause of the problem is (Camillus, 2008; Dentoni, Hospes, & Ross, 2012). There has also been a cognitive and mental shift, perceiving huge problems as opportunities rather than problems. There is also an economic opportunity for embracing and solving wicked problems and challenges, when these challenges are considered in both a *social* and *environmental* context. If we take a social problem such as poverty, for example, and teach impoverished women how to understand money and run a business and give them a micro-loan to get started, they then have the means to make money, educate their children and support their families, and adopt environmentally friendly behaviors such as recycling in their community and purchasing unpolluting stove cookers, for example. Nearly every social project has a loop back to the environment and almost every environmental problem, if not all, loops back to social. The community also prospers more as community members increasingly become customers of the loan provider, allowing the corporate provider to also prosper.

Agribusiness is an even clearer example, where financially helping and training impoverished farmers to grow better crops in an environmentally sustainable way returns nutrients to the soil. The farmers then achieve increased return on their money for the more sustainable crops they produce, while the corporate retailer who supports the farmer and buys the vegetables, has both a higher quality product and more product to sell. This then enters the argument for creating a shared value (CSV) methodology to implement these SIs or social projects, so that both society and the business benefit economically. Chapter 4 discusses the strengths and weakness of the shared value concept and provides numerous examples of how corporates and social enterprises have shaped their CSR SIs utilizing a CSV methodology, highlighting the need for corporates to take their CSR programs and initiatives to greater scale and to also achieve CSV type projects at greater depth.

Likewise, the mainstream movement toward the development of innovative social enterprises to co-create and deal with wicked problems as wicked challenges – and create 'change' in society through a business idea or mission – encompasses both an *environmental* and a *social* solution. Making 'change' and being a 'changemaker' is discussed as an opportunity for corporates to embrace this innovation as part of their CSR strategy, alongside millennial, Generation Z, and (soon to be) Alpha generation's involvement in this. As previously mentioned, corporates are key to funding millennial and Generation Z enterprise development and can provide entrepreneurial opportunities by incubating their innovative idea – within the safety net of the corporate enterprise – before unleashing their concept to the world. This is discussed further in Chapter 5.

The overall theme of this book acknowledges "business as usual is not an option" (Business and Sustainable Development Commission, 2017). Collaboration and SDG uptake is 'King' and sharing and integrating value between society and business will be the 'new normal'. However, knowing what people understand about CSR is crucial to determining how we communicate, develop, transition, and incorporate new themes. How people identify with and engage in some of these activities is key to unlocking the "doing" part of CSR and the social impact of its SIs, shared value (CSV) activities, and social entrepreneurial projects. This is explained further in Chapter 5, with a research paper example in Chapter 2.

Later chapters of this book examine the future of CSR and the new ecosystem required to inject 'purpose' into every part of that system. In Thomas Friedman's (2005) article, *"It's a Flat World, After All"* (New York Times), he defines succinctly the stages of globalization as a journey through time, commencing with Globalization 1.0 to Globalization 3.0 in 2000, which is now superseded since his 2005 article, by Globalization 4.0. While Globalization 3.0 allowed *"individuals all over the world to talk, work and enjoy leisure activities"* (Baker Mckenzie, 2018) online, none of this would have been possible without the spread of the World Wide Web and Internet. Globalization 4.0 has already begun and is the digital automation stage beyond 3.0. Many believe we are already vastly underprepared for this level of automation, clinging to an outdated way of thinking and only fixing parts of existing institutions and processes. It must be acknowledged that we need to:

> "…redesign them (the existing institutions and processes) from the ground up, so that we can capitalize on the new opportunities that await us, while avoiding the kind of disruptions that we are witnessing today" (Huffington Post, 2011).

If we consider CSR to be like Globalization, as a journey through time and different eras, the evolution of CSR and its surrogate and alternative terms and themes are also evolving as part of this journey. Therefore, rather than saying CSR (or CSR 1.0 or 2.0) is extinct, it is in fact, still evolving and transforming past CSR 3.0 to CSR 4.0, mapped on to new eras and social movements consistent with Globalization 4.0. As part of the Fourth Industrial Revolution, a more evolved CSR will play a key role in a new and integrated ecosystem which forces change and deep transformation in the way organizations and companies operate. This is discussed further in the final chapters of this book.

Conclusion

Some of our biggest fears are what the future will bring for this planet and whether there will be anything left for those who inhabit it. Whether it be automation and diabolical job loss or increasingly extreme weather conditions, *'change'* is inevitable. The United Nations call to action through global implementation of the SDGs must be at the core of this *change*.

Start-ups, social enterprises, SMEs, and especially global and multinational corporations (MNCs) and multinational enterprise (MNEs) all have the ability to scale up to make a difference. But it must be a difference that can be maintained in a new and evolved system. This book examines these issues and suggests ways to implement 'change' under both the traditional academic view and the evolving broader sector view, using definitions and labels that different fields of research and individuals are comfortable with. Whether it be CSR, sustainability, shared value, innovation, integration, social entrepreneurship, or 'purpose,' let us stop saying one school of thought is extinct or a lesser entity and just get on with the job. It is the task of this generation—right now—to rapidly implement the SDGs in a meaningful way and scale up in the Fourth Industrial Revolution, without worrying who can and cannot perform these tasks and what it should be called.

With the World Economic Forum's 2019 theme as *Globalization 4.0: Shaping a New Architecture in the Age of the Fourth Industrial Revolution,* this setting is unfolding before our eyes:

> "Its genesis is situated at the dawn of the third millennium with the emergence of the Internet. This is the first industrial revolution rooted in a new technological phenomenon—digitalization—rather than in the emergence of a new type of energy. This digitalization enables us to build a new virtual world from which we can steer the physical world" (Sentryo, 2017).

We are set for an entire ecosystem change of how the world lives, eats, and breathes. This book takes into consideration the escalation of innovation as part of this setting and covers the subject of innovation within an evolving setting (in Chapter 5) and considers different value systems and economic systems needed as part of a new and more sustainable ecosystem (in the final chapters of this book). Rather than creating a semantic war on terminology, this book discovers opportunities for future research in this area of academic literature, by being flexible with terminology while also incorporating perspectives from the business community, start-ups, global MNEs, their partners, and the current generation of employees and students (i.e., millennials and Generation Z). This book aims to provide a new generation of researchers and teachers with a greater depth of knowledge, of what has gone before on this subject, and determine what the future may bring.

To achieve the objectives of the 2030 Agenda, we need an integrated and transformed social policy and framework that aims:

> "…to progressively achieve universal coverage, while addressing the specific needs of vulnerable people through targeted policies and programmes … ultimately, leaving no one behind requires the transformation of deeply rooted systems — economic, social and

political, governance structures and business models at all levels, from local to global." (UNDESA, 2018).

Corporates are in a position to assist this evolution through placing their *stakeholders* (rather than their shareholders) at the center of their decision-making, by reaching out to their extensive supply chains and expanding their level of presence in the developing countries where they reside—whether it be labeled *creating* global citizenship, *creating* corporate SIs, *creating* shared value (CSV), integrated value *creation* (IVC), or *creating* new and inclusive innovative solutions to support entrepreneurs and social enterprises as part of a deeper transformation and new responsibility (CTV). This book explains how this is possible. Backed by literature and research, this book educates its audience, while also identifying gaps in the literature and outlining future emerging research opportunities to further the cause toward *'change'* and deep transformation.

Summary of Chapters

This book first examines a summary of definitions for CSR, its alternative, surrogate and competing terms, plus the historical development and evolution of its components and constructs over time. Traditional academic literature is presented to discuss the social side of CSR and introduce SIs as part of CSR activities and social projects. Extracts from a research paper developed from the traditional CSR literature is then presented to suggest future research possibilities, which can be adapted to the evolutionary aspects of CSR and the movement toward Globalization 4.0. Later chapters focus on recent innovations in CSR and terms that have emerged with the global movement toward CSR implementation of the SDGs alongside their impact and the possibility for a more integrated and deeply transformed ecosystem.

The transformation of CSR is also discussed, as a more inclusive and innovative CSR evolves alongside the addition of CSV projects in a more integrated value system. Further progression through social innovation and the development of social enterprises as part of CSR strategy is discussed and backed by emerging literature on these topics. The book ends with a thought toward future research opportunities, the future of CSR, and the possibilities that may emerge from both a research and theoretical sense, within a practical setting.

Chapter 1: CSR Historical and Emerging Themes and Related Terms

To determine the new responsibility and new form of CSR required in an evolving ecosystem, this chapter covers the historical evolution of CSR including the various additional labels CSR has attracted and its many surrogate, complementary, and alternative terms and themes. Some parties still view CSR as just a form of Philanthropy; however, current definitions for CSR involve many components, which have been adapted over time. The new CSR definition provided by the

European Commissions in 2011, for example, mirrors some of the changes created by the inclusion of the SDGs in 2015. The creation of shared and integrated value and the ongoing development of the social enterprise industry are further developments, alongside the growing trend toward B-Corp registration, the increasing emphasis on 'business-for-purpose' and the rise of the 'be the change' movement. This chapter discusses this journey and reveals how CSR has followed a cycle of social movements through several industrial revolutions. As we head toward the Fourth Industrial Revolution and usher in a new era of Globalization 4.0, this requires new business models, new labels, and new adaptations of CSR. These concepts are introduced in this chapter and developed further in later chapters.

Chapter 2: The Emergence of CSR Social Initiatives in a Research Setting

As part of discussing future research in the era of change for Globalization 4.0, this chapter examines the traditional academic CSR literature to determine a gap in current research. An academic literature search revealed limited literature on actual CSR activities, and more specifically SIs. It is important to expand on this area of research as it relates to an evolution of the original CSR definition by Carroll (1979, 1999). The literature review also revealed limited use of Social Identity Theory (SIT) in CSR studies: a theory which provides an excellent context to give 'purpose' and meaning to a more socially oriented form of CSR. It also provides a base to understand human 'identification' and 'identity' with CSR activities, in a new era of change. Recent research reveals the importance of understanding what employees and global citizens as *stakeholders* want, need, identify, and engage with. Following a literature review, this chapter introduces a new 'Social Initiatives Framework,' designed to incorporate the many terms and alternative themes associated with CSR. The chapter concludes with extracts from an example paper for this area of research, and provides a model to examine changing *stakeholder* perspectives in global settings. The findings behind the development of the model is discussed, revealing substantial opportunities for future research. The chapter highlights the development of CSR SIs to study the SDGs, while also supporting social enterprises to solve wicked challenges and create shared value (CSV) for both the host community and the company within the setting where the organization resides.

Chapter 3: The Universal Sustainable Development Goals for Purpose and Change

Since the 2015 introduction of the United Nations Global Goals, also referred to as the SDGs, we have witnessed a movement toward inclusion of goal-related initiatives listed under CSR strategy and in CSR sustainability reports. At the time of writing this chapter, the UN were presented a speech by young activist Greta Thunberg and many other activists commenced riots in major cities. All are pointing toward, what they perceive, as a lack of effort to solve issues related to climate warming. At the same time new research has revealed targets for the SDGs is falling behind levels expected for 2030. There has also been concern for the potential of 'SDG washing,' reported in the academic literature. This would greatly decrease the credibility of the goals over time. For this reason, it is vitally important to measure the impact of initiatives introduced to fit each SDG category and label. This will also assist with funding SDG implementation at a much faster rate. This chapter commences with a brief introduction of the SDG framework and discusses the United Nations and OECD methodology and the development and implementation of key global goals. Various research reports are discussed alongside a tracking study on uptake of the SDGs, and the need for SDG metrics to create transparency and evaluation. The chapter ends with example case studies of CSR strategy implementing and measuring the SDGs, alongside a discussion of financial vehicles released to support further development. The chapter also makes suggestions for future research opportunities to assist SDG progression.

Chapter 4: Creating Shared Value for Social Initiatives and Shared Purpose

A full and adequate *Systematic Quantitative Literature Research Analysis* of the academic literature and research on CSV is long overdue. This chapter commences this process by introducing some of the academic literature currently on CSV and examining the strengths and weaknesses of this literature, while identifying gaps for future research and providing a comparison with CSR literature and the debate of CSR versus CSV. The chapter builds on current academic literature to include writing and research from the business community in an attempt to make this chapter both topical and accessible to anyone interested in CSV, including practitioners interested in implementing these types of projects as direct CSV projects or as part of already existing CSR strategy. It is expected that the inclusion of this type of business literature will add value to academic research going forward. The Appendix brings the chapter together by presenting examples of a variety of CSV case studies to provide ideas for future project implementation and opportunities for future research in both implementation and measurement.

Chapter 5: Innovation, Entrepreneurship, and Solving Wicked Challenges through CSR and CSV

The Fourth Industrial Revolution has escalated Innovation to new heights unseen, creating an evolution of Innovation and CSR, and as a result, a more *'Innovative CSR.'* With this evolution comes also the evolution of the 'Preneur'—from social entrepreneur to corporate social entrepreneur and corporate social intrapreneur. It is therefore important to acknowledge that social entrepreneurship is not just for the social sector or start-up entrepreneur—corporations can also be social entrepreneurs. This chapter establishes an understanding of this possibility alongside solving wicked problems and challenges and how to provide collaborative networks and co-creation experiences to help others on this journey. More importantly, it is discussed how corporates can assist millennials (and Generation Z) by funding and incubating their Innovation or social enterprise idea under the umbrella of their CSR strategy, until its ready to be released. The chapter is supported by academic literature and business publications with suggestions for future research opportunities.

Chapter 6: The Future of CSR and the New Ecosystem for CSR 4.0

With the World Economic Forum's 2019 theme based on the new era – Globalization *4.0: Shaping a New Architecture in the Age of the Fourth Industrial Revolution* – this chapter takes into consideration innovation as defined in the previous chapter and builds on the escalation of innovation required for the Fourth Industrial Revolution and to reach the sustainable development goals (SDGs) deadline by 2030. Proposed is an entire ecosystem change of how the world lives, eats, makes money, sleeps and breathes. This chapter considers these changes with an explanation of CSR 1.0 and CSR 2.0 to CSR 3.0, providing case studies of these, plus discussing the transition from Globalization 3.0 to 4.0, and the various known and unknown system changes that may be required including integrated value creation (IVC). We live in exciting times where IVC and other systems, such as the well-being economy, exponential economy, shared economy, innovation and resilience economy, may be part of a new ecosystem. This chapter concludes with a discussion of these themes, and the development of CSR 4.0 mapped on to Globalization 4.0 within a deeply transformed systems approach to create transformed value (CTV). Emerging research opportunities as a result of these changes are discussed throughout this chapter.

Chapter 7: Overall Summary and Conclusion

As each chapter has its own independent conclusion, the overall book conclusion is provided as a snapshot aerial overview to further clarify key messages.

References

Are included after each chapter.

APPENDIX

Appendices are included throughout this book with case study examples of the following:

- Corporate case studies labeled as CSR in the Appendix of *Chapter 1*
- A 'Social Initiatives Framework' and extracts from a development research paper in the Appendix of *Chapter 2*

- Case Studies of SDG inclusion in CSR strategy in the Appendix of *Chapter 3*
- Case Studies Creating Shared Value (CSV) in the Appendix of *Chapter 4*
- Case Studies of CSR 2.0, CSR 3.0, and integrated value creation (IVC) in *Chapter 6*

References

Advameg. (2018). Reference for business. Retrieved from https://www.reference forbusiness.com/management/Tr-Z/Zero-Sum-Game.html#ixzz5WUvLZXkw

Aguinis, H., & Glavas, A. (2012). What we know and don't know about corporate social responsibility: A review and research agenda. *Journal of Management, 38*(4), 932–968. doi:10.1177/0149206311436079

Baker McKenzie. (2018). Globalization 3.0: A new era of trade, tax and political uncertainty. Retrieved from https://www.bakermckenzie.com/en/insight/publications/2018/01/globalization

Besharov, M. L., & Smith, W. K. (2014). Multiple institutional logics in organizations: Explaining their varied nature and implications. *Academy of Management Review, 39*(3), 364–381.

Boateng, A., Akamavi, R. K., & Ndoro, G. (2016). Measuring performance of nonprofit organisations: Evidence from large charities. *Business Ethics: A European Review, 25*(1), 59–74.

Business and Sustainable Development Commission. (2017). Better business, better world report. Retrieved from http://report.businesscommission.org/uploads/BetterBiz-BetterWorld_final.pdf

Camillus, J. C. (2008). Strategy as a wicked problem. *Harvard Business Review, 86*(5), 1–10.

Carroll, A. B. (1979). A three-dimensional conceptual model of corporate performance. *The Academy of Management Review, 4*(4), 497–505.

Carroll, A. B. (1999). Corporate social responsibility. *Business & Society, 38*(3), 268–295. doi:10.1177/000765039903800303

Carroll, A. B., & Brown, J. A. (2018). Corporate social responsibility: A review of current concepts, research and issues. In J. Weber & D. Wasleleski (Eds.), *Corporate social responsibility* (pp. 39–69). Bingley: Emerald Publishing.

Crane, A., Palazzo, G., Spence, L. J., & Matten, D. (2014). Contesting the value of "creating shared value". *California Management Review, 56*(2), 130–153. doi:10.1525/cmr.2014.56.2.130

Dentoni, D., Hospes, O., & Ross, R. B. (2012). Managing wicked problems in agribusiness: The role of multi-stakeholder engagements in value creation: Editor's introduction. *The International Food and Agribusiness Management Review, 15*(B), 1–12.

CSR Europe. (2018). Collaboration for Impact: Maturity and integration of sustainability in European sector associations. Retrieved from https://www.csreurope.org/collaboration-impact-maturity-and-integration-sustainability-european-sector-associations

European Commission. (2011). A renewed EU strategy 2011-14 for corporate social responsibility. Communication from the commission to the European parliament, the council, the European economic and social committee and the committee of the regions. Retrieved from https://eur-lex.europa.eu/legal-content/EN/TXT/?uri=CELEX%3A52011DC0681

Friedman, T. L. (2005). It's a Flat world, after all. *New York Times Magazine*. April 3, 2005. Retrieved from https://www.nytimes.com/2005/04/03/magazine/its-a-flat-world-after-all.html

Frynas, J. G., & Yamahaki, C. (2016). Corporate social responsibility: Review and roadmap of theoretical perspectives. *Business Ethics: A European Review, 25*(3), 258–285. doi:10.1111/beer.12115

George, J. M. (2014). Compassion and capitalism, implications for organizational studies. *Journal of Management, 40*(1), 5–15.

George, G., McGahan, A. M., & Prabhu, J. (2012). Innovation for inclusive growth: Toward a theoretical framework and a research agenda. *Journal of Management Studies, 49*(4), 661–683.

Hart, S., & Prahalad, C. K. (2002). The fortune at the bottom of the pyramid. *Strategy + Business, 26*, 54–67.

Ho, D. Y. (1995). Selfhood and identity in confucianism, Taoism, Buddhism, and Hinduism: Contrasts with the west. *Journal for the Theory of Social Behaviour, 25*(2), 115–139.

Huffington Post. (2011). Eric X. Li's globalization 2.0. November 1, 2011. Retrieved from https://www.huffingtonpost.com/nathan-gardels/eric-x-lis-globalization_b_10 69669.html

Illia, L., Zyglidopoulos, S. C., Romenti, S., Rodríguez-Cánovas, B., & del Valle Brena, A. G. (2013). Communicating corporate social responsibility to a cynical public. *MIT Sloan Management Review, 54*(3), 15–18.

Kim, R. C. (2018). Can creating Shared Value (CSV) and the United Nations Sustainable Development Goals (UN SDGs) collaborate for a better world? Insights from East Asia. *Sustainability, 10*(4128). doi:10.3390/su10114128

Kim, J. D., An, H. T., Myung, J. K., & Bae, S. M. (2016). Assessing CSV as a successful strategic CSR. *Korea Business Review, 20*, 291–318.

Korhonen, H. (2013). Organizational needs: A co-creation and human systems perspective. *Journal of Business Market Management, 6*(4), 214–227.

Laudal, T. (2018). Measuring shared value in multinational corporations. *Social Responsibility Journal, 14*(4), 917–933. doi:10.1108/srj-08-2017-0169

Marques, J. C., & Mintzberg, H. (2015). Why corporate social responsibility isn't a piece of cake. *MIT Sloan Management Review, 56*(4), 8–11.

Matten, D., & Crane, A. (2005). Corporate citizenship: Towards an extended theoretical conceptualization. *Academy of Management Review, 30*(1), 166–179.

Matten, D., & Moon, J. (2008). "Implicit" and "explicit" CSR: A conceptual framework for a comparative understanding of corporate social responsibility. *Academy of Management Review, 33*(2), 404–424.

Michelini, L., & Fiorentino, D. (2012). New business models for creating shared value. *Social Responsibility Journal, 8*(4), 561–577.

Mühlbacher, H., & Böbel, I. (2018). From zero-sum to win-win - organisational conditions for successful shared value strategy implementation. *European Management Journal. 37*(3), 313–324. doi:10.1016/j.emj.2018.10.007

Munro, V. (2017). *Identification of CSR micro social initiatives within a developed and developing country context*. PhD Thesis, Griffith University, Mount Gravatt, QLD. Retrieved from https://www120.secure.griffith.edu.au/rch/items/5e1def2f-25a0-4c9b-aa72-8c4b8761cb80/1/

Munro, V. (2018). Changing the boundaries of expectations: MNE uptake of universal principles and global goals. In S. A. Hipsher (Ed.), *Examining the private sector's role in wealth creation and poverty reduction*. Hershey, PA: IGI Global.

Munro, V., Arli, D., & Rundle-Thiele, S. (2016). CSR strategy at a crossroads: An example of a multinational corporation in a developing and developed society. Paper presented at the twenty-seventh annual meeting international association for business and society.

Porter, M. E., & Kramer, M. R. (2011). The big idea: Creating shared value. *Harvard Business Review, 89*(1–2), 1–17. Retrieved from http://www.nuovavista.com/SharedValuePorterHarvardBusinessReview.PDF

Rangan, K., Chase, L., & Karim, S. (2015). The truth about CSR. *Harvard Business Review, 93*, 42–49.

Schwab, K. (2018). The fourth industrial revolution will worsen inequality – But only if the world lets it. *South China Morning Post*. November 7, 2018. Retrieved from https://www.scmp.com/comment/insight-opinion/article/2171972/fourth-industrial-revolution-will-worsen-inequality-only-if

Sentryo. (2017). The 4 industrial revolutions. Retrieved from https://www.sentryo.net/the-4-industrial-revolutions/

Tamariz, M., & Kirby, S. (2016). The cultural evolution of language. *Current Opinion in Psychology, 8*, 37–43.

The Millennial Impact Report. (2017). Why do Millennials choose to engage in cause movements? Retrieved from http://www.themillennialimpact.com

The New York Times. (2008). Barack Obama's Feb. 5 speech. Retrieved from https://www.nytimes.com/2008/02/05/us/politics/05text-obama.html

Triandis, H. C., Robert, B., Marcelo, J. V., Masaaki, A., & Lucca, N. (1988). Individualism and collectivism. *Journal of Personality and Social Psychology, 54*(2), 323–338.

UNDESA. (2018). Leaving no one behind. Retrieved from https://www.un.org/development/desa/en/news/sustainable/leaving-no-one-behind.html

United Nations Sustainable Development Goals. (2015). Transforming our world: The 2030 agenda for sustainable development. Retrieved from https://sustainabledevelopment.un.org/post2015/transformingourworld

Visser, W. (2014). *CSR 2.0: Transforming corporate sustainability and responsibility*. New York, NY: Springer.

Visser, W., Matten, D., Pohl, M., Tolhurst, N., Bohmer, K., Ghebremariam, A. … Huble, S. S. (2007). *The A to Z of corporate social responsibility: A complete reference guide to concepts, codes and organisations*. Chichester: John Wiley & Sons.

Wei, Y.-C., Egri, P. C., & Yeh-Yun Lin, C. (2014). Do corporate social responsibility practices yield different business benefits in eastern and western contexts? *Chinese Management Studies, 8*(4), 556–576.

Chapter 1

CSR Historical and Emerging Themes and Related Terms

Abstract

To determine the new responsibility and new form of CSR required in an evolving ecosystem, this chapter covers the historical evolution of CSR including the various additional labels CSR has attracted, and its many surrogate, complementary, and alternative terms and themes. Some parties still view CSR as just a form of Philanthropy; however, current definitions for CSR involve many components, which have adapted over time. The new CSR definition provided by the European Commission in 2011, for example, mirrors some of the changes created by the inclusion of the sustainable development goals (SDGs) in 2015. The creation of shared and integrated value and the ongoing development of the social enterprise industry are further developments, alongside the growing trend toward B-Corp registration, the increasing emphasis on 'business-for-purpose' and the rise of the 'be the change' movement. This chapter discusses this journey and reveals how CSR has followed a cycle of social movements through several industrial revolutions. As we head toward the Fourth Industrial Revolution and usher in the new era for Globalization 4.0, this requires new business models, new labels, and new adaptations of CSR. These concepts are introduced in this chapter and developed further in later chapters.

Introduction

First, we need to remind ourselves that Corporate Social Responsibility (CSR) has a long history. In fact, CSR is centuries old and punctuated with consistent *change*. With any journey of time there is evolution – and therefore continued growth, expansion, threat, and opportunity. Different phases and different centuries inevitably provide different contexts over time, with many ways to perceive, define, and refine original concepts. Regardless of how you label and define CSR, society provides various challenges, checks, and balances to make sure CSR, or any term, for that matter, keeps pace with modern times. The 'be the change'

CSR for Purpose, Shared Value and Deep Transformation, 15–51
Copyright © 2020 Emerald Publishing Limited
All rights of reproduction in any form reserved
doi:10.1108/978-1-80043-035-820200004

movement provides one example of this, whereby the term may cease to exist when everyone is actioning 'change.' 'Change,' as a term is then integrated into society and morphed into other variants or adaptations of what has gone before. It is the same for CSR. New visions of CSR are recycled and revolutionized as social movements come and go. The era of Globalization 4.0 and the Fourth Industrial Revolution is the next social movement and cycle of innovation to arrive.

To understand this further, a quote comes to mind from CSR guru Archie Carroll, who has been studying CSR for more than 47 years. His first paragraph in his first ever published paper in 1974, provides an excellent illustration of 'time' and social revolutions that come and go:

> "Social revolution has been characterized by some as being paradoxical. It is paradoxical in the sense that it simultaneously casts the business institution in the role of villain and saviour. While on the one hand business organizations are thoroughly chastised for their philosophy, structure, and mode of operations, they are at the same time acknowledged to be an increasingly beneficial force in society" (Steiner, 1972, cited in, Carroll, 1974, p.75).

To illustrate this point further, Carroll takes a quote from the 1971 David Rockefeller (Jr) speech addressing the Advertising Council, and reported in the *Los Angeles Times*:

> "It is scarcely an exaggeration to say that right now American business is facing its most severe public disfavor since the 1930s. We are assailed for demeaning the worker, deceiving the consumer, destroying the environment and disillusioning the younger generation" (Rockefeller, 1971, cited in Carroll, 1974).

Roll forward to 2020, and it could be argued we still have the same disbelief or disfavor, albeit somewhat more magnified. Discussions of this nature have moved on to the Fourth Industrial Revolution and topics such as race and gender inequality, automation of jobs, rapid innovation, the development of a circular economy, implementing the sustainable development goals (SDGs), formalizing social enterprises through social entrepreneurship, and multilayered collaborations through partnerships and co-creation. This book covers many of these themes with this chapter introducing the evolution of CSR terminology, followed by the development of these themes.

Our choice of words and phrases to define an issue has a large impact on how we see and evaluate that issue (Hipsher, 2018; Imai, Kanero, & Masuda, 2016; Tamariz & Kirby, 2016). Initially corporate philanthropy, for example, was core to the CSR definition (e.g., Austin & Reficco, 2009), and this seems to have stayed in people's minds. However, from the various definitions of CSR later this chapter, it is clear discretionary activities and/or corporate philanthropy are just one of the many components of CSR. When the general business public and interdisciplinary academics from different fields, look at CSR with a less detailed lens, they still conjure up images of philanthropy and cash or cheque "giving" as the only form of CSR, forgetting its legal, ethical, environmental, and social components and subsequent developments.

As touched on above, over time CSR has gained additional labels and surrogate and competing terms, such as: 'purpose,' 'be the change', corporate citizenship (CC), corporate social performance (CSP), triple bottom line, sustainability, conscious capitalism, business ethics, corporate social entrepreneurship (CSE), creating shared value (CSV), integrated value creation (IVC), and other adaptations such as: Responsive CSR, Strategic CSR, Systemic CSR, among others (Carroll & Brown, 2018; Googins, Mirvis, & Rochlin, 2007; Porter & Kramer, 2011; Visser et al. 2007; Zadek, 2001).

To honor this perspective, key terms such as these are discussed in this chapter alongside the various social movements and activities moulding CSR through transition and change. Particular movements are introduced in this chapter and discussed further in the innovation chapter (Chapter 5), the SDG chapter (Chapter 3), and the CSV chapter (Chapter 4). Research opportunities are also identified as this chapter discovers ongoing gaps in the literature for CSR. In later chapters and also later this chapter, we discuss additional social revolutions and new innovations and trends, but to appreciate the overall evolution of CSR we must first revisit its historical past.

Historical Overview

The academic literature often commences historical discussions of CSR from the middle of the Industrial Revolution or during the time of the fallout post World War II. This chapter commences the journey of CSR from the fifth to fourth century BC and continues to contemporary times and to current deadlines expected for 2030, and beyond.

As stated in the introduction to this chapter, CSR has a centuries-long history and reflects a progression through various social movements to its current form, where some authors today still talk about what is yet to come, and "unleashing the 'long tail' of CSR" (e.g., Visser, 2011). The historical growth of CSR has been covered extensively in a number of books and papers and so a brief summary of the development of CSR will be covered here before moving on to newer and additional terms which, as stated above, can be alternative or surrogate terms, or as stated by Carroll and Brown (2018), complimentary and competing themes.

Unlike most academic literature therefore, the discussion on the history and development of CSR commences here from the fifth to fourth century BC.

Fifth and Fourth Century BC

The first written notions by CSR authors such as Eberstadt (1973) cite the origins of CSR back to the Classical Greek era in the fifth century (500 BC to the last day of 401 BC) to fourth century BC (400 BC to the last day of 301 BC). Business at this time was expected to be of social service to the community. During the medieval era from approximately 1000–1500 AD, businesses were expected to be honest and adhere to moral and legal obligations under the influence of the Catholic Church (Prafitri, 2017). During the Mercantile period from 1500 to 1800 AD and the Industrial Revolution in Europe from 1815 to 1848, the social obligation of business was to provide public service, with businessmen gaining respectability, dignity, and privileges for their services (Eberstadt, 1973; Prafitri, 2017). Businesses were also punished if they failed to provide social benefits to society (Prafitri, 2017). However, there was also exploitation of foreigners and unethical profit maximization (Eberstadt, 1973; Prafitri, 2017) leading to the era of "ethical business" arising from Bowen's work in the 1950s (Prafitri, 2017), with the publication of *The Social Responsibilities of the Businessman* (Bowen, 1953).

Pre-industrial Revolution to World War II

While much of the academic literature cites the history of CSR as commencing somewhere just prior to the middle of the First Industrial Revolution in Britain (1780–1850), many authors of modern-day CSR tend to cite World War II as the seed of CSR, and this is typically where academic papers commence a historical overview of CSR. Those quoting the beginning of CSR at the time of the First Industrial Revolution connect this with the transition to new manufacturing processes in the early 1700s–1840s. Some believe this to be the Western beginning of a documented and publicly demonstrated form of CSR. One example is the time of the Cotton Mills in Manchester, Northern England, providing community and staff with additional resources beyond that of the factory job. On a visit to the *Science and Industry Museum* in Manchester, I came across an entire exhibit explaining how one of the mill owners at this time had set-up additional facilities for workers and families in the mill and in the community where the mill resided. This gives an early indication of what CSR or at least 'social responsibility' was at this time.

Actual formal writing on CSR, however, is traced to the mid-to-late 1800s around the time of the Second Industrial Revolution. Industrialists such as American John H. Patterson of National Cash Register who started the industrial welfare movement is acknowledged at this time alongside well-known philanthropists such as John Rockefeller who set-up *The Rockefeller Foundation*, similar to the *Bill & Melinda Gates Foundation* today (Visser, 2012).

As part of this evolution of CSR and its complimentary themes, Wayne Visser, Professor of Integrated Value at Antwerp Management School and Fellow of Cambridge University's Institute for Sustainable Leaderships, authored a two-stream development approach to CSR, with his colleague Kymal (Visser & Kymal, 2015). The two streams they document evolving over time are: *responsibility* and *sustainability*. The *responsibility* stream they refer to originated in the 1800s, with industrialists Rockefeller and Carnegie promoting community philanthropy, followed by the employee welfare movement (Visser, 2017). The *sustainability* stream started with air pollution regulation in the UK and land conservation in the US in the 1870s (Visser, 2011) and moved on to the first Earth Day, Greenpeace and the first UN Stockholm meeting in the 1970s. As the two movements grew, so did the connection and integration between the two terms (Visser, 2011). This is discussed later this chapter.

In general, it is more common for Western authors to refer to CSR as a product of the twentieth century (January 1901–December 2000). However, if we dig deep into Eastern culture and developing countries, we may find examples of CSR existing much earlier and in different forms than its Western counterparts, and again with different versions of names, or labels for terms and themes. This is an opportunity for future research, as we discover the strength of CSR through the ages. This body of literature collected here, attempts to dispel the myth that CSR is becoming extinct, and is instead continuing to a more evolved form, through the journey of time.

1950s: The Idea of Social Responsibility

In Western academic literature, initial discussions on businesses assuming responsibility beyond their direct shareholders, commenced in the 1950s. At this time CSR momentarily caught the attention of the general public, but this was not embedded into mainstream thought till the 1960s. In an era where the modern corporate was yet to be unveiled, the term 'social responsibility' did not include the term corporate and spoke of businesses and businesspeople in general.

As mentioned earlier, the early 1950s lays claim to the often quoted, landmark and seminal work of Howard Bowen – *The Social Responsibilities of the Businessman* (Bowen, 1953). A sign of the times with few businesswomen, his definition of *social responsibility* refers to the obligations of businessmen – "to pursue those policies, to make those decisions, or to follow those lines of action which are desirable in terms of the objectives and values of our society" (Bowen, 1953, p. 6). Bowen is recognized by many academics as the founding father of CSR and the one who started the discussion of 'social responsibility' at this time. His work today is seen as visionary and holds the belief that social responsibility should be "a basic foundation of human interaction" (Bowen, 1953).

Both academia and businesspeople took great interest in advocating this perspective; however, not all were entirely taken by his argument. A Harvard Business School paper, for example, wrote of the *The Dangers of Social Responsibility* (Levitt, 1958), emphasizing the primary goal of business to be long-term profit maximization, arguing that it should be the government that takes care of general welfare, so businesses can address aspects of material welfare (Carroll & Brown, 2018). Today it is more acknowledged as a collaboration of both.

In the late 1950s and early 1960s, Milton Friedman was cited in many academic texts regarding his perspectives on CSR. Quoted as the twentieth century's most prominent advocate of free markets he stated that 'social issues' as such, were not the concern of businesspeople and should be handled by the unrestrained workings of a free market system. He is well known for his statement that management should "make as much money as possible" (Friedman, 1970). Carroll and Brown (2018), however, draw attention to the rest of Friedman's quote, where he states the purpose of business is "to make as much money as possible while conforming to the basic rules of society, both those embodied in the law and those embodied in ethical customs" (p. 43). Hence, he refers to society, law, and ethics, which became part of the many definitions given for CSR, which later evolved to include 'social issues' and helping people in society, alongside dealing with environmental issues.

The 1960s: Growth of CSR Research

Research on CSR developed considerably in the 1960s. It was also in the 1960s when researchers began in a more formal sense to suggest that businesses take their responsibilities beyond that owed to their *stakeholders.* The 1960s also saw the development of four "social movements": the civil rights movement and the environmental, consumer and women's rights movements. These movements were seen to address the expectation that businesses were expected to deliver on issues related to these movements in addition to their responsibility of an investment return to *stakeholders* (Carroll & Brown, 2018).

As a sign of the times, new thought and types of publications began to appear. In the spring of 1960, academic Keith Davis published *Can Business Afford to Ignore Its Responsibilities?* and commenced defining what these might be. He suggested that social responsibility refers to both what he defined as socioeconomic (primarily external) obligations and sociohuman (primarily internal) responsibilities. This argument also stressed the beginning of concerns which were to arise, such as the threats of the external environment as we have come to know them, but also arising internal social issues such as "making work meaningful, developing people to their fullest capacities, preserving freedom and creativity, and fulfilling expectations of human dignity" (Carroll, 1974, p. 85).

This suggests that these social and very human-related issues were coming to the foreground of thinking and 'purpose' at the time and were beginning to be thought of at a corporate level in the late 1960s and more definitely in the early 1970s.

The 1970s: Expansion of the CSR Definition

Toward the end of the 1960s and beginning of the early 1970s, the Third Industrial Revolution began to unfold. At the same time an expansion of academic writing on CSR and a growing acceptance toward CSR began to develop. Researchers suggest that the 1970s was the time of real movement for CSR in business. Exactly 100 years after air pollution regulation in the UK and US in the 1870s, the first Earth Day was held in April 1970. Greenpeace was founded in 1971, and the UN Stockholm Conference on Environment and Development mentioned earlier was held in June 1972 (Visser & Kymal, 2015).

The definition by Keith Davis in 1973 set the scene for development of CSR definitions going forward. He saw CSR as: "the firm's consideration of, and response to, issues beyond the narrow economic, technical, and legal requirements of the firm" (Davis, 1973, p. 312). Further, Davis goes on to say "it is a firm's acceptance of a social obligation beyond the requirements of laws" (p. 313). In his 1973 article in the *Academy of Management Journal*, Davis discusses the for and against arguments for 'social responsibility' and concludes that by this stage, businesses have assumed a "certain minimum role of social responsibility" (Davis, 1973, p. 321). What is queried is whether businesses should assume a more significant role or not. However, he states once the "direction" has been decided for social responsibility "businesses must move vigorously to integrating social values into their decision-making machinery." He saw social responsibility as "necessary for an interdependent one world" (Davis, 1973, p. 321). This integration today is still a key component of CSR.

There was also an expansion of the literature with more detailed definitions of CSR. Carroll's four-part component definition was developed at this time:

> "The social responsibility of business encompasses the economic, legal, ethical, and discretionary expectations that society has of organizations at a given point in time" (Carroll, 1979, p. 500, p. 500).

"Discretionary" expectations were later referred to as "philanthropic." Philanthropic activities, as mentioned previously, gradually became more than just straight cash or cheque "giving." It instead involved an input of skills to causes or social projects that needed assistance at different levels, and voluntary assistance was provided by employees for the same purpose. Carroll's 1979 definition, however, is an important starting point to discuss the evolution of CSR and how it is understood as a concept, because it considers the business case for CSR, by mentioning the firm's economic responsibility, alongside the three other components.

Although academic writing on CSR and a growing acceptance toward the concept of CSR began to expand in the 1970s, a number of concerns remained, such as the discussion on where the emphasis should be placed: responsibility, accountability, or corporate action (Carroll & Shabana, 2010). This query was addressed in the writings of Ackerman and Bauer (1976), who thought the term 'social responsibility' placed too much emphasis on motivation rather than performance and preferred the term 'social responsiveness' to 'social responsibility.' Frederick (1978) built on this to distinguish between CSR 1, the more standard understanding of CSR entailing accountability, and CSR 2, which they suggest be labeled corporate social "responsiveness," focusing on the literal act of responding (Carroll & Brown, 2018, p. 44).

Frederick's CSR 1 and CSR 2 should not be confused with Visser's CSR 1.0 and CSR 2.0, where one is an evolution of the other, and not separate items of the same thing. CSR 1.0 and CSR 2.0 are discussed in more detail in Chapter 6. In contrast to Frederick (1978), Ackerman and Bauer (1976) extended the CSR definition itself to raise issues of accountability, measurement, responsiveness, and performance. Soon after mention of accountability and responsiveness, corporate social performance (CSP) developed a following, whereby the 'performance' part of CSR was the new focus, and Carroll (1979) developed a CSP model to depict this. The model included three dimensions: the basic *definition* of CSR (which includes his four components), a statement of the firm's philosophy of *responsiveness* (e.g., reaction, defense, accommodation or proaction), across the *social issue arenas* involved (e.g., consumerism, environment, discrimination, product safety, occupational safety, *shareholders*), which could then be played out or implemented (Carroll, 1979). The movement of terms toward a CSP focus shows some of the complexity creeping into the CSR dialogue at the time. This meant discussions of the definition of CSR were to become a key theme of academic research for a number of decades.

In the late 1970s, the 1977 Sullivan Principles also existed for social responsibility (Visser, 2012). More formally, known as the Global Sullivan Principles, launched in 1977 by the Philadelphia civil rights leader and faith-based activist, Leon Sullivan. This movement was seen as one of the twentieth century's most powerful attempts to represent social justice through economic leverage. To do so, Sullivan used the power of American investment to bear down on key issues, such as the Apartheid situation in South Africa (The Encyclopedia of Greater Philadelphia, 2013).

Another business revolution in the 1970s was the arrival of total quality management (TQM) and ISO 9001, introduced by US-based statistician Edwards Deming. At the core of the TQM model and ISO standard is "continual improvement," a principle now key to management systems and approaches for performance. The most popular environmental management standard, ISO 14001, is also built on this principle (Visser, 2012). According to Visser (2012) there is nothing wrong with continuous improvement per se (for safety and reliability of products and services), but when used as the main approach for social and environmental problems, it fails on speed and scale. Visser (2012) termed this the "incremental approach of CSR". This was not enough to fail CSR however, and a move toward more innovative approaches was in the not too distant future.

The 1980s: Refining Definitions and Introducing Related Themes

Meanwhile the 1980s saw the continued discussion of the definition of CSR as a key theme in academic literature. Not surprisingly, CSR along its historical progression, developed multiple dimensions. The 'performance' component of CSR touched on above, continued in the 1980s, allowing for further consideration toward the measurement of CSR. Wartick and Cochran (1985), for example, expanded on Carroll's CSP model. They listed the three dimensions as: *principles* (with CSR reflecting a philosophical orientation); *processes* (responsiveness, reflecting an institutional orientation); and *policies* (social issues reflecting an organizational orientation). Later, Wood (1991) elaborated on both the above models. Wood proposed that CSP include a business organization with principles of social responsibility, including "processes of social responsiveness and policies, programs and other observable outcomes as they related to the firm's societal relationships" (Carroll & Brown, 2018, p. 44).

In the 1980s, themes such as *stakeholder theory* and *business ethics* began to be discussed in the literature (Carroll, 1999). These are discussed below.

1980s: Business Ethics

Both business ethics and CSR have been used to address conduct in business or businesses, and are considered complementary to each other (Carroll & Brown, 2018). They are also considered as separate fields. Business ethics was widely accepted in the US in the 1970s, arising in Europe and Japan in the 1980s (De George, 2011). It moved to the forefront of people's minds again in the late 1980s due to the rise of various corporate business scandals of an ethical nature (Carroll & Brown, 2018), followed by later scandals of bribery, insider trading, false advertising, and the stories of Enron, Arthur Andersen, and Bernard Madoff's Ponzi scheme spring to mind (De George, 2011).

Some believe business ethics developed as a second strand of the way corporates must behave. Others see it as part of business ethics (De George, 1987) or as a part of CSR, in particular, Carroll's (1979) definition incorporating the four components of CSR: economic, legal, ethical, and discretionary.

Joyner and Payne (2002) also suggest both terms, CSR and business ethics can be used interchangeably. Distinguished Professor and Co-Director of the International Center for Ethics in Business (University of Kansas), Richard De George succinctly explains the overlap between CSR and Business ethics. He also stresses companies can have two separate roles, a CSR officer for external and an ethical officer for internal issues:

> The emphasis on CSR, however, in some instances has become equated with business ethics, even though only some of a corporation's social obligations are ethical... Corporations can have exemplary CSR programs and be ethically deficient in other areas of their operations, as the case of Enron demonstrated.
> De George (2011)

To combat these deficiencies in corporate culture, many multinational companies have adopted codes that cover their practices throughout the world in their various locations. Some have signed on to the Caux Principles 16 or the principles contained in the UN Global Compact (UNGC; De George, 2011). The UNGC is discussed in Chapter 3, and contains 10 principles dealing with the environment, corruption labor standards, and human rights, providing a framework for corporations to commit themselves to these principles and implement them.

Hence, as mentioned previously, both business ethics and CSR have been used to address questionable conduct in business and have become complementary to each other (Carroll & Brown, 2018), but are also listed as separate fields. One distinction that helps is to refer to CSR at the 'business level,' whereas business ethics may pertain more to 'individual behaviors' and actions within the organizational framework (Carroll & Brown, 2018).

1980s: Stakeholder Theory

With Business Ethics first mentioned in the era of Bowen, the 1980s saw it taught in business schools alongside CSR, Corporate Governance and *Stakeholder Theory*. *Stakeholder Theory* (or *stakeholder management* as it is also known), therefore also became popular at this time. It is well acknowledged in the literature that Edward Freeman (1984, p. 40) introduced the *stakeholder concept* to the CSR debate and he is listed as its modern pioneer (Carroll & Brown, 2018; Prafitri, 2017). Freeman, however, first proposed the theory as a way of approaching strategic management. He believed it would help firms be more responsive to their environment and deal with triple bottom line issues. Triple bottom line here refers to a framework with three parts: social, environmental, and financial. The social part takes account of fair and beneficial business practice toward labor and the community; environmental is related to sustainable environmental practice; and profit refers to the economic value created by the business (Elkington, 1997). As part of his definition, Freeman defined *stakeholders* as "groups and individuals who can affect, or are affected by, the achievement of an organisation's mission" (Freeman, 1984, p. 52).

This definition also encompassed the concept of a win-win situation (referred to in later chapters of this book) and is at the front of the 'business-for-purpose' discussions today. Sturdivant (1979), for example, believed that understanding the attitudes and behaviors of *stakeholders* would assist managers build win-win solutions for their companies and *stakeholders*. Managers then came to learn that there are different categories of *stakeholders* that vary in legitimacy and power (Carroll & Brown, 2018). Two key types of *stakeholders* were then labeled primary and secondary (Clarkson, 1995), with primary *stakeholders* having high levels of interdependency with the company, and secondary *stakeholders* with no active engagement with the company (Clarkson, 1995). This led to a *stakeholder* management framework which was seen as consistent with both CSR and business ethics and institutionalized the role of the *stakeholder manager* to take care of *stakeholders* (Carroll & Brown, 2018).

In contrast, the neoclassical notion of value creation suggests that CSR distracts company management from its main 'purpose': serving the interests of *shareholders* and/or *stakeholders*. In this regard, managers have to minimize costs and maximize efficiency for *shareholder* value. This was proposed by Michael Jensen from Harvard Business school in the mid-1980s (Jensen, 1986). However, Friedman was already writing that individual managers may have a personal responsibility to society and give to charity but not on behalf of the company (Friedman, 1970) and this perspective continued into the early 1980s (Carroll & Brown, 2018).

Late 1980s: Sustainability

Toward the end of the 1980s, the Valdez Principles (CERES Principles) were released in 1989. Previous to this the World Commission on Environment and

Development (1987) released the Brundtland definition of "sustainable development." Before the release of this definition, sustainable development had been defined in many ways, but the most frequent quoted definition became the Brundtland Report definition:

> "Sustainable development is development that meets the needs of
> the present without compromising the ability of future generations
> to meet their own needs" (Brundtland, 1987).

While sustainable development appears grounded in the continuous satisfaction of human needs, as mentioned above, it is more often aligned with concerns for the natural environment. Many research studies state that the concept of sustainability from this strongly "environmental" perspective is now the key focus. The language of environmental sustainability is also increasingly used to describe a company's CSR overall including their socially responsible initiatives and activities.

In this vein, sustainability is often equated with eco-efficiency (Dyllick & Hockerts, 2002) which is based on high efficiency production technology and methods, and less use of natural resources and energy for the same amount of production, alongside less waste (UNIDO Eco-efficiency, 2018). It is noted that eco-efficiency is a valuable part of corporate strategy, but as a sole concept it is considered insufficient (Dyllick & Hockerts, 2002). Eco-efficiency is therefore different from CSR, which includes every efficiency, not just environmental. Dyllick and Hockerts (2002) therefore demonstrate in their research that eco-efficiency is only one part of corporate sustainability criteria. Also involved should be socio-efficiency, and therefore also *social sustainability* and or the organization's "socially responsible" initiatives and activities.

Instead, the reliance on eco-efficiency is reflected in the overall term for sustainability which focuses on environmental sustainability and not social sustainability. Even in business schools today who teach sustainability, there is an emphasis on environmental and little if anything on *social* under the sustainability umbrella. In contrast, the use of the term CSR allows the organization to focus on all aspects of responsibility – social, environmental, legal, ethical – and make sure all components are ongoing and sustainable for the next generation.

The use and understanding of the term 'sustainability' also varies across global regions. As mentioned in the preface of this book, some countries are more attuned to using the term 'sustainability' as a priority, and Australian business terminology, for example, uses the term to override the use of CSR as a term. Hence, different regions of the world and different countries emphasize different aspects of CSR (Munro, 2013).

Another reason suggested by researchers for the term 'sustainability' being used "interchangeably" with CSR in the UK and Europe (rather than "instead of" as in Australia) has been likened to the use of the concept for 'triple bottom line' mentioned earlier. First introduced by John Elkington, the emphasis for triple bottom line is meant to be placed simultaneously on economic prosperity, environmental quality, and social equity (*The Economist*, 2009). The social bottom line emphasizes people, quality of life, and equity between people, communities, and nations. The environmental bottom line refers to conservation and natural environment protection (Carroll & Brown, 2018) and this is what 'sustainability' seems to get related to most, due to the strong use of the term 'sustainability' in environmental studies. Hence, if 'sustainability' is the preferred term for CSR or in addition to CSR – then *environmental* sustainability and *social* sustainability needs to be clearly differentiated. This is because if you are using the term sustainability in a sustainability biased country such as Australia, the mainstream understanding will default to just the 'environmental' aspects of CSR and therefore label CSR as sustainability. CSR, however, allows for a framework where we are able to refer to both *social* and *environmental* simultaneously.

In terms of sustainability being a replacement term for CSR, the often quoted Herman Aguinis, Professor of Organizational Behavior and Management (at the George Washington University School of Business in Washington), adds triple bottom line to his definition of CSR. He does this by defining CSR as "context-specific organizational actions and policies that take into account *stakeholders'* expectations and the triple bottom line of economic, social, and environmental performance" (Aguinis, 2011, p. 855). Aguinis refers to CSR as the key term, and not sustainability as its replacement term.

The reliance on eco-efficiency in sustainability, mentioned earlier, strengthens the argument of why it is difficult to understand how sustainability could replace CSR. Regardless, sustainability has become a mantra for the twenty-first century (Dyllick & Hockerts, 2002). This is understandable given the urgency of climate change, but the term was initially part of CSR rather than a replacement for CSR. In the last half decade, however, these terms are coming together under the umbrella of the United Nations Sustainable Development Goals (UN SDGs) when these SDGs are included in CSR strategy. The UN SDGs are discussed further in Chapter 3.

The 1980s–1990s: CSR Definitions Revisited and Institutionalized

From the 1980s and into the 1990s the discussion regarding the definition of CSR continued to be a main topic in academic literature on CSR.

1980s–1990: CSR Definitions Revisited

In 1991, Carroll revisited his original definition of CSR proposed in 1979: "The social responsibility of business encompasses the economic, legal, ethical, and discretionary expectations that society has of organizations at a given point in time" (Carroll, 1979, p. 500). On revisiting his four-part definition of CSR in 1991, he states "... by this time, I was referring to the discretionary component as philanthropic and suggesting that it embraced "corporate citizenship" (Carroll, 1999, p. 289). Carroll created the "Pyramid of CSR" – taking the four components of this 1979 definition and explaining them in a hierarchical nature. If you picture a pyramid, at the pointed peak of the pyramid was *Philanthropic*

Responsibilities, followed by *Ethical Responsibilities,* at the next level, then *Legal Responsibilities* with *Economic Responsibilities* at the pyramid's base.

The hierarchical nature of the four components is best explained here by Carroll: "The pyramid of CSR depicted the economic category as the base (the foundation upon which all others rest), and then built upward through legal, ethical, and philanthropic categories" (Carroll, 1991, p. 42). Further, with philanthropic being at the top of the pyramid, Carroll explains, "...all of these kinds of responsibilities have always existed to some extent, but it has only been in recent years that ethical and philanthropic functions have taken a significant place" (p. 40).

In 1991, Carroll's original 1979 model and definition of CSP was expanded on by Wood (1991) who created a CSP model that captured CSR concerns. Wood's model was built on past CSP models and included "the principles of CSR, the processes of corporate social responsiveness (including *stakeholder* management), and the outcomes of corporate behaviour" (Schwartz & Carroll, 2008, p. 155).

1990s: The Institutionalization of CSR
In the 1990s, CSR was described as becoming "institutionalized". Companies began to adopt standards such as SA 8000 (a labor standard) and ISO 14001 (an environmental standard). They also increasinly adopted corporate governance codes and guidelines such as the Global Reporting Initiative (GRI). The 1900s also saw the first series of social responsibility codes begin to emerge. As previously mentioned, the Sullivan Principles existed for social responsibility in 1977, followed by SA 8000 in 1997, Charter for Sustainable Development in 1992, and the UNGC in 2000. The UNGC is discussed further in Chapter 3.

The 1990s also saw the development of the 1992 Rio Earth Summit and the development of standards such as ISO 14001 in 1996 (Visser, 2011). By the mid-1990s the 'Triple bottom line' of economic, social, and environmental performance by John Elkington (1994) was followed in the late 1990s by the 1999 UNGC 10 principles. The UNGC principles plus a summary of the UNGC is discussed further in Chapter 3.

Integration of both social responsibility and sustainability reporting also started to happen. The ISO 9001 quality standard (1987) became the design template for ISO 14001 on environmental management (developed in 1996) and OHSAS 18001 on occupational health and safety (first published in 1999) was to be replaced by ISO 45001 (published in March 2018). Previous to this, the GRI (founded in 1997), and the Dow Jones Sustainability Index (launched in 1999) adopted the triple bottom line lens (economic, social, and environmental) and Fair-Trade certification became popular (Visser & Kymal, 2015). These developments highlighted the increasing importance and the practicalities of reporting CSR.

1990s: Corporate Citizenship and Political CSR
Embracing CC in his revamped 1991 definition of CSR, Carroll changed discretionary to philanthropy as part of a more active form of philanthropy. Following this, CC became increasingly popular from the late 1990s into the

early 2000s. Carroll and Brown (2018) state that at this time, CC was used by the business community as a substitute term for CSR for some of the same reasons that sustainability became a popular term. It was thought to provide a simpler, more "palpable" explanation.

As discussed in Chapter 2, a simple definition of CC involved "business taking greater account of its social, environmental and financial footprints" (Zadek, 2001, p. 7), and therefore being a good corporate citizen with a more "social" and human side to it. This also included people relating to individuals as being good corporate citizens, just like a business, and without mention of particular responsibilities or obligations. As mentioned above, Carroll and Brown (2018), likened this to *sustainability*, being simpler with less obligations, and therefore a more neutral term. However, CC with its more human side relates more to the pure definition of CSR than sustainability. Although CC was popular first, sustainability became the more popular term, with the narrow view of CC more akin to "community relations" and community projects. This is discussed further in Chapter 2.

The four faces of CC published by Carroll (1998) included the economic face, the legal face, ethical face, and philanthropic face, which were closely aligned with the CSR definition for Carroll in 1979. Fombrum (1998), around the same time, proposed a broader and more complex CC definition in three parts:

- a reflection of shared *ethical* principles
- a vehicle for *integrating* individuals into the communities in which they work
- a form of enlightened self-interest that balances *all stakeholders'* claims and enhances a company's long-term *value*.

Source: Carroll & Brown (2018).

Other conceptions of the CC definition become even broader as companies increasingly became more global (Scherer & Palazzo, 2007). Carroll and Brown (2018) refer to a more global definition, which existed in the mid-2000s, presented by Wood et al., (2006):

> "A global business citizen is a business enterprise (including its managers) that responsibly exercises its rights and implements its duties to individuals, *stakeholders*, and societies within and across national and cultural borders."

Hence, CC was increasingly referred to both as a "business" and a "person," and this is what makes it appealing to not only businesses and their employees but also the general public, or public citizens, where the business is located.

Political CSR
With the expansion of global business, referred to above, political CSR became increasingly popular (Carroll & Brown, 2018). It is suggested that Political CSR was in fact first introduced by Matten and Moon under the CC framework and

developed by Palazzo and Scherer (Palazzo & Scherer, 2008). Research in political CSR examines corporations as political actors that have social and political responsibilities beyond their legal responsibilities (Carroll & Brown, 2018). Activities associated with political CSR incudes responsible leadership styles, the level of which differs in different political contexts and countries (e.g., Maak, Pless, & Voegtlin, 2016). This level of leadership is becoming increasingly important and is discussed further in Chapter 7.

Other researchers at this earlier time believed that corporations should not act as supervising authorities or take on a policymaking role (e.g., Hussain & Moriarty, 2018).

A detailed focus on this topic is beyond the scope of the current book but is touched on here to give meaning to later discussions on the globalization of CSR by highlighting CSR differences in various countries and regions, and therefore government structures, institutional infrastructures, regulatory requirements, and sociopolitical contexts that exist in different countries. This is discussed further later this chapter (see the *Regional Differences* section, Matten and Moon). This perspective considers that "the changing role of business corporations in society requires that we take new measures to integrate these organizations into society-wide processes of democratic governance" (Palazzo & Scherer, 2008, cited in Hussain and Moriarty, 2018, p. 159). This will indeed be the case as we head to the new decade, 2020 and beyond. Many researchers already see partnerships between CSR and political activity as an enabler for companies to respond to *stakeholders'* concerns and broader societal issues (e.g., Hond, Rehbein, Bakker, & Lankveld, 2014, cited in, Carroll & Brown, 2018). With *Stakeholder Capitalism* as the revised mantra for the 2020 *World Economic Forum*, political CSR provides a renewed research opportunity to look at both sides of the argument for political CSR, to determine if inclusion of political activity provides the best advantage. This also provides an additional research opportunity examining how multinational corporations are involved in patching institutional gaps in the different global business contexts and emerging country settings where they reside.

Late 1990s: The Second Wave

By the early of 2000s, CSR was experiencing a second phase. CSR initiatives in the philanthropy phase of the 1960s and 1970s began to receive criticism for being static and unrelated to context (Beaulieu & Pasquero, 2003). CSR was also increasingly criticized for what now has become a famous phrase, of being merely "bolted on" and not integrated (Grayson & Hodges, 2004; Weaver et al., 1999).

In response a more *strategic* approach emerged (Burke & Logsdon, 1996; Porter & Kramer, 2006; Van de Ven & Jeurissen, 2005), with CSR becoming a way to achieve competitive advantage, by shifting company focus toward CSR activities that were different from competitors but also lowered costs while enhancing customer service (Porter, 1985). This more strategic approach was labeled *Strategic CSR* and, in some cases, *Responsive CSR* (Porter & Kramer, 2006). Visser refers to *Strategic CSR* as CSR activities related to the company's core business alongside CSR codes and implementation of social and environ-mental management systems. CSR became more strategic in that it involved "cycles of CSR policy development, goal and target setting, programme imple-mentation, auditing and reporting" (Visser, 2010, p. 3). Visser (2011) lists the period as "rising from 1977, with the launch of the Global Sullivan Principles, to a peak in 2010, when the ISO 26000 social responsibility standard was launched" (p. 96). *Strategic CSR* is discussed further in Chapter 6.

2000s: The Era of Innovation and Additional Themes

The beginning of the first century of the third millennium (i.e., the twenty-first century from 2001 to 2100) coincided with the transition to Globalization 3.0 around 2000 (Friedman, 2005). This time is often credited with the emergence of a shift in world consciousness. With a changing world came changing CSR prac-tices, and an increasing number of investors became attracted to sustainable and responsible investment opportunities (Mishra, 2017). Innovation and additional themes of CSR began to appear, and definitions of CSR at this time typically involved mention of business and society.

Nine years after Carroll's formal and second definition of CSR in 1999, Dahlsrud (2008) conducted a literature review of CSR definitions by recording a frequency google count and conducting a content analysis to determine five common dimensions across definitions. He found 37 definitions of CSR, from 27 authors over a time span of 1980–2003.

The top five definitions (based on frequency of google counts) and the five dimensions (based on commonality of themes) are shown in Table 1.1.

Of interest to the previous discussion on sustainability, Dahlsrud (2008) found the environmental dimension received a significantly lower ratio than other dimensions. This might be because the environment was not included in earlier definitions (Carroll, 1999), which then may have influenced subsequent definitions. In addition, some organizations like the WBCSD had two definitions, one for CSR and one for corporate environmental responsibility. It would therefore be inter-esting to recreate this study today by examining definitions in future research, from where Dahlsrud (2008) ended his research in 2003 to the present day.

2000s: Regional Differences

With the new era of globalization in the 2000s, regional differences in CSR around the world became apparent. In 2008, Matten and Moon published their landmark paper in the *Academy of Management Review* on the existence of two types of CSR. This also provided a framework to consider CSR in different regions around the world and in particular, developing countries. They defined CSR as:

> "policies and practices of corporations that reflect business responsibility for some of the wider societal good. Yet the precise manifestation and direction of the responsibility lie at the discretion of the corporation" (Matten & Moon, 2008, p. 411).

Table 1.1. The Top Five CSR Definitions and Five Dimensions from 1980 to 2003.

The leading definition: *A concept whereby companies integrate social and environmental concerns in their business operations and in their interaction with their stakeholders on a voluntary basis* (Commission of the European Communities, 2001)	**The fourth definition:** *Business decision making linked to ethical values, compliance with legal requirements and respect for people, communities and the environment* (Business for Social Responsibility, 2000)
The second definition: *Corporate social responsibility is the continuing commitment by business to behave ethically and contribute to economic development while improving the quality of life of the workforce and their families as well as the local community and society at large* (The World Business Council for Sustainable Development, 2000)	**The fifth definition:** *Operating a business in a manner that meets or exceeds the ethical, legal, commercial and public expectations that society has of business. Social responsibility is a guiding principle for every decision made and in every area of a business* (Business for Social Responsibility, 2000)
The third definition: *Corporate social responsibility is essentially a concept whereby companies decide voluntarily to contribute to a better society and a cleaner environment* (Commission of the European Communities, 2001)	**The content analysis found five dimensions reflected in definitions:** 1. Environmental – i.e., natural environment 2. Social – i.e., relationship between business and society 3. Economic – i.e., socioeconomic or financial aspects 4. *Stakeholder* – i.e., *stakeholder* groups 5. Voluntariness – i.e., actions not prescribed by law

Source: Dahlsrud (2008).

The definition by Matten and Moon (2008) for CSR, may also contribute to the regional differences the authors suggest.

Matten and Moon (2008), for example, argue that CSR is more "explicit" in the US and consists of voluntary, self-interest-driven policies, programs, and strategies typical of a US-based understanding of CSR. In contrast, "implicit" CSR of the UK and Europe embraced the country's formal and informal institutions with an agreed-upon share of responsibility (Carroll & Brown, 2018). Further, Matten and Moon (2008) explain that Implicit CSR involves the values, norms, and rules of the local culture. Therefore, CSR is more implicitly *understood and accepted* in Europe because it is part of their governments and cultural institutions, where particular aspects of CSR are imposed. In contrast, in the US (and Australia), CSR was described as being more discretionary, or voluntary, and often in response to pressure from special interest groups or an independent management style.

The above argument becomes extremely helpful when we move the discussion on CSR away from the US, UK, and Western societies to the developing countries. With regards to this, Matten and Moon (2008) suggested that explicit CSR is more often found in liberal market economies, and implicit CSR in coordinated market economies, where collectivism is more evident (Matten & Moon, 2008, p. 411). Previous research has shown that CSR in developing Eastern countries comes from a collective base, and therefore strong identification with CSR as part of the "group" or the organization (Munro, 2017). This is discussed further in Chapter 2.

In the interim, Wayne Visser in 2008 coined the term CSR 2.0 which he later labeled *Systemic CSR* in his Ages and Stages model (Visser, 2011). He considers CSR 2.0 to be the transformation phase of CSR with the commencement of *Systemic CSR* under a new era labeled the Age of Responsibility from 1994. He defined *Systemic CSR* as focusing on:

> "identifying and tackling the root causes of our present unsustainability and irresponsibility, typically through innovating business models, revolutionizing their processes, products and services and lobbying for progressive national and international policies" (Visser 2010, p. 3).

CSR was indeed changing and becoming more innovative. CSR 2.0 and other innovative CSR developments are discussed in more depth in Chapter 6.

2000s: Conscious Capitalism and Political CSR
As mentioned previously, increasing globalization saw a spread of changing concepts around the year 2000. One of these being conscious capitalism, which was thought to be first articulated by John Mackey, cofounder of Whole Foods (Carroll & Brown, 2018). Whole Foods was set-up in 1978, and culminated in his book *Conscious Capitalism* with Professor Raj Sisodia in 2013. Conscious capitalism, described as a way of thinking that was different toward capitalism and business, took into account the human journey and the current state of the world (Conscious Capitalism, Inc, 2018).

Perceived as another emerging form of capitalism, conscious capitalism followers developed a set of principles to guide businesses (Mackey & Sisodia, 2013). These include: a higher purpose, *stakeholder* orientation, conscious leadership, and a conscious culture (Conscious Capitalism, Inc, 2018). This movement maintained a *stakeholder* orientation, while also providing a win-win proposition. It also fosters a "we" rather than "I" culture and "builds trust between a company's team members and its other stakeholders" (Conscious Capitalism, Inc, 2018).

Carroll and Brown (2018) suggest that the many themes of CSR are also part of conscious capitalism and that the same companies that identify with conscious capitalism are the same companies that identify with CSR and the other terms and themes examined in this chapter.

This also suggests the use of the term CSR or any surrogate, alternative, or complementary or competing term – by corporates, managers, or the general public – is based solely on the decision to do so. Rosanas (2013) provides an academic perspective on CSR, conscious capitalism, and *stakeholder theory* with regards to decision-making, and this is discussed in the conclusion of this chapter.

2010s: Social Projects, Shared Value, Integrated Value, and a New Definition for CSR

The emerging area of research for developing and developed countries touched on in the 2000s began to gather momentum and reveal further issues regarding regional differences in the definition and understanding of CSR. During this era a number of industry associations got on board to determine CSR direction and definition. The European Commission (EC), responsible for drawing up proposals for European legislation (and implementing the decisions of the European Parliament), developed what they called a 'new' definition for CSR focusing on the *impacts* on society, as follows:

> "To fully meet their corporate social responsibility, enterprises should have in place a process to integrate social, environmental, ethical, human rights and consumer concerns into their business operations and core strategy in close collaboration with their stakeholders" (European Commission, 2011).

Around this time, *CSR Europe* developed its *Enterprise 2020 Initiative* (CSR Europe). *CSR Europe*, as the leading European business network for CSR, represents over 3,000 companies in Europe. They foster collaborative action and shape the business contribution toward the European Union's *Enterprise 2020* strategy for smart, sustainable, and inclusive growth under the umbrella of CSR (CSR Europe, 2011). Based on the EC's announcement and report in 2011, *CSR Europe* made a statement respecting the EC's global influence on CSR and asked for assistance to review their *Enterprise 2020 Initiative*. This initiative seeks to provide guidelines for companies developing *innovative* business practices within their CSR programs by 2020, while involving *stakeholders* in solutions to emerging societal needs (CSR Europe, 2011).

The reporting of CSR also became more prominent in this era. Reporting of social responsibility evolved into a more holistic concept through the ISO 26000 established in 2010 (Visser & Kymal, 2015). The ISO 26000 details seven core constructs from organizational governance, human rights, and labor practices through to the environment, fair operating practices, consumer issues, and community involvement and development. The GRI, founded in 1997, also launched its first global standards in 2016, highlighting the globalization of CSR.

During this era many additional CSR guidelines, codes, and standards were released, helping to explain the ongoing rigor of measurement and reporting that continues to surround CSR.

2011: Creating Shared Value

About the same time the EC released its new definition of CSR, Porter and Kramer (2011) released their landmark article 'Creating Shared Value' in the *Harvard Business Review*. Creating shared value (CSV) as a concept is discussed in more detail in Chapter 4. However, as part of the discussion for this chapter on overlapping and complementary definitions and related concepts to CSR, CSV is discussed briefly here. The founders that coined the term CSV define it as follows:

> "Policies and operating practices that enhance the competitiveness of a company while simultaneously advancing the economic and social conditions in the communities in which it operates" (Porter & Kramer, 2011, p. 66).

In relation to CSR, Porter and Kramer admit that CSV "overlaps" with CSR, but state CSV is different (Carroll & Brown, 2018; Crane, Palazzo, Spence, & Matten, 2014). They quote CSR as more of a "cost center," focused on *responsibility*, whereas CSV is more about *new opportunities and new markets* – and therefore more of a "profit center" (Porter & Kramer, 2011). One key difference acknowledged therefore between CSR and CSV by its founders is financial. For example, the social project "costs" the company as a social project through CSR but "profits" the company as a social project through CSV. Porter and Kramer also explain a transition in mindset whereby shared value is created when companies treat social problems as business opportunities and then innovate toward addressing these opportunities. This could also be described as a "corporate mentality shift," a change that is possible if commitment comes from the top-down as it has in several companies such as Unilever and Tesla. Authors such as Carroll and Brown (2018) and Crane et al. (2014), for example, suggest that the idea promoted by CSV, such as integrating social issues with "strategic management" is not new. Porter and Kramer, however, state CSV has contributed to a real shift in management thinking (Porter & Kramer, 2011).

Without entering the debate as to whether CSR and CSV refer to the same or different phenomena, or if one is an evolution of the other, both terms are acknowledged here as being beneficial to business and society. Archie Carroll, as previously mentioned in this chapter, and as one of the founders of the first definition of CSR, believes the two concepts share considerable commonality and are therefore overlapping (Carroll & Brown, 2018). Future research would be helpful to determine if this is the case, and to discuss if or where the overlaps exist and how one term can benefit the other. CSV and the CSR versus CSV debate are discussed in more detail in Chapter 4.

2014: Integrated Value Creation

Following CSV in 2011, Visser coined the term integrated value creation (IVC) in 2014 and claims the concept has roots in CSR, CC, business ethics, and corporate sustainability (Visser & Kymal, 2015). Visser proposes that IVC combines many of the ideas and practices already in circulation – like CSR, sustainability, and CSV – but signals important shifts, focused on integration and value creation (Visser & Kymal, 2015).

Much of what is required for IVC to succeed is a change of the current economic system, and accordingly the way we produce and do business. Professor Visser's current definition of IVC is:

> "the simultaneous building of multiple 'non-financial' capitals (notably infrastructural, technological, social, ecological and human capital) through synergistic innovation across the nexus economy (including the resilience, exponential, access, circular and wellbeing economies) that result in net-positive effects, thus making our world more secure, smart, shared, sustainable and satisfying" (Huffpost, 2017c).

IVC is discussed further in Chapter 6.

2015 and beyond: A Topical Focus and the Introduction of the Sustainable Development Goals

First and foremost, 2015 saw the UN SDGs and Global Goals introduced. The Global Goals are discussed further in Chapter 3. In addition, at this time the EC who proposed their 'new' CSR definition in 2011 held their 2015 Multi Stakeholder Forum on CSR. The forum attracted participants from an array of sectors and *stakeholder* groups. This also clarified the merge of responsible business conduct across civil society, governments, and international organizations. Research findings from the forum concluded that CSR is used as a synonym to reference everything from 'sustainability' and "responsible business conduct" to "business and human rights." This is similar to the argument proposed in this book, that the definition of CSR is interchangeable and evolving, rather than dead or becoming extinct. Further, the EC forum found that the drivers of these definitions addressed their key definition of CSR, as mentioned in the previous section.

The research findings from the EC forum also revealed that the differences in CSR definitions and other selected terms must also be acknowledged in order to speak the same language as the business community. By way of example, the sheer variety of topics areas considered as part of CSR at the forum, included: *International Market Access; Education and Human Capital; SMEs; International Development Cooperation; Business and Human Rights; Public Procurement; Innovation, Competitiveness and Growth; Human Rights and Access to Remedies;*

Responsible Investment; Responsible Supply Chains; National and Regional Policies on CSR; and Financial Institutions (ACCA Global, 2015).

A similar broad array of subject areas was discussed at the CSR Asia Summit 2017 that I attended in Bangkok. Similar themes were acknowledged at the CSR Asia Summit 2018 and 2019. The 2017 event, for example, recognized many of the components under the umbrella term for CSR, shown in Table 1.2.

Hence, the *CSR Europe Enterprise 2020* initiative referred to above provides a European example, alongside the global UN SDG target expectation by 2030, meaning all things CSR, innovative, and sustainable are on the move in the decade from 2020 to beyond.

Toward 2020: The Corporate 'Purpose-driven Business'

The corporate 'purpose-driven business' concept is also sometimes considered a competing and complementary term with CSR, by many authors, for example, Kanter (2011), Carroll and Brown (2018), and touched on by Hoffman (2018).

However, others perceive the 'purpose-driven business' as a theme or movement for all organizations to follow, not just corporates through CSR strategy. It is difficult to put a date to the phenomena of purpose or the 'purpose-driven businesses.' 'Purpose' conferences have been held in the business community for a number of years and although a general theme for organizations, 'business for purpose' as the term is now expressed in wider society, is a prominent theme in the social enterprise 'business-for-purpose' trend.

Table 1.2. CSR Asia 2017 Topics.

1. Corporate Social Performance	10. Unlocking Business Value from the Circular Economy
2. Future Proofing Your Business	
3. Making the SDGs Your Business	11. The Marine Plastics Problem
4. From Social Compliance to Factory Improvements	12. The Business Case for Investing in Gender Rights in Supply Chains
5. Eco-Towns and Sustainable Lifestyles of the Future	13. Climate Resilience
	14. Women's Empowerment
6. Unlocking the Value of Corporate Sustainability	15. Children's Rights
	16. Reporting (GRI)
7. Community Investment: Development and Use of Technology	17. Partnering with Social Enterprises for Scalability and Impact, e.g., AVPN, B Corp, Credit Suisse
8. Human Rights Due Diligence and Human Trafficking	
9. Creating Value from *Stakeholder* Engagement	

This trend is also gathering increasing momentum in university curriculums and social projects for millennials and Generation Z (henceforth referred to as millennials). Millennial start-up businesses are mentioned later in this chapter and defined further in Chapter 5.

Academic research such as Hower (2016) refers to the 'purpose-driven business' as a business focused on a societal need while also operating as a profitable enterprise (Carroll & Brown, 2018). Identification of a 'social purpose' is therefore seen as the key difference of a 'purpose-driven business,' in comparison to other enterprises. Beyond this difference, Carroll and Brown (2018) state that the notion of a 'purpose-driven business' doesn't seem to be that different from concepts such as sustainability, shared value, and CC. However, they suggest that with the 'purpose-driven business,' there is a clearer emphasis on "the idea that the enterprise can get behind and be energized by the idea that it has a clearly stated 'purpose' that extends beyond the usual" (p. 54). With regards to CSR, the *CSR Wire*, a largely subscribed Internet site based in the US incorporates topics such as embedding 'purpose' in organizations as a key theme for CSR (CSR Wire, 2018).

In contrast, an academic literature search on *EBSCOhost Business Support Complete* in early 2019 revealed limited academic research literature discussing the 'purpose-driven business.' Just two articles were discovered on a 'purpose-driven business', and these articles only appeared when CSR was added to the search. The first of the articles is Professor Rosabeth Moss Kanter at the Harvard Business School, writing about great or 'purpose-driven' companies, in *American Lawyer* (2011). Kanter refers to great companies as not only generating incomes but also creating frameworks for societal value. The article also mentions Kanter's six facets of institutional logic which include: 'common purpose'; emotional engagement; and innovation; as a way forward – all of which are connected to CSR. The other article found on *EBSCOhost* under the same search headings is a 2014 *Harvard Business Review* article by Christoph Lueneburger. His article suggests 'purpose-driven' initiatives and a company's good deeds and social responsibility can inspire employees and improve business results. He also connects 'purpose' strongly with CSR and found it was supported under a CSR strategy framework.

It is therefore evident that there is a gap in the academic literature examining 'purpose-driven' businesses, suggesting an excellent opportunity for future research on this topic area. This is extremely important given the extent that 'business for purpose' is discussed in the wider business literature, the business community, and in social media at present. A discussion regarding Larry Fink's recent letters to BlackRock investors and the importance of 'purpose' and the relocation of funds for *all stakeholders* is mentioned in the Preface of this book, signaling the current importance of these movement in the wider business community.

In addition, millennials are particularly focused on 'business for purpose' and the setting up of social enterprises which are 'purpose driven' and also part of the 'be the change' movement. This is discussed briefly below and in more detail in Chapter 5.

Be the Change

As mentioned in the introduction to this chapter, 'be the change' is part of the ongoing social revolution or evolution of CSR, rather than the death or extinction of CSR.

If we look at the present and discuss CSR in the context of 'change' – or more commonly termed under the theme 'be the change' – it is as if suddenly we all have a 'purpose' which also relates to 'business-for-purpose.' 'Be the change' and the shift toward every one of us becoming a 'changemaker' is top of mind in current society. This new role has reached developing countries of which I have seen and assessed firsthand, 'changemakers' in emerging markets. Millennials and Generation Z, in particular, are encouraged to be their own changemaker in everything they do in life, but also set-up social projects and social enterprises as their primary employment, for the betterment of society.

This, however, does not replace CSR for companies or corporates, MNEs, or SMEs. Millennials and 'changemakers' may still need a job in a company, corporate, MNE, or SME, or at least need to know how to approach them for funding and/or supporting a social enterprise or innovation under the company's CSR banner. This is discussed further in Chapter 5. Companies, corporates, MNEs, or SMEs are also a part of the 'be the change' movement through their CSR programs, their innovation of products and employees, and their determination to allocate resources to a selection of core or relevant SDGs.

Examples of the 'for-purpose organizations' often gets mixed with the label 'for-benefit organizations.' This leads to a discussion on social entrepreneurialism, corporate entrepreneurialism, and 'for-purpose' and benefit organizations such as the B-Corp. Social entrepreneurialism and corporate entrepreneurialism are discussed in Chapter 5; however, the B-Corp is briefly discussed here in relation to CSR.

The B-corporation and CSR

Related to 'Purpose' and the social enterprise movement is the B-Corp. Some researchers say "the benefit corporation has emerged as a new organizational form dedicated to legitimizing the pursuit of CSR" (Andre, 2012, p. 133). Others describe it as a new legal form for the governance of public corporations (Mickels, 2009). Carroll (2015) provides an interesting slant on social entrepreneurship in the corporate sector using B-Corps as an example. This is covered further in Chapter 4.

B-Corp as a social enterprise is more closely related to CSR than what is often realized. It is recognized that organizations more than ever now are focusing on their commitment to achieving 'social purpose' beyond philanthropy and on reporting their CSR performance and impact as a means of accountability. By way of understanding this further, Gilbert, Houlahan, and Kassoy created B-Lab, as a 501(c)3 nonprofit organization, to develop structures that could be used to build the fourth sector (Wilburn & Wilburn, 2015). The B-Lab they created then formed the B-Corporation certification program in 2007 to recognize corporations that meet established standards for social and environmental performance, accountability, and transparency (Wilburn & Wilburn, 2014). A B-Corp therefore is the organization that has completed the certification process through the nonprofit B-Lab (Wilburn & Wilburn, 2015).

While some see B-Corp as a movement, others view it as just another form of measurement or a certification program as mentioned above, suggesting that B-Lab is just one way to certify a company's CSR achievements. There is also: GRI, the International Standardization Organization (ISO) ISO 2600 (or ISO SR). Wilburn and Wilburn (2015) also list the Underwriters Laboratories (built upon third-party verifiable standards such as UL 880); the Food Alliance and Sustainable Agriculture Network (SAN) provide certifications for sustainable practices; the Food Green Seal Business certification; and 4 Earth, a Sustainability Accounting and Management System framework for products and services (Wilburn & Wilburn, 2014).

In relation to this, researchers see the B-Corp as pursuing CSR missions because they describe their responsibilities and suggest impact for *shareholders*, customers, employees, communities, and the environment. In this respect, the B-Ratings system includes sections on: accountability (governance, transparency); employees (compensation and benefits, job creation, employee ownership); the work environment, consumers (beneficial products and services); community (suppliers, local involvement, diversity, community impact, investor base); charity and service, environment (facilities, energy usage, supply chain, manufacturing inputs and outputs); and beneficial business models (for employees, consumers, community, environment) (Source: B Impact Assessment, 2010).

Hence, some researchers have suggested that instead of taking away from CSR, the benefit corporation is there to enhance CSR and does so by: *providing legal protection to managements that want to both maximize shareholder income and pursue a social or environmental agenda. This form (is) also referred to as the "b-corporation"* (Andre, 2012, p. 133). Wilburn and Wilburn (2015) suggest that for small companies the Certified B Corporation (B-Corp) is an option. GRI is more commonly applied to sustainability reports for large corporations and multinationals (Munro, 2013). Future research needs to determine to what extent the B-Lab measurement and/or the B-Corp certification program has spread to multinationals and larger corporate organizations, replacing current CSR and ESG measures.

Conclusion

Over time, the landscape for CSR has painted a picture of various surrogate, competing, alternative, and complementary terms and branches of themes. By way of concluding this chapter, a discussion of the expectations for 2020 and beyond is acknowledged here.

2020 and Beyond: Toward Social Innovation, the Rise of the Social Enterprise, and a New Phase of Business

Terms such as: 'be the change' at a corporate and social entrepreneurial level, plus the Fortune annual *Change the World* list, reveals many corporations and collaborations are following the direction of 'change' and 'purpose.' Some argue that business schools are slower to catch up on these separate movements. When William Fredrick released his book in 2006 titled *Corporation, be good!: the story of corporate social responsibility*, he questioned the relevance and ethical commitment in business school education and refers to the 'New Millennium' as the hope for improved ethical performance of business in the future.

The business community and university business schools and curriculum, have come a long way since Fredrick's book was published. Many developments have also been made by the United Nations, and corporates have become more operational on these themes. The EC's more evolved definition of CSR in 2011 (discussed previously in this chapter) and the introduction of the SDGs in 2015 have seen a flood of SDG-related material and lingo on to social media and business sites, and across communications materials produced by companies of different sizes, not just large corporates. This has been the case in Western countries primarily, but also Eastern countries have commenced at a courageous pace in some of their industries and especially investment in youth training and youth research, to understand the SDGs and what the future may bring.

As previously mentioned, business schools have picked up on new and alternative themes, and have created environments and youth-learning hubs conducive to the spirit and needs of millennials and Generation Z. As mentioned in Chapter 5 of this book, by 2025, millennials will make up over half of the workforce and they will seek *changes* in society, they will 'be the change' and they will have the power to effect *change*. In addition, the SDGs are expected to be sorted by 2030. An update on the SDGs with current case studies is provided in Chapter 4.

The "New Phase of Business" outlined by Andrew Hoffman in his *Stanford Social Innovation* article (2018) acknowledges this new phase and includes many of the items *CSR Europe* draw attention to with regards to new conceptions for: optimizing supply chains, developing partnerships, collaborations, and new conceptions of government engagement and transparency. He also includes new ways of conceiving business including new conceptions of a corporate's 'purpose' and one's own consumption. He also discusses new business models and metrics, moving away from neoclassical economics and agency theory selfishness and maximization of profit, to Doughnut Economics and shared value as a way of redefining capitalism as conscious capitalism, to serve *all stakeholders* (Hoffman, 2018).

Conscious capitalism and shared value have been discussed already in this chapter and are discussed further in later chapters in this book. Doughnut Economics is referred to as a model of economic growth that links social justice to efforts to stay within the planetary boundaries of the Anthropocene epoch (Hoffman, 2018, p. 38). It is argued here that many academics, business commentators, and global citizens already feel this urgency. The concern for the increase in human deprivation and poverty and the issues surrounding climate change escalation already exists. Increased steps are now being made by governments, corporations, and various collaborations involving many different organizations, entities, and platforms, but much more needs to be done to conceptualize Globalization 4.0.

It would therefore be a weak argument to suggest that contrasting opinions do not exist on the rise and fall of CSR. As in every field there are advocates and non-advocates. In regard to the former, Laudal (2018) recently released an article in the *Social Responsibility Journal* citing an increasing number of firms around the world referring to CSR. He justifies this by the increasing use of global CSR standards and the increase in references related to CSR on the Web. He also cites the number of companies submitting "communications on progress" to the UNGC with growing significance in the past decade (UN Global Compact, 2017), and a similar increase in the number of firms submitting sustainability reports following the GRI template (Laudal, 2018). Further he states that in 2004, four years after the first GRI guidelines were published, 300 submitted a GRI report. In 2014, more than 5,000 (90% of the world's largest 250 corporations) report on their sustainability performance (Laudal, 2018). As a measure of CSR uptake, he also refers to the number of *google* hits to provide a sign that CSR receives an increasing amount of attention, stating a search in 2008 for "corporate social responsibility" gave 170 hits, but in 2014, the number of Google hits was more than two million. In February 2019, I did a similar search and found 730 million hits and 760 million hits in February 2020.

This chapter began with a discussion regarding various surrogate, alternative, complementary, and sometimes competing terms, themes, and frameworks for CSR, many evolving from CSR, and therefore also often overlapping. CSR, CC and sustainability, for example, have each grown in use, but also significantly overlap. Other researchers seem to agree with this, such as Pohl and Tolhurst (2010) where CSR, sustainability, and CC are now seen as essential elements of modern business, synonymous as one, and in one package. CSV, for example, first proposed in 2011 by Kramer and Porter, is also seen as an evolution of CSR in parts, while other researchers say it is more committed to developing projects that have both an economic benefit to the community plus a return of income to the business.

Rosanas (2013) provides an academic perspective on the blurring of the boundaries across CSR, sustainability, conscious capitalism, and *stakeholder theory* verging on aspects of CC, with regards to decision-making. While some say CSR is the predecessor to many terms including CC, Rosanas also suggests interest in CSR has revived in recent years. The merging of CSR, sustainability, and conscious capitalism challenges business leaders "to re-think why their organizations exist." Further, "trust, compassion, collaboration, and value-creation are essential elements of healthy, functioning economies" (Rosanas, 2013, p. 171). Rosanas therefore concludes that CSR, conscious capitalism, and *stakeholder theory* are all pointing in the same direction.

A Final Retrospective

As mentioned in the introduction to this chapter, CSR has followed a cycle of social movements and industrial revolutions through a journey of time. The need for greater innovation and models depicting social entrepreneurialism has evolved out of both the 'be the change' and the 'business-for-purpose' movements, as discussed above. Chapter 5 discusses this further alongside the need for social enterprises to be incorporated under CSR strategy.

As we are usher in the new era of Globalization 4.0, it would be interesting to recreate the research of Dahlsrud (2008) from where he ended examining the terminology for CSR in 2003 and extend this to beyond 2020, to determine how the definition of CSR and sustainability and its social and environmental components have evolved in more recent years. With the 2015 Paris Agreement and current climate change issues, alongside the 2015 UN SDGs, some of the SDG and climate-related terminology will have crept into the evolving extensions of CSR definitions since Dahlsrud's (2008) study. In addition, the new EC definition proposed in 2011 has shifted the emphasis of CSR to innovation, co-creation, and collaboration. This is discussed further in the following chapters of this book.

In summary, today it is "a given" that we take a long-term view for future generations – this being at the forefront of the original sustainability definition. It is also an underlying theme of CSR. This overlap needs to be clarified further in future research to determine if companies have the same or different perception of CSR and sustainability and other related terms, and to also determine whether CSR components and complementary themes are more 'identified' with, within an *environmental* or *social* context. While Friedman's (1970) perspective of creating maximum shareholder value is no longer thought to be a proper (or even a normal) response in current times, this notion is thought to sometimes still dominate corporate thinking and actions (Prafitri, 2017). The strength of this notion needs to be tested and replicated in new research formats. There have been many changes to corporate thinking backed by noticeable actions since Friedman's era, such as the adoption of the UN SDGs – the ongoing work of the UNGC, and the commencement of a new era – Globalization 4.0 – requiring a new ecosystem. As a consequence, we are seeing the development of new terms and conditions for CSR. A focus on *all stakeholders* that make up a company's ecosystem, not just its direct *shareholders,* and the adoption of new themes such as CSV, IVC, and creating transformed value (CTV). These themes are discussed further in the following chapters.

References

ACCA Global. (2015). The European Commission's multi-stakeholder forum on corporate social responsibility. Retrieved from https://www.accaglobal.com/an/en/technical-activities/technical-resources-search/2015/february/ec-forum-on-csr.html

Ackerman, R., & Bauer, R. A. (1976). *Corporate social responsiveness: Modern dilemma.* Reston, VA: Reston Publishing Company.

Aguinis, H. (2011). Organizational responsibility: Doing good and doing well. In S. Zedeck (Ed.), *APA handbook of industrial and organizational psychology* (Vol. 3, pp. 855–879). Washington, DC: American Psychological Association.

Andre, R. (2012). Assessing the accountability of the benefit corporation: Will this new gray sector organization enhance corporate social responsibility? *Journal of Business Ethics, 110*(1), 133–150. doi:10.1007/s10551-012-1254-1

Austin, J., & Reficco, E. (2009). Corporate social entrepreneurship. *International Journal of Not-For-Profit Law, 11*(4), 305.

Bowen, H. R. (1953). *Social responsibilities of the businessman*. New York, NY: Harper & Row.

Brundtland, G. H. (1987). Our common future - report of the world commission on environment and development. Retrieved from http://conspect.nl/pdf/Our_Common_Future-Brundtland-Report_1987.pdf

Carroll, A. B. (1974). Corporate social responsibility: Its managerial impact and implications. *Journal of Business Research, 2*(1), 75–88.

Carroll, A. B. (1979). A three-dimensional conceptual model of corporate performance. *The Academy of Management Review, 4*(4), 497–505.

Carroll, A. B. (1991). The pyramid of corporate social responsibility: Toward the moral management of organizational stakeholders. *Business Horizons, 34*(Generic), 39–48. doi:10.1016/0007-6813(91)90005-G

Carroll, A. B. (1998). The four faces of corporate citizenship. *Business and Society Review, 100*(1), 1–7.

Carroll, A. B. (1999). Corporate social responsibility. *Business & Society, 38*(3), 268–295. doi:10.1177/000765039903800303

Carroll, A. B. (2015). Corporate social responsibility. *Organizational Dynamics, 44*(2), 87–96. doi:10.1016/j.orgdyn.2015.02.002

Carroll, A. B., & Brown, J. A. (2018). Corporate social responsibility: A review of current concepts, research and issues. In J. Weber & D. Wasleleski (Eds.), *Corporate social responsibility* (pp. 39–69). Bingley: Emerald Publishing Co.

Carroll, A. B., & Shabana, K. M. (2010). The business case for corporate social responsibility: A review of concepts, research and practice. *International Journal of Management Review, 12*(1), 85–105. doi:10.1111/j.1468-2370.2009.00275.x

Clarkson, M. E. (1995). A stakeholder framework for analyzing and evaluating corporate social performance. *Academy of Management Review, 20*(1), 92–117.

Conscious Capitalism. (2018). Opportunities. Retrieved from https://www.consciouscapitalism.org/about/opportunities

Crane, A., Palazzo, G., Spence, L. J., & Matten, D. (2014). Contesting the value of "creating shared value". *California Management Review, 56*(2), 130–153. doi:10.1525/cmr.2014.56.2.130

CSR Europe. (2011). New EU definition on CSR mirrors enterprise 2020 aspirations. Retrieved from https://www.csreurope.org/new-eu-definition-csr-mirrors-enterprise-2020-aspirations

CSR Wire. (2018). Program. Retrieved from http://www.3blforum.com/program

Dahlsrud, A. (2008). How corporate social responsibility is defined: An analysis of 37 definitions. *Corporate Social Responsibility and Environmental Management, 15*(1). doi:10.1002/csr.132

Davis, K. (1973). The case for and against business assumption of social responsibilities. *The Academy of Management Journal, 16*(2), 312–322. doi:10.2307/255331

De George, R. (2011). A history of business ethics. Retrieved from https://www. bbvaopenmind.com/en/articles/a-history-of-business-ethics/

DeGeorge, R. T. (1987). The status of business ethics: Past and future. *Journal of Business Ethics, 6*(3), 201–211.

Dyllick, T., & Hockerts, K. (2002). Beyond the business case for corporate sustainability. *Business Strategy and the Environment, 11*(2), 130–141. doi:10.1002/bse.323

Eberstadt, N. N. (1973). What history tells us about corporate responsibility. *Business and Society Review/Innovation, 76*(7), 76–82.

Elkington, J. (1994). Towards the sustainable corporation: Win-win-win business strategies for sustainable development. *California Management Review, 36*(2), 90–100.

Elkington, J. (1997). *Cannibals with forks: The triple bottom line of 21st century business.* Gabriola Island, BC: New Society Publishers.

European Commission. (2011). A renewed EU strategy 2011-14 for corporate social responsibility. Communication from the commission to the European parliament, the council, the European economic and social committee and the committee of the regions. Retrieved from https://eur-lex.europa.eu/legal-content/EN/TXT/?uri= CELEX%3A52011DC0681

Fombrum, C. J. (1998). Three pillars of corporate citizenship. In N. M. Tichy, A. R. McGill, & L. S. Clair (Eds.), *Corporate global citizenship* (pp. 27–61). San Francisco, CA: New Lexington Press.

Frederick, W. C. (1978). From CSR1 to CSR2: The maturing of business-and-society thought. Working Paper No. 279. University of Pittsburgh, Graduate School of Business.

Freeman, R. E. (1984). *Strategic management: A stakeholder approach.* Boston, MA: Pitman.

Freeman, R. E. (2017). The new story of business: Towards a more responsible capitalism. *Journal of the Center for Business Ethics Bentley University, 122*(3), 449–465.

Friedman, M. (1970, September 13). The social responsibility of business is to increase its profits. *The New York Times Magazine, 32–33*, 122–126.

Friedman, T. L. (2005, April 3). It's a flat world, after All. *The New York Times Magazine.* Retrieved from https://www.nytimes.com/2005/04/03/magazine/its-a-flat-world-after-all.html.

Googins, B. K., Mirvis, P. H., & Rochlin, S. A. (2007). *Beyond "good company": Next generation corporate citizenship.* New York, NY: Palgrave Macmillan.

Hipsher, S. A. (2018). *Examining the private sector's role in wealth creation and poverty reduction.* Hershey, PA: IGI Global.

Hoffman, A. J. (2018). The next phase of business sustainability. *Standford Social Innovation Review,* (Spring 2018).

Hond, F. d., Rehbein, K. A., Bakker, F. G. A. d., & Lankveld, H. K. v. (2014). Playing on two chessboards: Reputation effects between corporate social responsibility (CSR) and corporate political activity (CPA). *Journal of Management Studies, 51*(5), 790–813. doi:10.1111/joms.12063

Hower, M. (2016). The rise of the purpose-driven business. *Greel1bil, January 28.* Retrieved from https: //www.green biz.com/article/rise-purpose-driven-business

Hussain, W., & Moriarty, J. (2018). Accountable to whom? Rethinking the role of corporations in political CSR. *Journal of Business Ethics, 149*(3), 519–534. doi: 10.1007/s10551-016-3027-8

Imai, M., Kanero, J., & Masuda, T. (2016). The relation between language, culture, and thought. *Current Opinion in Psychology*, *8*, 70–77. doi:10.1016/j.copsyc. 2015.10.011

Jensen, M. C. (1986). Agency cost of free cash flow, corporate finance, and takeovers. *The American Economic Review*, *76*(2), 323–329.

Joyner , B. E., & Payne, D. (2002). Evolution and implementation: A study values, business ethics, and corporate social responsibility. *Journal of Business Ethics*, *41*(4), 297–311.

Laudal, T. (2018). Measuring shared value in multinational corporations. *Social Responsibility Journal*, *14*(4), 917–933. doi:10.1108/srj-08-2017-0169

Levitt, T. (1958). The dangers of social responsibility. *Harvard Business Review*, *36*(5), 41–50.

Maak, T., Pless, N. M., & Voegtlin, C. (2016). Business statesman or shareholder advocate? CEO responsible leadership styles and the micro-foundations of political CSR. *Journal of Management Studies*, *53*(3), 463–493. doi:10.1111/joms.12195

Mackey, J., & Sisodia, R. (2013). *Conscious capitalism: Liberating the heroic spirit of business*. Cambridge, MA: Harvard Business School Press.

Matten, D., & Moon, J. (2008). "Implicit" and "explicit" CSR: A conceptual framework for a comparative understanding of corporate social responsibility. *Academy of Management Review*, *33*(2), 404–424.

Mickels, A. (2009). Beyond corporate social responsibility: Reconciling the ideals of a for-benefit corporation with director fiduciary duties in the U.S. And Europe. *Hastings International and Comparative Law Review*, *32*(1), 271–304.

Mishra, D. R. (2017). Post-innovation CSR performance and firm value. *Journal of Business Ethics*, *140*(2), 285–306.

Munro, V. (2013). Stakeholder preferences for particular corporate social responsibility (CSR) activities and social initiatives (SIs): CSR initiatives to assist corporate strategy in emerging and frontier markets. *The Journal of Corporate Citizenship*, *51*(September 2013), 72–105.

Munro, V. (2017). *Identification of CSR micro social initiatives within a developed and developing country context. PhD Thesis. Griffith University, Australia.* Retrieved from https://www120.secure.griffith.edu.au/rch/items/5e1def2f-25a0-4c9b-aa72-8c4b8761cb80/1/

Palazzo, G., & Scherer, A. G. (2008). Corporate social responsibility, democracy, and the politicization of the corporation. *Academy of Management Review*, *33*(3), 773–775. doi:10.5465/amr.2008.32465775

Pohl, M., & Tolhurst, N. (Eds.). (2010). *Responsible business: How to manage a CSR strategy successfully*, Hoboken, NJ: John Wiley & Sons.

Porter, M. E. (1985). *Competitive advantage: creating and sustaining superior performance*. New York: The Free Press.

Porter, M. E., Hills, G., Pfitzer, M., Patscheke, S., & Hawkins, E. (2013). Measuring shared value: How to unlock value by linking social and business results Retrieved from http://www.fsg.org/publications/measuring-shared-value

Porter, M. E., & Kramer, M. R. (2006). Strategy and society: The link between competitive advantage and corporate social responsibility. *Harvard Business Review*, *84*(12), 78–92.

Porter, M. E., & Kramer, M. R. (2011). The big idea: Creating shared value. *Harvard Business Review, 89*(1–2), 1–17. http://www.nuovavista.com/Shared ValuePorterHarvardBusinessReview.PDF

Prafitri, R. (2017). Creating shared value (CSV) in East Java, Indonesia: A critical analysis of CSV impacts on dairy farming communities. PhD thesis, Murdock University. Retrieved from http://researchrepository.murdoch.edu.au/id/eprint/42583

Rosanas, J. (2013). *Decision-making in an organizational context: Beyond economic criteria*. Basingstoke: Palgrave MacMillan.

Scherer, A. G., & Palazzo, G. (2007). Toward a political conception of corporate responsibility: Business and society seen from a Habermasian perspective. *Academy of Management Review, 32*(4), 1096–1120. doi:10.2307/20159358

Schwartz, M. S., & Carroll, A. B. (2008). Integrating and unifying competing and complementary frameworks the search for a common core in the business and society field. *Business & Society, 47*(2), 148–186.

Steiner, G. A. (1972). Social policies for business. *California Management Review, 15*(2), 17–24. doi:10.2307/41164414

Tamariz, M., & Kirby, S. (2016). The cultural evolution of language. *Current Opinion in Psychology, 8*, 37–43. doi:10.1016/j.copsyc.2015.09.00

The Economist. (2009). Triple bottom line. Retrieved from https://www.economist.com/news/2009/11/17/triple-bottom-line

The Encyclopedia of Greater Philadelphia. (2013). Sullivan principles. Retrieved from https://philadelphiaencyclopedia.org/archive/sullivan-principles/

UNIDO Eco-efficiency. (2018). What is Eco-efficiency? Retrieved from http://www.ecoefficiency-tr.org/?cat=4

Visser, W. (2010). The age of responsibility: CSR 2.0 and the new DNA of business. *Journal of Business Systems, Governance and Ethics, 5*(3), 7–22.

Visser, W. (2011). *The age of responsibility: CSR 2.0 and the new DNA of business*. London: Wiley.

Visser, W. (2012, May 13). CSR 2.0: Reinventing corporate social responsibility for the 21st century. Management eXchange.

Visser, W. (2017). Integrated value: What it is, what it's not and why it's important. *HuffPost*.

Visser, W., & Kymal, C. (2015). Integrated value creation (IVC): Beyond corporate social responsibility (CSR) and creating shared value (CSV). *Journal of International Business Ethics, 8*(1), 1–14.

Visser, W., Matten, D., Pohl, M., Tolhurst, N., Bohmer, K., Ghebremariam, A. ... Huble, S. S. (2007). *The A to Z of corporate social responsibility: A complete reference guide to concepts, codes and organisations*. Chichester: John Wiley & Sons.

Wartick, S. L., & Cochran, P. L. (1985). The evolution of the corporate social performance model. *Academy of Management Review, 10*(5), 758–769.

Wilburn, K., & Wilburn, R. (2014). The double bottom line: Profit and social benefit. *Business Horizons, 57*(1), 11–20. doi:10.1016/j.bushor.2013.10.001

Wilburn, K., & Wilburn, R. (2015). Evaluating CSR accomplishments of founding certified B Corps. *Journal of Global Responsibility, 6*(2), 262–280.

Wood, D. J. (1991). Corporate social performance revisited. *Academy of Management Review, 16*(4), 691–718.

Zadek, S. (2001). *The civil corporation: The new economy of corporate citizenship*. Sterling, VA: Earthscan.

Case Study Appendix

Corporate Case Study Examples Labeled as 'CSR': by a collection of Associations, Journals, and Business Magazines.
A broad list of companies labeled as practicing CSR is provided by various organizations, publications, and websites. Included here are CSR companies listed by *CSR Hub, Fortune magazine,* the *Hiring Success Journal*, and *Forbes*.

CSR Hub provides Sustainability and CSR ratings for more than 18,500 public and private companies and measures a combination of ESG and CSR ratings and generates consensus ratings across organizations and industries using big data algorithms to provide an overall score. The top 10 listed on their website include:

1. Bain & Company (International Management Consultancy Firm)
2. ABB in India (Multinational operating in robotics, power, heavy electrical equipment and automation technology)
3. McKinsey & Company (International Management Consultancy firm)
4. United Services Automobile Association (Financial services to military community)
5. Clifford Chance LLP (International Law firm)
6. SWECO AB (European Engineering Consultancy)
7. KPMG International (International Accountancy firm)
8. Hogan Lovells US LLP (International Law firm)
9. Engineers India Ltd. (Engineering consultancy and Engineering, Procurement and Construction services across the globe)
10. Baker & McKenzie LLP (International Law firm)

Source: CSR Hub (2018).

As many of these organizations are consultancy service firms, they are not household names to the general public. The Fortune *World's Most Admired Companies* (2018) top 10 list, however, shows a more rounded list of industries which are better known to the general public.

Fortune *World's Most Admired Companies* (2018) top 10 list:

(1) Apple (Computers)
(2) Amazon (Internet Services and Retailing)
(3) Alphabet (Internet Services and Retailing)
(4) Berkshire Hathaway Specialty Insurance (Property Casualty Insurance)
(5) Starbucks (Food Services)
(6) Walt Disney (Entertainment)
(7) Microsoft (Computer Software)
(8) Southwest Airlines (Airlines)
(9) FedEx (Delivery)
(10) JP Morgan Chase (Megabanks)
Source: Fortune (2018).

Most research on the *Fortune* magazine rankings has tended to focus on financial performance; however, recent research by Jeffrey, Rosenberg, and McCabe (2018) has shown that CSR behaviors (measured by MSCI ESG STATS), also affects company's membership on this list. They argue that CSR behaviors are of growing importance as shown by the increasing number of S&P 500 firms that release sustainability reports and the importance of sustainability reporting to younger investors. The *World's Most Admired Companies* (2018) top 10 list is similar to the leading CSR Initiatives list below.

The *Hiring Success Journal* lists what they consider to be the top 20 leading corporates based on each company's CSR Initiatives for 2018:

(1) Marc Jacobs – the fashion label partners with SATO to rescue abandoned dogs
(2) Indigo.ca – provides a platform for educational, athletic, and groups to fundraise
(3) IKEA – supports communities in crises, by building schools and donating/facilitating water access and safe child areas in war zones
(4) Abercrombie & Fitch – teen clothes label launched a partnership with SeriousFun Children's Network, to support community camps and programs for ill children
(5) Equinox – the gym hosts *spin marathons to raise money* for charitable causes
(6) Bosch – through its foundation, focuses on peace, integration, inclusion, and dialogue
(7) LinkedIn – provides economic opportunities for refugees through partnering with governments, nonprofits, and their own users
(8) Ben & Jerry's – their foundation awards more than $1.8 million per year to fund community action, social change, and sustainability initiatives
(9) Starbucks – its foundation started a global literacy campaign
(10) Apple – provided an easy way to follow the elections from a trusted source
(11) Coca-Cola – its foundation donates to causes such as: prioritizing women's empowerment, access to clean drinking water, and the development of disadvantaged youth.
(12) Twitter – uses online communities to help nonprofits and NGOs build audiences for their work
(13) Adidas – hosts running events to turn the public's attention toward the effect of plastic pollution on marine life
(14) Alaska Airlines – customers donate air miles to charitable organizations
(15) Levi's – significantly reduces water use in manufacturing, up to 96% for some styles
(16) GE – its foundation contributes to community educational/health programs, while also matching contributions by employees and retirees
(17) Salesforce – launched a philanthropy cloud to connect corporations, employees, and nonprofits at scale
(18) BMW – focuses on education, wellness, and intercultural understanding, teaching youth basic computer and English skills.

(19) Dell – addresses community challenges, global supply-chain responsibility, hiring diversity, bringing computer knowledge to Ethiopian classrooms
(20) Walt Disney Company – gave more than $400 million to nonprofit organizations (2016) while employees have donated 2.9 million hours (since 2012)

Source: Adapted from *Hiring Success Journal* (2018).

Missing from the 2018 list is: Apple (stated as unwilling to unlock its iPhone to assist law enforcement during a shooting investigation), Samsung (problem with Galaxy combusting and a bribery scandal), and Volkswagen (cheating in emissions testing in 2015) (*Hiring Success Journal*, 2018).

Others missing from the 2018 list, are included below in order of their ranking out of 20 companies (e.g., *ranked 8th or 10th*):

- *Virgin Atlantic's Change (ranked 8th)* – air sustainability initiative: environment, sustainable design and sustainable buying, reduced emissions, and community investment (donates annually to Entrepreneurship Caribbean and raises onboard collection for charity partner)
- *Alphabet (Google) (10th)* – supports initiatives based on innovative use of technology to achieve social goals, e.g., using data to uncover racial injustice; translating books through an open-sourced platform to improve education; and connecting people with jobs to enhance economic mobility worldwide
- *TOMS (14th)* – donates one pair of shoes for every pair purchased, but has since expanded to programs supporting a wide range of services for people in need, investing in jobs, social entrepreneurship, and integration with other charitable organizations
- *Cisco (15th)* – makes use of technology and resources to aid underserved communities with education, healthcare, economic empowerment, and disaster relief
- *Zappos (16th)* – their charity works with charitable organizations to donate goods such as shoes, books, and school supplies to those in need
- *3M (17th)* – gave $67 million funds in 2016 focused on community and the environment, plus educational initiatives that helps boost student interest in science and technology
- *IBM (18th)* – supports education, disaster relief, diversity, economic development, global health, and more. In 2016, The World Community Grid combined the computing power of idle PCs and mobile devices to support projects such as cancer treatment research.
- *Deloitte (19th)* – works on innovative solutions along with government and nonprofit organizations, and encourages its employees to donate time to pro bono work

Source: Adapted from *Hiring Success Journal* (2017).

Some of these companies may have been dropped from the 2018 list as their initiatives are philanthropic, or "static' with related employee volunteering activities, rather than *building innovation in ecosystem solutions to examine grass roots problems.* So, while there are *partnerships and collaborations to solve wicked problems* and global challenges, existing in these CSR examples, some of these initiatives are not scaled up. In addition, some are not targeting the root cause of the problem or collaborating more extensively on the intricate micro and macro layers including government and cross-border partnerships to engage the entire ecosystem.

Of interest, some of the organizations listed above for the top 20 CSR initiatives are also on the *Forbes* (2017) top 10 list, which is an analysis of 170,000 company ratings from respondents in 15 countries, regarding consumers' selection of the most 'socially responsible'. The annual survey compiled by the Reputation Institute (RI), a Boston-based reputation-management consulting firm, examines consumer perception of company governance, positive influence on society, and treatment of employees, scoring each with its proprietary RepTrak Pulse system. In order of scoring for most socially responsible are: Lego, Microsoft, Google, Walt Disney Company, BMW Group, Intel, Bosch, Cisco, Rolls-Royce Aeropsace, Colgate-Palmolive.

Companies on the *Forbes list (2017)* top 10 list, which are different from the *Hiring Success Journal (2017, 2018)* include: Lego, BMW, Intel, Cisco, Rolls-Royce Aeropsace, Colgate-Palmolive. Companies on the *Forbes list (2017)* top 10 list, which are the same as the *Hiring Success Journal (2017, 2018)* include: Walt Disney Company, BMW Group, Bosch. Of note, is the Lego example below.

Lego Case Study: Lego tops the *Forbes list (2017)*

Lego tops the list for CSR reputation for its 'Build the Change' (with children) initiative. Sustainable Materials Center initiatives, and World Wildlife Fund partnership are part of this. In June 2015, the Lego Group established their Sustainable Materials Center, with expectations to employ more than 100 staff to forward their 2030 ambition of using sustainable alternatives in the product's entire lifecycle, including the social conditions where the raw materials are produced. The biggest challenge they face will be to ensure its fossil fuel–based bricks are recycled or replaced with recyclable materials (The Conversation, 2018, March). In March 2018, Lego announced that all its vegetation (leaves, bushes, and trees) will now be made from plant-based plastic sourced from sugarcane (Lego, 2018b. In addition, Lego has three key priority areas:

- Supporting children's rights with UNICEF and also helping to include play into the curriculum
- Embedding the 10 Principles of the United Nations Global Compact (2000)
- Improving energy efficiency in partnership with the World Wildlife Fund to reduce greenhouse gas (GHG) emissions by working with suppliers to identify opportunities to improve the sustainability of products, using fewer materials, increasing recyclability, and decreasing energy

Source: Adapted from Lego (2018a).

Case Study References

CSR Hub. (2018). CSR home page. Retrieved from https://www.csrhub.com/

Hiring Success Journal. (2017). Top 20 corporate social responsibility initiatives of 2017. Retrieved from https://www.smartrecruiters.com/blog/top-20-corporate-social-responsibility-initiatives-for-2017/

Hiring Success Journal. (2018). Top 20 corporate social responsibility initiatives of 2018. Retrieved from https://www.smartrecruiters.com/blog/top-20-corporate-social-responsibility-initiatives-of-2018/

Forbes. (2017). The 10 companies with the best CSR reputations in 2017. *Forbes.* September 13, 2017. Retrieved from https://www.forbes.com/sites/karstenstrauss/2017/09/13/the-10-companies-with-the-best-csr-reputations-in-2017/#28e0d805546b

Fortune. (2018). World most admired companies. September 13, 2017. Retrieved from http://fortune.com/worlds-most-admired-companies/

Jeffrey, S., Rosenberg, S., & McCabe B. (2018). Corporate social responsibility behaviors and corporate reputation. *Social Social Responsibility Journal, 14*(5), 2–15. doi: 10.1108/srj-11-2017-0255

Lego. (2018a). About us. Retrieved from https://www.lego.com/en-us/aboutus/responsibility/our-partnerships

Lego. (2018b). Newsroom. Retrieved from https://www.lego.com/en-us/aboutus/newsroom/2018/march/pfp

The Conversation. (2018). 'Sustainable' Lego: Plastics from plants won't solve a pollution crisis. Retrieved from https://theconversation.com/sustainable-lego-plastics-from-plants-wont-solve-a-pollution-crisis-92953

United Nations Global Compact. (2000). Who we are. Retrieved from https://www.unglobalcompact.org/what-is-gc

Chapter 2

The Emergence of CSR Social Initiatives in a Research Setting

Abstract

As part of discussing future research in the era of change for Globalization 4.0, this chapter examines the traditional academic CSR literature to
determine a gap in current research. An academic literature search
revealed limited literature on actual CSR activities, and more specifically,
Social Initiatives (SIs). It is important to expand on this area of research
as it relates to an evolution of the original CSR definition by Carroll
(1979, 1999). The literature review also revealed limited use of Social
Identity Theory in CSR studies: a theory which provides an excellent
context to give 'purpose' and meaning to a more socially oriented form of
CSR. It also provides a base to understand human 'identification' and
'identity' with CSR activities, in a new era of change. Recent research
reveals the importance of understanding what employees and global citizens as *stakeholders* want, need, identify, and engage with. Following a
literature review, this chapter introduces a new 'Social Initiatives
Framework,' designed to incorporate the many terms and alternative
themes associated with CSR. The chapter concludes with extracts from an
example paper for this area of research, and provides a model to examine
changing *stakeholder* perspectives in global settings. The findings behind
the development of the model is discussed, revealing substantial opportunities for future research. The chapter highlights the development
of CSR SIs to study the sustainable development goals, while also supporting social enterprises to solve wicked challenges and create shared
value (CSV) for both the host community and the company within the
setting where the organization resides.

Introduction

As mentioned in the preface, corporates and businesses have the power to take on
board the 'challenge' of solving wicked systemic issues or problems, through their

CSR for Purpose, Shared Value and Deep Transformation, 53–83
Copyright © 2020 Emerald Publishing Limited
All rights of reproduction in any form reserved
doi:10.1108/978-1-80043-035-820200005

core CSR strategy, and include *all stakeholders* including their employees, supply chain, and host communities. To do so, the Business Roundtable (2019) signed a (new) modern standard for CSR. This acknowledges employees and their communities:

> "CEOs work to generate profits and return value to *shareholders*, but the best-run companies do more. They put the customer first and invest in their employees and communities. In the end, it's the most promising way to build long-term value" (Tricia Griffith, President and CEO of Progressive Corporation, cited in the press release for Business Roundtable, 2019).

To take up the challenge to solve wicked challenges, corporates must also acknowledge their 'social purpose' by inclusion of community-related Social Initiatives (SIs) and social projects as part of CSR strategy. This chapter shows how research can provide a framework to evaluate this methodology. In doing so, this chapter goes beyond the definition debate and evolution of CSR presented in Chapter 1 to examine the development of research associated specifically with CSR activities and SIs.

As discussed in chapter 1, understanding the definition of CSR and its many components constituted much of the early traditional academic research literature for CSR. More recently, a body of CSR literature has emerged that seeks to understand how organizations can best address the *'needs'* of *stakeholders* in society and satisfy their economic self-interest at the same time (Munro, 2017, p. 20). The largest development in CSR literature in the last decade has been the movement away from how do we 'define' CSR and its many related terms to how do we 'conduct' and action CSR (Luo & Bhattacharya, 2006; Margolis, Elfenbein, & Walsh, 2007). A part of conducting CSR is defining and acknowledging CSR strategy and its contents, i.e., the CSR activities that are implemented as part of the strategy (Munro, 2017, p. 20).

As reported previously, the academic research for CSR activities and SIs reveals a number of gaps in the literature, providing numerous research opportunities. Examining the literature in depth provides a setting to develop this research and examine more specifically corporate micro SIs in both an academic and theoretical context and also within the practical setting of the global multinational organization. This chapter commences with a review of the literature examining CSR activities and SIs in multinational corporations and acknowledges their transition from the original definition of CSR (Carroll, 1979, 1999) to a more inclusive and integrated definition.

Academic Research Development

Chapter 1, refers to, the development of CSR having a long history and evolving alongside surrogate and complementary terms and in some cases competing and alternative terms. CSR is therefore accepted as an intertwined definition in a setting which is forever evolving (Munro, 2017). In traditional CSR research literature, the definition of CSR is selected for each research paper and listed to provide clarity of the term and to determine the type of CSR and stage of evolution. This is typically referred to in the introduction or methodology section of CSR research papers and is also referred to in the extracts of the research paper, listed later this chapter.

The focus for this chapter evolved from the original discretionary and social component part of Carroll's (1979, 1999) definition. As shown in Fig. 2.1, Leisinger (2007) later followed a similar format confirming Carroll's definition and placing philanthropic activities at the top of his "corporate pyramid" as the "can" dimension, listing legal and regulatory as the "must" dimension and going beyond "legal norms" as an "ought to" dimension (Munro, 2013a, p. 60). The philanthropic component then developed to go beyond cash donations and cheque signing to include core corporate involvement in underlying activities. This includes the implementation of activities which are socially and community-oriented initiatives and are labeled as SIs (Munro, 2013b). These are shown in the 'Social Initiatives Framework' in Fig. 2.1 as active, nonstatic, and embedded in 'corporate actions,' measurement, and outcomes and also the workplace and marketplace within an overall 'systems outcome' or ecosystem change.

In order to explain this type of research further, it is necessary to outline the development of SIs and their grounding in the academic literature. Following the discretionary components and definition of CSR (Carroll, 1979, 1999), there was a further transition from 'corporate philanthropic activities' to CSI or corporate social involvement (Hess, Rogovsky, & Dunfee, 2002a, 2002b) and CCI as in corporate community investment (Margolis & Walsh, 2003; Munro, 2017). CSI has already been discussed in Chapter 1 and is listed as a 'corporate action' in the 'Social Initiatives Framework' in Fig. 2.1. The term CCI is often used alongside CSR strategy development as part of the community aspects of the discretionary component of the CSR definition (Carroll, 1979 and 1998). As discussed previously, 'corporate philanthropy' evolved into CCI programs to include a number of CSR activities, which at a micro level can be described as SIs (Munro, 2013b). In contrast, corporate community initiatives (CCI) encompasses the overall financial investment in initiatives and CSR activities in the communities where corporates operate (Muthuri, 2007). Chapple and Moon (2005) refer to CCI as the origin of the wider concept of CSR and is a core part of an organization's CSR agenda, especially in developing countries (cited in Munro, 2017, p. 18). CCI is listed as a 'corporate action' in the 'Social Initiatives Framework' in Fig. 2.1.

As discussed in chapter 1, corporate social performance (CSP) refers to "the actions of the organization (usually a for-profit business) and the consequences of those actions on the broader society in which the organization is embedded" (Mahon, 2002, p. 427). In this context, CSR refers to the programs a firm engages in, whereas CPS refers to a *shareholder's* assessment of those programs (Luo & Bhattacharya, 2009; Munro, 2017, p. 17). To summarize this, CSP is listed as a 'corporate measure' in the 'Social Initiatives Framework' in Fig. 2.1.

Corporate citizenship (CC) as discussed in Chapter 1 can also be referred to as CSR. Zappala (2004) refers to CSR and CC, as one or the other, defining both as the understanding and management of an organization's influence on society and all its *stakeholders*. For this reason, empirical research examining CSR often uses CC scales as a measure (e.g., Maignan & Ferrell, 2000a, 2000b), which maps on to CSR scales (e.g., Turker, 2009a). CC strategies also underpin the movement from philanthropy and charity giving to more engaged SIs (or social and community) type activities in the community (Munro, 2017). This relationship is often described as the organization's duty as a corporate citizen. CC is listed as a 'corporate outcome' in the 'Social Initiatives Framework' in Fig. 2.1.

Hence, CC, CSP, and CCI are referred to in the following discussion in relation to these aspects of CSR to provide a setting to understand the literature coverage of CSR activities and SIs. By way of summary, Fig. 2.1, depicting the 'Social Initiatives Framework' referred to, combines these terms and develops them into a framework touched on in the research paper presented later this chapter. The framework is adapted from Munro (2017, p. 19) and has been further developed to include the themes and topic areas covered in the following chapters of this book.

The CSR literature earlier this decade saw a movement toward examining CSI or community social involvement (Hess et al., 2002a, 2002b). This initially involved corporate donations to NGOs and various CSR initiatives, including cause-related marketing and employee volunteerism. Increasingly today, we see support and mentoring of grass roots innovative social and development projects (Lichtenstein, Drumwright, & Braig, 2004; Munro, 2017), related to core business (Munro, 2013a) and a shared value format (Porter & Kramer, 2011). CSI, social projects and shared value projects, all fit as 'corporate actions' in the 'Social Initiatives Framework' in Fig. 2.1.

Previous to this, CCI-based activities were considered to be evolving as long-term strategies for companies (Hess et al., 2002a, 2002b). Examples of CCI include Intel donating computers to schools in developing countries and engaging their staff to train teaches on computer use; Nestlé helping farmers produce better milk cows in northern India; and Coca-Cola provides retail training and jobs to unemployed youth in Brazil (Lichtenstein et al., 2004; Munro, 2017; Porter, Hills, Pfitzer, Patscheke, & Hawkins, 2013, p. 20). These projects also return profit back to the corporates that support them and are also referred to as creating shared value (CSV) projects as discussed in Chapter 4.

A variety of corporates at the higher level now engage in these more integrated types of initiatives (Sen and Bhattacharya 2001). This has evolved further with the introduction of the sustainable development goals (henceforth SDGs) in 2015 (Munro, 2018) and their ongoing implementation. These are listed as SIs (for corporate action) and grouped as SDG categories (for 'corporate outcomes') in the 'Social Initiatives Framework' in Fig. 2.1, alongside solving systemic wicked challenges (also included in Fig. 2.1 and discussed in Chapters 3 and 5, respectively). An overall summary of the framework is discussed overleaf. In the following section, research related to CSR activities and SIs is discussed to further illustrate the context for this framework.

From Definition to Action: Research Focused Social Initiatives and CSR Activities

As previously mentioned, understanding the definition of CSR and its many components constituted much of the early traditional academic research literature on CSR. More recently, a body of academic literature has emerged that seeks to understand how organizations can best address the *'needs'* of *stakeholders* and society and satisfy their economic self-interest at the same time (Munro, 2017, p. 20). As mentioned in the introduction to this chapter, the largest development in the CSR literature in the last decade has been the movement away from how do we 'define' CSR to how do we 'conduct' and action CSR (Luo & Bhattacharya, 2006; Margolis et al., 2007). A part of conducting CSR is defining and determining the CSR strategy and its contents, i.e., the CSR activities that are implemented as part of this strategy (Munro, 2017, p. 20).

As previously mentioned, an *EBSCOhost* search at the time of developing this body of research revealed a scarcity of literature examining CSR activities, related to individual SIs, and *stakeholder* perceptions of these activities and initiatives. An examination of literature related to CSR activities revealed that researchers tend to talk about these activities as a general concept, rather than identifying the 'micro' initiatives (individual social and community activities) within the 'macro' concept of CSR strategy (Bauman & Skitka, 2012; cited in Munro, 2017, p. 21). This is surprising given the majority of Fortune 500 companies not only engage in social responsibility initiatives but also devote considerable resources to reporting them as part of their CSR activities (KPMG, 2011; cited in Munro, 2017).

An additional difficulty throughout the academic literature examining CSR is how to define CSR activities and these types of corporate social causes and activities. While Kotler and Lee's overall definition of CSR is "a commitment to improve community well-being through discretionary business practices and contributions of corporate resources" (2005, p. 3, cited in Munro, 2017, p. 22), their definition of an organization's CSR initiatives is very broad and considered to be *anything* that reflects elements of 'social responsibility,' (where) corporate resources (e.g., money, labor) are allocated to activities intended to improve societal welfare (Munro, 2017). Numerous scholars have listed various definition of CSR activities (e.g., Munro, 2017, p. 22–24), with no conclusive definition, and refer to these activities under general labels and broad categories.

There is also limited research and literature providing a definition of CSR initiatives specifically (i.e., *individual* CSR micro initiatives). There is also to date no standardized list, scale, or questionnaire in the CSR research for micro initiatives within these broad CSR categories (Munro, 2017, p. 24). With limited research available on individual initiatives and a lack of available definitions and scales for individual initiatives, the term SIs was developed:

> "SIs are defined as the micro 'social and community initiatives'
> (and activities) an organization adopts and supports in an ongoing
> and sustainable fashion, and relates to the 'needs' of the society
> and the community surrounding the organization's geographical
> location and market areas" (Munro, 2013b, p. 73).

As explained earlier, these CSR activities and micro SIs arose from the discretionary component of the original CSR definition (Carroll, 1979) and are socially and community oriented. They relate to '*needs*' in society and are depicted in the 'Systems Outcome' box in the 'Social Initiatives Framework' in Fig. 2.1.

The examination of individual SIs fits with the request for micro constructs and CSR frameworks in the academic literature, as requested by Aguinis and Glavas (2012) and Bauman and Skitka (2012). This also assists with the gap in the literature regarding a lack of tools available for testing underlying CSR mechanisms and micro initiatives (Aguinis & Glavas, 2012), such as the lack of a list of SIs in current research literature and/or a rated scale or available questionnaire regarding this type of CSR activity. The extracts from the research paper listed in the next section of this chapter provides a list of actual micro SIs specific to an organization and is therefore a development in the literature, with a list of general (generic) SIs across organizations previously listed in Munro (2013a, 2013b).

A New Framework to Understand CSR Social Initiatives and Corporate Outcomes

The development of this area of CSR literature is illustrated by the 'Social Initiatives Framework' (Fig. 2.1). This includes areas of research mentioned in the previous section of this chapter regarding CC, CCI, corporate social investment (CSI), and SIs.

By way of summary, this framework depicts the evolution of CSR SIs and subsequent changes in a flow diagram with a series of boxes describing corporate 'corporate actions'; 'corporate measurement'; and 'corporate outcomes'; culminating in a 'systems outcome'. This framework was especially designed for this area of CSR research and is adapted to provide a new framework for inclusion in this book.

In doing so, the 'Social Initiatives Framework' in Fig. 2.1 portrays an important development of one of the discretionary (i.e., Philanthropic) components of CSR, identified by Carroll (1979, 1999), as shown in the first level of the framework under CSR components. The addition to the SIs area of research includes the potential to examine SIs supporting social enterprises; SIs as shared value or integrated value projects; SIs related to SDGs (as 'corporate actions'); Social Impact Assessment of SIs (as 'corporate measurement'); transforming micro SIs to become macro social projects, and SIs solving systemic wicked problems and challenges (as 'corporate outcomes'). These are shown in the second level of the framework (Fig. 2.1). This leads to global corporations assisting local host communities in the developing countries where they reside and it is part of the creation of shared value (CSV) or an integrated value creation (IVC) or creating a transformed value system (CTV), as part of a new ecosystem (and 'systems outcome'), as shown in the third layer of the framework. These developments are highlighted (**) in the second and third layers of the 'Social Initiatives Framework' (Fig. 2.1).

As shown in the 'Social Initiatives Framework,' the new 'systems outcome' for creating a shared (CSV) or integrated value creation (IVC) or creating a transformed value system (CTV) as part of a new ecosystem, for Globalization 4.0, is

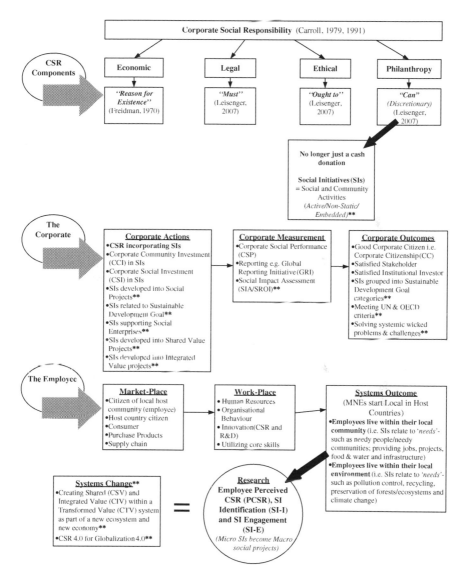

Fig. 2.1.   The 'Social Initiatives Framework' (*Source:* Adapted from
Munro, 2017**, embargoed till 2021).

discussed further in Chapter 6. The 'Social Initiatives Framework,' is also listed in
this chapter to specifically understand better the potential areas for research on
CSR SIs. The extracts from the research paper in the following sections will touch
on earlier forms of SIs and provide examples of how the area of SI research can be
developed further.

Research Inclusion of Employee Perspectives of CSR Social Initiatives

Beyond the literature focusing on CSR definitions, and a lack of research focusing on CSR activities and SIs, the literature review revealed a third understudied area regarding employee perceptions of CSR. The academic research literature confirms and notes on a number of occasions the importance in understanding *stakeholder* and in particular employee perceptions of CSR initiatives (e.g., Bhattacharya, Korschun, & Sen, 2009; Klein & Dawar, 2004; Lichtenstein et al., 2004; Munro, 2013a). However, it is also documented that there is limited research on understanding the underlying factors, which lead to this assessment (Aguinis & Glavas, 2012; Munro, 2017). While it is important for *stakeholders* to be aware of CSR initiatives (Sen, Bhattacharya, & Korschun, 2006), the literature refers to awareness and familiarity with CSR initiatives as low among stakeholders (e.g., Sen et al., 2006). Further evidence of this is provided in the extract below:

> Despite the lack of research at this level, studies in the past have provided support for the benefits that CSR initiatives provide companies, particularly in terms of enhanced consumer perceptions of the organization (e.g., Brown & Dacin, 1997; Drumwright, 1996; Sen & Bhattacharya, 2001). There is also evidence that employee-organization type relationships are also enhanced through CSR activities and initiatives. This can happen through employee identification with the organization whereby there is an overlap in the employee's self-concept (i.e., compassion, or caring for a community project), but more detailed research is needed (Lichtenstein et al., 2004) (cited in Munro, 2017, p. 21).

With the current social and environmental turmoil witnessed around the globe, organizations are increasingly concerned about how their actions affect environmental and social welfare (Bode, Singh, & Rogan, 2015; Sprinkle & Maines, 2010). In response, corporations need to be extremely knowledgeable of *stakeholder* (and in particular employee) perspectives and levels of understanding. Based on the results from the Edelman Trust Barometer (2019), the evidence indeed shows trust has moved to employers to do what is right, creating an even bigger responsibility to do this through the corporate perspective:

> "... people have shifted their trust to the relationships within their control, most notably their employers. Globally, 75 percent of people trust "my employer" to do what is right, significantly more than NGOs (57 percent), business (56 percent) and media (47 percent)" Edelman (2019).

These results also signify an excellent time for employers to select CSR initiatives and strategy which are aligned with employee understanding of CSR and employee identification and preferences for CSR SIs with regard to saving the planet environmentally and socially and to incorporate social 'purpose-for-business,' as discussed in Chapter 1. The Edelman (2019) results suggest it is more vital than ever, that corporates, companies, and organizations make the perspectives and knowledge of their employees a priority, especially the multinational companies, where employees are often 80%–99% citizens of the host of developing or developed country where the company resides (Munro, 2017). Understanding and acknowledging their employees' perspectives will therefore assist in future embedded trust.

An interesting survey by Gartenberg, Prat, and Serafeim (2018) examined over 500,000 employee perceptions of their employers and found that companies showing both high levels of *purpose* and clarity had systematically higher future accounting and stock market performance. They also found that this perception was driven by middle management and professional staff rather than senior executives or hourly commissioned workers. They concluded that companies with mid-level employees who had strong beliefs in the 'purpose' of their organization and clarity in the path toward that 'purpose,' experience better performance (Gartenberg et al., 2018).

To provide an example of research in this area, extracts from a developing paper are provided in the next section. The paper examines employee perspectives of micro SIs in multinational corporations (MNCs) through a Social Identity Theory (SIT) lens. In doing so, this paper provides a model suitable for adoption in future research. From a theoretical sense, SIT is not often used in the International Business (IB) literature or CSR literature setting (Munro, 2017). This therefore provides an excellent backdrop for both fields of literature and a unique opportunity to explore this body of research. In addition, SIT helps further unpackaging of the social side of CSR, which is relevant to the future direction CSR research needs to take.

Extracts from a Paper: A Proposal for Future Social Initiatives Research

As mentioned directly above, this section provides an example research paper, which is a development of a conference proceedings paper (e.g., Munro, Arli, & Rundle-Thiele, 2016), examining employee perspectives in relation to CSR SIs, and makes suggestions for future research aligned to the development of research in this field. The paper extracts presented here provide an opportunity for readers of this book to further this research. Presenting this paper also allows for illustration of SIT use in CSR research and International Business (IB) studies. A glossary of terms for this area of research can be found in Table 2.1 (Appendix).

The example paper abstract with extracts included here, provides an examination of an alternative model to the original theoretical model reported in Munro et al. (2016). This allows us to examine the mediating effect of employee identification with Social Initiatives (SI-I) in two multinational law firm subsidiaries. As Munro et al. (2016) found a difference in identification of SIs between countries for the original precursors in the model, the current paper

**The Mediation Effect of Social Initiatives Identification
Incorporating Social Identity Theory in US-based
Multinational Law Firms**
Munro, V., Arli, D., and Rundle-Thiele S.

Abstract: CSR has been found to vary in definition, meaning, and importance across employees and citizens from different countries (Munro, 2013a, 2013b), and different national systems for levels of identification with CSR Social Initiatives (SIs) and activities (Munro et al., 2016). Much of the research and resulting academic literature on CSR has been predominately conducted in Western settings with limited research comparing national systems of host countries where multinational corporations (MNCs) subsidiaries are based. Social Identity Theory (SIT) provides a lens in which to examine this and understand identification within national systems and across 'corporate outcomes'. As MNCs typically take with them their CSR strategy from head office, when expanding into foreign countries, and host environments, they also typically employ 80 to 99% local citizens (Munro, 2017) from that host country. It is therefore important that these settings are understood. The first part of this study investigates this by examining a theoretical model for a US headquartered MNC (Munro et al., 2016). Structural Equation Modeling revealed significant differences between Indonesian Law firm employees and their Australian counterparts for how they perceive their organization's CSR (PCSR), plus the importance that organizations practice CSR generally (ICSR) and their identification with the organizations Social Initiatives (SI-I), relative to their engagement in these initiatives (SI-E). The current paper provides an alternative model to the previous theoretical model in Munro et al. (2016), by examining SI identification as a mediator between perceived CSR and engagement in CSR activities (or SIs) to determine the significance of this across employees in one multinational law firm in two different countries, societies and social settings.*

adds the mediation model shown as Fig. 2.2 (in the Paper Appendix). The additional two hypotheses related to this model are listed overleaf. Please refer to Munro et al. (2016) for a discussion regarding the original model and a definition of its constructs. Unique to these research papers is use of the 'actual' SIs of the organization (rather than a generic list). These are included in the survey and employees are asked which of the SIs they identify and engage with.

As identification of SIs is core to the model for this paper, SIT is discussed in the following paper extract:

Social identity theory proposes that identity salience leads to behaviors consistent with identity and appropriate norms (Tajfel & Turner, 1986) and is based on the premise that the individual has knowledge that "he (or she) belongs to certain social groups" and experiences "emotional and value significance" relative to this group membership (Munro et al., 2016; Tajfel, 1978). Hence, if an employee is proud of being a member of a socially responsible organization, his or her work attitudes are also influenced positively (Ashforth & Mael, 1989; Brammer, Millington, & Rayton, 2007; Maignan & Ferrell, 2001; Munro et al., 2016; Peterson, 2004; Turker, 2009b). Mowday, Porter, and Steers (1982), in particular claim that work attitudes are a significant aspect of organizational commitment and the psychological identification that an individual feel toward his or her employing organization. Under this framework it could also be assumed that not only work attitudes but attitudes to extra-curricular work activities will be entertained and enhanced by employees becoming more engaged in extra-work activities such as CSR social and community activities. These are identified as SIs in the current study. The extent of this identification and SI engagement may therefore differ depending on country context and level of country development (Azmat & Zutshi, 2012; Matten & Moon 2008; Munro & Arli, 2019; Visser, 2008). This approach and the use of Social Identity Theory is relatively new to the International Business Literature and the CSR literature (Adapted from Munro, 2017).

To examine the mediating effect of identification with SIs, i.e., Social Initiatives-Identification (SI-I), for employees in two multinational law firm subsidiaries, SI-I is removed from the model to determine its impact. The research paper discussed here includes two new hypotheses not previously discussed in the Munro et al. (2016) paper.

The two hypotheses proposed for the current paper are:

- *Hypothesis 4 (H4): SI Identification (SI-I) will have a mediating effect between Perceived CSR (PCSR) and SI Engagement (SI-E) for law firm employees of the developed country (1) Australia but will have no mediating effect for the law firm employees of the developing country (2) Indonesia*
- *Hypothesis 5 (H5): SI Identification (SI-I) will have a mediating effect between the Importance of CSR (ICSR) and SI Engagement (SI-E) for the law firm employees of the developed country (1) Australia and will have no mediating effect for the law firm employees of the developing country (2) Indonesia*

The codes and questions, sample collection, and methodology are discussed in more depth in Munro et al. (2016), alongside the literature examining the precursors for CSR. The precursors and constructs, however, are listed briefly here as how they perceive their organization's CSR (PCSR), the importance that organizations practice CSR generally (ICSR) and their identification with the organizations SIs (SI-I), relative to their engagement in these SIs (SI-E). Table 2.1 in the Appendix provides further clarification of these definitions. In addition, the definition of CSR provided to respondents to refer to while completing the survey is also included in Table 2.1.

As previously mentioned, the survey sent to respondents, also lists the micro SIs for each organization, for respondents to refer to when answering questions in the survey regarding the organization's micro SIs. An example of these specific to both law firms include: *Mentoring high school students at risk of disengaging from school/learning; Program to assist with literacy and reading in school students in remote areas; Program to provide training workshops for university students and firm mentoring; Employee/Firm donation to natural disasters.*

The analysis and results for the first model are discussed in Munro et al. (2016), including the demographic analysis, reliability and validity of measures, precursors of CSR, identification of SIs and engagement in Sis, and the model fit. The analysis for the current paper is shown in Appendix B, of this chapter, and the results are shown in Tables 2.2 and 2.3, in Appendix C of this chapter. An extract from the results section of the current paper summarizes the findings briefly as follows:

The results from the mediation effect of SI Identification suggest that it is important for Indonesian law firm employees to identify with their SIs in order for perception of their own organization's CSR to effect their engagement in these SI activities. In contrast, for Australian law firm employees, identifying with SIs mediates the effect between how important it is that organizations practice CSR in general and engagement in their SIs. We would therefore reject hypothesis 4 for Indonesia as there is a mediating effect for Indonesia as a developing country and we would also reject hypothesis 4 for Australia as there is no mediating effect for Australia as the developed country. In contrast we would accept hypothesis 5 for Australia as there is a mediating effect between ICSR and SI-E for the developed country, and we would accept hypothesis 5 for Indonesia as there is no mediating effect of SI-I between ICSR and SI-E, as the developing country. We however support the overall premise of this paper that there are differences for the mediating effect of SI-I between the developed (Australia) and developing country (Indonesia).

To understand the results of this paper, it is important to understand individualistic and collective societies and in-group and out-group comparisons. The in-group and out-group phenomena of SIT, for example, allow one to identify with the in-group and reject the out-group and position individuals against other members of society and other social groupings (Munro, 2017). An aspect of the SIT in-group out-group phenomena is reflected in belonging to different groups, for example, different *country groups*. The in-group out-group phenomena also allows us to understand the individualism and collectivism dimension as a key construct of *country context* (Aguinis & Henle, 2003; Hofstede, 2001; House, Javidan, Hanges, & Dorfman, 2002; Schwartz, 1994; Søndergraad, 1994; cited in; Munro, 2017, p. 37).

The extract below provides an example of this for *country context*:

> *As part of the definition, for collectivism, the collectivist nation, culture, or country does not separate the individual from his or her respective groups. The perception of the self is blurred, intertwined, and interdependent with that of the other in-group members (Ma, Huang, & Shenkar, 2011). Individualist societies, in comparison, are thought to cherish the individual and his or her aspirations. These societies are thought to celebrate his or her uniqueness, free will, and nondeterminism and legitimize his or her search for recognition and advancement.*
>
> *Hence, a key difference between nationalities, cultures, and countries is how individuals define and understand their relationship with others. Individuals participate with in-group members to project a higher degree of trust and are under moral and social pressures to act in the interest of the group (Triandis, Robert, Marcelo, Masaaki & Lucca, 1988). Where the interests of the in-group reign supreme, individuals are expected to subsume their own interests to that of the group (Triandis, 1995). In contrast 'individualist' based societies are given autonomous and independent self-perception and are therefore less concerned with their group membership (Triandis et al., 1988). While individualist societies may also differentiate between in-group and out-group members, the differences and impact are mitigated by strong emphasis on the self and respect for self-interests (Chen & Miller, 2010).*
>
> *As a result, Triandis (1972) suggests individual understanding of who is in the in-group may vary across countries and cultures. In 'collectivist' societies, for example, the in-group is defined as 'family and friends and other people concerned with my welfare' (Triandis et al., 1988, p. 326). The in-group for this research would therefore be the family members and community members of the employee (as internal stakeholder). Based on strong connections, individuals are more likely to be treated and perceived as in-group members and more strongly identify with the in-group. (Adapted from Munro, 2017, p. 38).*

The paper proposes that these strong connections will therefore differ in different countries and cultures:

> *If we take Indonesia, for example, this country is traditionally referred to as a collectivist society (Jetten, Postmes, & McAuliffe, 2002; Leung, 2008; Markus & Kitayama, 1991; Triandis et al., 1988; Wei, Egri, & Yeh-Yun, 2014) whereby 'collectivism' is "a situation in which people belong to in-groups, which look after them in exchange for loyalty," and 'individualism' is "a situation in which people look after themselves and their immediate family only" (Hofstede & Bond, 1984, p 419). This relates well to the "I" and "we" of Social Identity Theory relative to in-groups (Ma et al., 2011), with Indonesia from a collective society (identifying with the group) versus Australia, for example, which is a country from an individualistic society (identifying with the individual). (Adapted from Munro, 2017).*

An extract from the findings of this work supports a SIT framework as follows:

> *The fact that Indonesian law firm employees in comparison to Australian law firm employees need to know that their own organization's PCSR is good in order to identify in the micro SI activities of their organization and be engaged in them, supporting a SIT framework. This suggests that Indonesian employees need to know their overall key group (their organization) has good PCSR in order to identify with the in-group which is the micro Social Initiatives (SIs) relating to their families and community. Under a SIT framework, they therefore identify with the in-group for SIs, which is the 'needy' group in society as illustrated by their selection of SIs. Indonesia's strong historical and cultural history, Javanese values, and following Islamic principle also lean them more toward the need to identity with the dominate group or in-group as does the collectivist nature of Indonesian society. This study confirms that within an 'Identification framework,' country context must be taken into account where and when an MNC sets up business in foreign lands. An MNC must acknowledge that a "one-size-fits-all" CSR systems based on Western codes and regulations should not necessarily be implemented in the East or in developing countries (Munro, 2013a, 2013b; Munro et al., 2016; Peters, Miller, & Kusyk, 2011; Adapted from Munro, 2017).*

Future research should examine the following:

(1) *Future research should examine further the employee's preference for particular SI activities in different local communities and settings.*

(2) *Future research should consider the examination of employee perspectives in each country where the law firm is based. Future research should also compare and contrast more than one international Law firm in the region.*

(3) *There is also an opportunity to develop SIT further in this paper by measuring the collective, individualistic, and in-group individual character trait of each individual employee in a multilevel analysis rather than a macro group analysis.*

(4) *With the introduction of the SDG framework by the United Nations in 2015, future research should examine corporate activities and SIs within an SDG context (Munro & Arli, 2019). A further element for future research, however, is to systematically analyze the grouped SIs or microactivities in a cross-category SDG analysis.*

(5) *Future research should also examine SIs and social projects within a shared value context as discussed in Chapter 4. Porter and Kramer (2011) define 'creating shared value' (CSV) as:*

...policies and operating practices that enhance the competitiveness of a company while simultaneously advancing the economic and social conditions in the communities in which it operates. CSV also focuses on identifying and expanding the connections between societal and economic progress (p. 6).

Point 5 above, is not only consistent with the movement toward examining CCI or 'community involvement and investment' (Hess et al., 2002a, 2002b) in CSR strategy, but includes making a profit in return from the Social Initiative (SIs) or social projects. This research could therefore be replicated utilizing the same model as this study but examining identification with the organization's CSV initiatives instead of the organization's micro Social Initiative (SIs).

Note: Extracts from this paper have been adapted from parts of Munro (2017). The 'theoretical model' mentioned in the extracts of this research paper is derived from Munro et al. (2016). The 'alterative model,' which is a development of this, is shown in the Appendix of this chapter, at Fig. 2.2. PCSR and SI-E are also referenced in a different model for Munro and Arli (2019), across different sectors and countries, and a second model with different constructs is explored in Munro, Arli and Rundle-Thiele (2018). A glossary of terms can be found in Table 2.1 (Appendix) and are expanded and adapted from Munro (2017) to assist understanding of the current model for this paper, alongside the Munro (2017) adapted 'Social Initiatives Framework' mentioned earlier this chapter.

The ideas for future research listed here are elaborated further in the conclusion of this chapter. Points 4 and 5 above are discussed further in Chapters 3 and 4, respectively.

Introspective: A Summary of the Example Research Paper

Extracts from the example paper in this chapter provide a base in which to examine employee perspectives from a multinational corporation (MNC) and international law firm.

The research paper example presented here, is a good start toward examining employee perspectives of CSR and CSR SIs, but much more needs to be considered in terms of understanding MNC collaborations with governments, NGOs, entrepreneurial start-ups, development banks, and private funding partnerships, across sectors, borders, and countries. Emphasizing MNC strategists and employees as potential 'changemakers' or intrapreneurs will make a real difference to the universal transition toward the SDG uptake by 2030 (Munro, 2018), as discussed in Chapter 3. There is also a need to study actual social projects beyond micro SIs and to study social projects such as CSV projects and creating integrated value (CIV) projects and measure their overall impact in the countries where MNCs operate.

Future research should therefore examine SIs and social projects as CSV projects and IVC projects. IVC projects are discussed further in Chapter 6. The primary focus of Chapter 4 is CSV, which provides case study examples of organizations utilizing CSV initiatives. In particular, the academic research by Prafitri's (2017), discussed in Chapter 4, is based on a case study for Nestlé in Java (Indonesia) and suggests that the CSV initiatives should *"not be a one size fits all"* strategy for all situations and countries. This has also been suggested in past research for CSR Initiatives (e.g., by Munro, 2013a, 2013b). The findings from Prafitri (2017) suggest Nestlé's CSV initiatives (designed and approved by Nestlé Global and implemented by Nestlé in several countries), may need to be adapted to each country setting. Future research should therefore test if the same CSV projects (like the CSR SIs in the current paper) can be replicated in different countries. The current research paper in this chapter touches on this by examining different CSR initiatives across at least two countries for one multinational corporation (MNC). The current model could easily be adapted to assess CSV case study examples across multiple countries and organizations. This presents an emerging opportunity for future research.

An additional emerging opportunity from this research is to measure the *social impact* of these initiatives in larger-scale macro SIs and social projects. Future research using the model outlined above should therefore combine all these measures to determine both internal and external *impact* directly in relation to targeted SIs and social projects.

With the development of the SDG framework in 2015, future research should examine the SIs in this study within an SDG context. As previously mentioned, the SIs can be grouped into one or more of the 17 SDG categories proposed by the United Nations (Munro & Arli, 2019). The SIs could then be compared and analysed across each SDG category. The following chapter, Chapter 3, provides a review of the SDGs and their categories. In the current example paper, the organizations 'actual' SIs are listed in the survey. This allows employees to identify with them and confirm identification directly with their organization's SIs and therefore their direct engagement in these SIs. A further research development would be to examine different stakeholder preferences for particular SDG categories (e.g. SDG 1: End Poverty versus SDG 4: Quality Education).

Although the organization's micro SIs in the current research paper refer to wicked problem and challenges (henceforth wicked challenges) such as poverty and hunger, they are not necessarily co-creating or actively collaborating to solve these issues as required for macro social projects. Future research needs to examine SIs or larger social issues in terms of wicked challenges and explain how large corporates, MNCs, and SMEs can assist in solving the problem at a deeper level under the umbrella of their CSR or shared value program. As mentioned earlier, the third layer of research suggested in the Social Initiatives Framework (figure 2.1), in relation to CSV, CIV and CTV social projects, could also explain the *social impact*, highlighting the *impact* for wider beneficiaries and how this impact could be improved.

In summary, the example paper presented here, provides a foundation toward filling some of the research gaps in current literature. The context of different regions and countries needs to be further considered, utilizing SIT. Although religious beliefs are touched on in this paper, an individual employee's *Altruistic* belief (e.g., Clary & Clark, 1991; Ellen, Webb, & Mohr, 2006; Graff Zivin & Small, 2005) should also be considered in this context. Knowledge of an employee or stakeholder's Altruistic nature as an additional construct in this model is an emerging research opportunity and would assist corporates in making better managerial decision for particular *stakeholders*.

By examining the perception and importance of CSR, plus identification of SIs, the employees are identifying with the 'good' CSR of the company and therefore also the 'purpose' of the company, if it is related to the organization's core business. Hence, the model for this paper provides an opportunity to add a *purpose measure* to this body of literature, as Gartenberg et al. (2018) suggest in the introductory sections of this chapter. This should be given priority in future research utilizing the current model.

Chapter Conclusion

The Need to Develop CSR Social Initiatives Research

According to Beaulieu and Pasquero (2002), CSR initiatives have been criticized for being static and not giving sufficient attention to their context. In addition, CSR initiatives have also been increasingly criticized for not being integrated into company strategy and operations and therefore looking as though they are bolted on (Grayson & Hodges, 2004; Preuss, 2011; Weaver, Trevino, & Cochran, 1999) instead of a core and integral part of CSR. This chapter proposes the examination of less static SIs that are more integral to core business and in addition be mapped on to the SDGs. More developed SIs, referred to as social projects, need to be studied alongside CSV projects and are an emerging research opportunity in current academic literature.

As discussed in the Chapter 5, various social enterprise initiatives can also be supported and adapted as a SIs or social projects within CSR strategy. From a theoretical perspective which utilizes SIT, it would also be interesting to see if these innovative social enterprises as corporate SIs and social projects can become interwoven into the everyday activities of the company. If so, do they become a part of the company's identity as Berger, Cunningham, and Drumwright (2007) suggest? Do they do so more than the philanthropic static CSR initiatives of the past? As a result of this, do employees identify more with these types of SIs? These research questions are an emerging opportunity for future research utilizing the current model.

In summary, the SIs examples provided in this research paper are micro initiatives, pitched at the local level and by a single company. These initiatives need to 'scale up' to have greater *impact* in society and be integral to the organization's function and 'purpose.' The model and methodology utilized in this paper could easily be adapted to examine interconnected social projects at a macro level. The micro SIs incorporated in this paper could therefore be developed into larger macro social projects or CSV projects utilizing the same model. This would allow measurement of the *social impact* of each of these macros SIs and social projects and make possible the interpretation of actual uptake and therefore *impact* of these projects in different countries.

Scaling up CSR micro SIs to fix complex wicked challenges within a poorly functioning supply chain or a systemic system already in place, requires reaching out at a higher level and a more inclusive level, while also co-creating and collaborating with partners to achieve additional funding. This means companies need to become more inclusive in this process, calling for a more 'Inclusive CSR' approach, so SIs and social projects can scale up and include a CSV delivery. An innovative collaborative component is required to do this, while creating a more 'Innovative CSR.' This is discussed further in the following chapters of this book.

If we single out co-creation as a vehicle for 'change,' as defined by Ramaswamy (2009) in Chapter 5, there is much more to examine with regard to employee identification connected to co-creation. If identification of SIs enhances engagement of SIs, as the results of the model reported in Munro (2017) suggests, identification of such would also enhance co-creation and therefore collaboration of everything from SDGs to implementing of social projects. The study of co-creation within the research model presented in this chapter, is therefore an emerging opportunity for future research.

To conclude, it is evident from this body of academic research examining MNCs and a corporate's micro SIs under the umbrella of the CSR framework, that the importance of designing and implementing SIs related to community 'needs' in the host country, town, or city where the MNC resides is of utmost importance. Further research should examine larger macro social projects as an extension of the MNC's SIs.

Future research should also examine this model based on these 'needs' and with a 'business-for-purpose' theme, by including a *purpose measure* as previously mentioned. This research could also therefore incorporate the 'be the change' movement mentioned in Chapter 1, by incorporating SIs and social projects central to tackling wicked challenges. CSR strategy, utilizing entrepreneurial employees throughout their entire supply chain, is increasingly important as we usher in Globalization 4.0.

Corporates are expected to take up this challenge. The Prince of Wales at the *Corporate Leaders Group on Climate Change Conference* in 2010 made an example of this:

> "The challenge that I would like to lay before every single member of the Corporate Leaders Group on Climate Change is simple. Will you stand up and be counted? At every opportunity will you confront the sceptics and tell them they are wrong? Will you challenge your in-house economists with the urgent need to define a new paradigm – in other words a macroeconomics for sustainability? Will you use the power of your brands and the power of your communications and, most of all, your marketing teams to support what the science tells us, and if necessary be prepared to take risks with your reputation to ensure you are on the right side of the debate? If you don't pick up this challenge and inspire many others, particularly those in your supply chains, then I fear the battle will be lost." (The Prince of Wales, 2010, also cited in Visser, 2011).

At the most recent *World Economic Forum* (2020), his message is still relevant and represents even more so, the increasing public sentiment toward corporates taking on board one of the most wicked of all problems: climate change.

Overall, the current research model presented in this chapter provides a method to implement and test SIs which can accommodate larger social projects and environmental wicked challenges. This research example here suggests many gaps in the literature to provide new opportunities to measure 'purpose' within the current research model. The inclusion of SIT in this research area also allows us to unpack the social identity side of CSR and examine the facts within an overall national, individualistic, or collective system (with a 'systems outcome') as part of a new framework. The CSR 'Social Initiatives Framework' as shown in Fig. 2.1 provides a framework to develop this research area further. In addition, the inclusion of the SIs analyzed across SDG category groups is a unique research opportunity. The next chapter covers the SDGs to assist with understanding this methodology. The 'Social Initiatives Framework' shown in

Fig. 2.1 and the current research model can assist with building 'identification' and 'engagement' in SIs, with a more integrated and transformed system for 'systems change' in the new era for Globalization 4.0. These topics are developed further in the following chapters of this book.

Chapter Appendix

Table 2.1. Glossary of Terms.

Construct	Source/Author(s)	Definition
Corporate Social Responsibility (CSR)	World Business Council for Sustainable Development (2000)	CSR is the continuing commitment by business to behave ethically and contribute to economic development while improving the quality of life of the workforce and their families, as well as the local community and society at large.
Social Identity Theory	Tajfel (1978)	The individual's knowledge that he/she belongs to certain social groups together with some emotional and value significance to him/her of this group membership.
Sustainable Development	Brundtland Report (Brundtland Commission, 1987)	Sustainable development is development that meets the needs of the present without compromising the ability of future generations to meet their own needs.
Integrated Value Creation (IVC)	Visser (2014)	Integrated value is the simultaneous building of multiple capitals (notably financial, infrastructural, technological, human, social, and ecological) through synergistic innovation across the

Table 2.1. *(Continued)*

Construct	Source/Author(s)	Definition
		resilience, exponential, access, circular, and well-being economies that result in a world that is more secure, smart, shared, sustainable, and satisfying.
Creating Shared Value (CSV)	Porter and Kramer (2011)	The policies and operating practices that enhance the competitiveness of a company while simultaneously advancing the economic and social conditions in the communities in which it operates. Shared value creation (therefore) focuses on identifying and expanding the connection between societal and economic progress.
Social Initiatives (SIs)	Munro (2013b)	Defined here as micro *social and community activities* and grouped into SIs related to the environment, employment/training, needy people/community, volunteer staff, health, local, and global.
Organizational Identification (OI)	Ashforth and Mael (1989)	A specific form of social identification and the perception of oneness with or belongingness to the organization.
Social Initiatives Identification (SI-I)	(Munro, 2017)	A specific form of social identification and the perception of oneness with or belongingness to the organization's *social and community activities*.

Table 2.1. *(Continued)*

Construct	Source/Author(s)	Definition
Perceived CSR (PCSR)	Waddock (2004)	Waddock (2004) singles out 'perception' as a key component: "The perception *stakeholders* hold of an organization impacts on an organization's strategies and operating practices as well as the well-being of all its key *stakeholders* including the natural environment" (p. 10). Glavas and Godwin (2013) claim to have developed the term perceived CSR (PCSR) relevant to employees, as a way forward in the organizational identification literature. They use Waddock's (2004) CSR definition above to define their definition of PCSR.
Importance of CSR (ICSR)	Korschun, Bhattacharya, and Swain (2014)	How 'important' employees think CSR is for organizations to practice. The current research model utilizes the 'importance' scale as the Korschun et al. (2014) study, which was first implemented by Vogel (2005).
Job Engagement	Bakker, Hakanen, Demerouti, and Xanthopoulou (2007)	A positive, fulfilling work-related state of mind that is characterized by vigor, dedication, and absorption.
Social Initiatives Engagement (SI-E)	(Munro, 2017)	A positive, fulfilling *social and community activities* related state of mind that is characterized by vigor, dedication, and absorption.

Source: Adapted from Munro, 2017, embargoed till 2021.

References

Aguinis, H., & Glavas, A. (2012). What we know and don't know about corporate social responsibility: A review and research agenda. *Journal of Management, 38*(4), 932–968.

Ashforth, B. E., & Mael, F. (1989). Social identity theory and the organization. Academy of management. *Academy of Management Review, 14*(1), 20.

Bakker, A. B., Hakanen, J. J., Demerouti, E., & Xanthopoulou, D. (2007). Job resources boost work engagement, particularly when job demands are high. *Journal of Educational Psychology, 99*(2), 274.

Bauman, C. W., & Skitka, L. J. (2012). Corporate social responsibility as a source of employee satisfaction. *Research in Organizational Behavior, 32*, 63–86.

Beaulieu, S., & Pasquero, J. (2002). Reintroducing stakeholder dynamics in stakeholder thinking: A negotiated-order perspective. In B. Husted, J. Andriof, S. S. Rahman, & S. Waddock (Eds.), *Unfolding stakeholder thinking: Theory, responsibility and engagement* (pp. 101–118). Sheffield: Greenleaf Publishing.

Berger, I. E., Cunningham, P. H., & Drumwright, M. E. (2007). Mainstreaming corporate social responsibility: Developing markets for virtue. *California Management Review, 49*(4), 132–157.

Bhattacharya, C. B., Korschun, D., & Sen, S. (2009). Strengthening stakeholder company relationships through mutually beneficial corporate social responsibility initiatives. *Journal of Business Ethics, 85*(S2), 257–272. doi:10.1007/s10551-008-9730-3

Bode, C., Singh, J., & Rogan, M. (2015). Corporate social initiatives and employee retention. *Organization Science, 26*(6), 1702–1720. doi:10.1287/orsc.2015.1006

Brown, T. J., & Dacin, P. A. (1997). The company and the product: Corporate associations and consumer product responses. *Journal of Marketing, 61*(1), 68–84. doi:10.2307/1252190

Brundtland Commission. (1987). *Our common fFuture - Report of the world commission on environment and development.* Retrieved from http://conspect.nl/pdf/Our_Common_Future-Brundtland-Report_1987.pdf

Business Roundtable. (2019). Business roundtable redefines the purpose of a corporation to Promote 'an economy that serves all Americans'. Retrieved from https://www.businessroundtable.org/business-roundtable-redefines-the-purpose-of-a-corporation-to-promote-an-economy-that-serves-all-americans

Carroll, A. B. (1979). A three-dimensional conceptual model of corporate performance. *Academy of Management Review, 4*(4), 497–505. doi:10.2307/257850

Carroll, A. B. (1991). The pyramid of corporate social responsibility: Toward the moral management of organizational stakeholders. *Business Horizons, 34*(Generic), 39–48. doi:10.1016/0007-6813(91)90005-G

Carroll, A. B. (1998). The four faces of corporate citizenship. *Business and Society Review, 100*(1), 1–7.

Carroll, A. B. (1999). Corporate social responsibility. *Business & society, 38*(3), 268–295. doi:10.1177/000765039903800303

Chapple, W., & Moon, J. (2005). Corporate social responsibility (CSR) in asia: A seven-country study of CSR web site reporting. *Business & Society, 44*(4), 415–441. doi:10.1177/0007650305281658

Chen, M.-J., & Miller, D. (2010). West meets east: Toward an ambicultural approach to management. *Academy of Management Perspectives, 24*(4), 17–24. doi:10.5465/AMP.2010.24.4.3651479.a

Clary, E. G., & Clark, M. S. (1991). A functional analysis of altruism and prosocial behavior: The case of volunteerism. In M. S. Clark (Ed.), *Review of personality and social psychology* (Vol. 12, pp. 119–148). Newbury Park, CA: SAGE Publications.

Drumwright, M. E. (1996). Company Advertising with a social dimension: The role of noneconomic criteria. *Journal of Marketing, 60*(4), 71–87.

Edelman. (2019). 2019 edelman trust barometer. Retrieved from https://www.edelman.com/trust-barometer

Ellen, P. S., Webb, D. ., J., & Mohr, L. A. (2006). Building corporate associations: Consumer attributions for corporate socially responsible programs. *Journal of the Academy of Marketing Science, 34*(2), 147–157. doi:10.1177/0092070305284976

Friedman, M. (1970, September 13). *The social responsibility of business is to increase its profits.* The New York Times Magazine.

Gartenberg, C., Prat, A., & Serafeim, G. (2018). Corporate purpose and financial performance. Harvard Business School Working Paper, No. 17-023, September, 2016, 1–40

Glavas, A., & Godwin, L. N. (2013). Is the perception of "goodness" good enough?: Exploring the relationship between perceived corporate social responsibility and employee organizational identification. *Journal of Business Ethics, 114*(1), 15–27. doi:10.1007/s10551-012-1323-5

Graff Zivin, J., & Small, A. (2005). A modigliani-miller theory of altruistic corporate social responsibility. *B.E. Journal of Economic Analysis and Policy: Topics in Economic Analysis and Policy, 5*(1), 1–19. Retrieved from http://www.bepress.com/bejeap/topics/

Grayson, D., & Hodges, A. (2004). *Corporate social opportunity! Seven steps to make corporate social responsibility work for your business.* Sheffield: Greenleaf Publishing.

Hess, D., Rogovsky, N., & Dunfee, T. W. (2002). The next wave of corporate community involvement: Corporate social initiatives. *California Management Review, 44*(2), 110–125.

Klein, J., & Dawar, N. (2004). Corporate social responsibility and consumers' attributions and brand evaluations in a product–harm crisis. *International Journal of Research in Marketing, 21*(3), 203–217. doi:10.1016/j.ijresmar.2003.12.00.

Korschun, D., Bhattacharya, C. B., & Swain, S. D. (2014). Corporate social responsibility, customer orientation, and the job performance of frontline employees. *Journal of Marketing, 78*(3), 20–37.

Kotler, P., & Lee, N. (2005). *Corporate social responsibility: Doing the most good for your company and your cause.* Hoboken, NJ: John Wiley & Sons.

KPMG (2011). Reporting at record levels worldwide. *Business and the Environment, 22*(12), 6–7.

Leisinger, K. M. (2007). Corporate philanthropy: The "top of the pyramid". *Business and Society Review, 112*(3), 315–342. doi:10.1111/j.1467-8594.2007.00299.x

Lichtenstein, D. R., Drumwright, M. E., & Braig, B. M. (2004). The effect of corporate social responsibility on consumer donations to corporate-supported nonprofits. *Journal of Marketing, 68*(4), 16–32. doi:10.1509/jmkg.68.4.16.42726

Luo, X., & Bhattacharya, C. B. (2006). Corporate social responsibility, customer satisfaction, and market value. *Journal of Marketing, 70*(4), 1–18. doi:10.1509/jmkg.70.4.1

Luo, X., & Bhattacharya, C. B. (2009). The debate over doing good: Corporate social performance, strategic marketing levers, and firm-idiosyncratic risk. *Journal of Marketing, 73*(6), 198–213. doi:10.2307/20619069

Mahon, J. F. (2002). Corporate reputation: A research agenda using strategy and stakeholder literature. *Business & Society, 41*(4), 415–445.

Maignan, I., & Ferrell, O. C. (2000). Measuring corporate citizenship in two countries: The case of the United States and France. *Journal of Business Ethics, 23*(3), 283–297. doi:10.1023/A:1006262325211

Maignan, I., & Ferrell, O. C. (2001). Antecedents and benefits of corporate citizenship: an investigation of French businesses. *Journal of Business Research, 51*(1), 37–51. doi:10.1016/S0148-2963(99)00042-9

Margolis, J. D., & Walsh, J. P. (2003). Misery loves companies: Rethinking social initiatives by business. *Administrative Science Quarterly, 48*(2), 268. doi:10.2307/3556659

Margolis, J. D., Elfenbein, H. A., & Walsh, J. P. (2007). *Does it pay to be good? A meta-analysis and redirection of research on the relationship between corporate social and financial performance*. Working Paper. Harvard University.

Matten, D., & Moon, J. (2008). "Implicit" and "explicit" CSR: A conceptual framework for a comparative understanding of corporate social responsibility. *Academy of Management Review, 33*(2), 404–424.

Munro, V., & Arli, D. (2019). Corporate sustainable actions through United Nations sustainable development goals: The internal customer's response. *International Journal of Nonprofit and Voluntary Sector Marketing, 24(4)*, 1–15.

Munro, V. (2013a). Stakeholder understanding of corporate social responsibility (CSR) in emerging markets with a focus on Middle East, Africa (MEA) and Asia. *Journal of Global Policy and Governance, 2*(1), 59–77. doi:10.1007/s40320-013-0026-3

Munro, V. (2017). *Identification of CSR micro social initiatives within a developed and developing country context*. PhD Thesis, Griffith University. Retrieved from https://www120.secure.griffith.edu.au/rch/items/5e1def2f-25a0-4c9b-aa72-8c4b8761cb80/1/

Munro, V. (2018). Changing the boundaries of expectations: MNE uptake of universal principles and global goals. In S. A. Hipsher (Ed.), *Examining the private sector's role in wealth creation and poverty reduction*. Hershey, PA: IGI Global.

Munro, V., & Arli, D. (2019). Corporate sustainable actions through UN sustainable development goals: The internal customer's response. *International Journal of Nonprofit and Voluntary Sector Marketing, 24*(4), 1–15.

Munro, V., Arli, D., & Rundle-Thiele, S. (2018). CSR engagement and values in a pre-emerging and emerging country context. *International Journal of Emerging Markets, 13*(5), 1251–1272. doi:10.1108/IJoEM-04-2018-0163

Muthuri, J. N. (2007). Corporate citizenship and sustainable community development. *Journal of Corporate Citizenship, 2007*(28), 73–84. doi:10.9774/GLEAF.4700.2007.wi.00008

Porter, M. E., & Kramer, M. R. (2011). Creating shared value. *Harvard Business Review*, *89*(1/2), 62–77.

Porter, M. E., Hills, G., Pfitzer, M., Patscheke, S., & Hawkins, E. (2013). *Measuring shared value: How to unlock value by linking social and business results* (pp. 1–20): Boston, MA: FSG.

Prafitri, R. (2017). *Creating shared value (CSV) in East Java, Indonesia: A critical analysis of CSV impacts on dairy farming communities*. PhD Thesis, Murdoch University, Perth. Retrieved from http://researchrepository.murdoch.edu.au/id/eprint/42583

Preuss, L. (2011). Innovative CSR: A framework for anchoring corporate social responsibility in the innovation literature. *The Journal of Corporate Citizenship*, *42*(Summer 2011), 17–33.

Ramaswamy, V. (2009). Co-creation of value—Towards an expanded paradigm of value creation. *Marketing Review St*, *26*(6), 11–17.

Sen, S., & Bhattacharya, C. B. (2001). Does doing good always lead to doing better? Consumer reactions to corporate social responsibility. *Journal of Marketing Research*, *38*(2), 225–243. doi:10.2307/1558626

Sen, S., Bhattacharya, C. B., & Korschun, D. (2006). The role of corporate social responsibility in strengthening multiple stakeholder relationships: A field experiment. *Journal of the Academy of Marketing Science*, *34*(2), 158–166. doi:10.1177/0092070305284978

Sprinkle, G. B., & Maines, L. A. (2010). The benefits and costs of corporate social responsibility. *Business Horizons*, *53*(5), 445–453. doi:10.1016/j.bushor.2010.05.006

The Prince of Wales. (2010). A speech by HRH the Prince of Wales to the "deal or No deal" corporate Leaders group on climate change conference. Retrieved from https://www.princeofwales.gov.uk/speech/speech-hrh-prince-wales-deal-or-no-deal-corporate-leaders-group-climate-change-conference

Triandis, H. C., Robert, B., Marcelo, J. V., Masaaki, A., & Lucca, N. (1988). Individualism and collectivism. *Journal of Personality and Social Psychology*, *54*(2), 323–338. doi:10.1037/0022-3514.54.2.323

Turker, D. (2009a). Measuring corporate social responsibility: A scale development study. *Journal of Business Ethics*, *85*(4), 411–427. doi:10.1007/s10551-008-9780-6.

Turker, D. (2009b). How corporate social responsibility influences organizational commitment. *Journal of Business Ethics*, *89*(2), 189–204. doi:10.2307/40295049

Visser, W. (2008). Corporate social responsibility in developing countries. In A. Crane, D. Matten, A. McWilliams, J. Moon, & D. Siegel (Eds.), *The Oxford handbook of corporate social responsibility* (pp. 473–479). Oxford: Oxford Handbooks Online.

Visser, W. (2011). *The age of responsibility: CSR 2.0 and the new DNA of business.* London: Wiley.

Visser, W. (2014). *CSR 2.0: Transforming corporate sustainability and responsibility.* New York, NY: Springer.

Waddock, S. (2004). Parallel universes: Companies, academics, and the progress of corporate citizenship. *Business and Society Review*, *109*(1), 5–42. doi:10.1111/j.0045-3609.2004.00002.x

Weaver, G. R., Trevino, L. K., & Cochran, P. L. (1999). Integrated and decoupled corporate social performance: Management commitments, external pressures, and corporate ethics practices. *Academy of Management Journal, 42*(5), 539–552. doi: 10.2307/256975

World Business Council for Sustainable Development. (2000). Geneva. Retrieved from https://www.wbcsd.org

Zappala, G. (2004). Corporate citizenship and human resource management: A new tool or a missed opportunity? *Asia Pacific Journal of Human Resources, 42*(2), 185–201. doi:10.1177/1038411104045362

Paper Appendix

Paper Appendix A

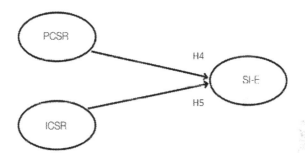

Fig. 2.2.   Alternative Model—Direct Path from PCSR and ICSR to SI-E for Employees from Multinational Law Firms.

Appendix B: Research Paper Analysis and Results

The analysis and results for the mediating effect of SI identification for the research paper discussed in this chapter is included below as an extract from the current paper:

Analysis: For the Alternative Model

> *To examine the mediating effect of SI-I, the three-step analysis recommended by Hair et al. (2010) was adopted. A correlation analysis was first used to examine the relationships between PCSR, ICSR, SI-I, and SI-E. The direct*

(Continued)

effects for all variables were significant at p <0.05, except for PCSR → SI-I when SI-E is the dependent variable (and SI-I is the mediator) for Australia (p =0.07). To further examine the mediating effect of SI-I, an alternative model was created for analysis (Lee & Lee, (2015)). The alternative model contains only the f = direct path from PCSR and ICSR to SI-E, shown in Fig. 2.2 in Appendix A.

As shown in Table 2.2 in Appendix C, when a direct path is created in the 'alternative' model from the precursors to SI-E, PCSR still does not have an effect on SI-E for Australia; however, ICSR now does not have a significant effect on SI-E for Indonesian employees. According to Hair et al. (2010), this proves the mediating effect of SI-I. A bootstrapping method was then used to check for mediating effects (Hayes, 2009). Simulation research has shown that bootstrapping is one of the more valid and powerful methods for testing intervening variable effects (MacKinnon, Lockwood, & Williams, 2004; Williams & MacKinnon, 2008) and for this reason should be the preferred method of choice over other methods (Hayes, (2009)). Bootstrapping in AMOS found that the p-values of the indirect effects of PCSR are significant for Indonesia and that the indirect effects for ICSR are not significant for Indonesia at 0.11. In contrast the indirect effects of PCSR are not significant for Australia at 0.40 but the indirect effects for ICSR are significant, confirming the different mediating effect of SI-I across variables and countries. Based on this we would accept the p-values that SI-I has a mediating effect between PCSR and SI-E for Indonesia but not for ICSR and SI-E for Indonesia. We would also accept the p-values that SI-I does not have a mediating effect with PCSR and SI-E for Australia but does for ICSR and SI-E for Australia.

As the lower an upper range does not include zero, for PCSR → SI-E for Indonesia there is a mediation effect, but not for Australia. However, there is a mediating effect between ICSR → SI-E for Australia but not for Indonesia, as the range includes zero. Based on the reported bootstrapping, we would accept the p-values that SI-I has a mediating effect between PCSR and SI-E for Indonesia but does not have a mediating effect between ICSR and SI-E for Indonesia. We would also accept the p-values that SI-I does not have a mediating effect between PCSR and SI-E for Australia but does have a mediating effect between ICSR and SI-E for Australia. Please see Table 2.2 and Table 2.3 in Appendix C.

Paper Appendix C

Table 2.2. SEM Results for the Alternative Model – of Indonesia (IND) and Australia (AUST) Employees from Multinational Law Firms.

Path	Standardized Estimate		CR		*p*	
	IND	AUST	IND	AUST	IND	AUST
PCSR→ SI-E	0.08	0.10	5.71	−0.85	***	0.40NS
ICSR → SI-E	0.17	0.12	1.60	5.28	0.11NS	***

**p <0.05 ***, p <0.001, CR = critical ratio, NS = not significant.
Variable pathways listed above: Perceived CSR (PCSR) → Social Initiatives Identification (SI-I), Importance of CSR (ICSR) → Social Initiatives Identification (SI-I), SI-Identification (SI-I) → Social Initiatives Engagement (SI-E).

Table 2.3. Bootstrapping Results of the Alternative Model—for Indonesia (IND) and Australia (AUST) Employees from Multinational Law Firms.

Pathway	Indonesian Employees					Australian Employees				
	R	*p*	SE	Lower	Upper	R	*P*	SE	Lower	Upper
PCSR → SI-E	0.46	0.001	0.09	**0.30**	**0.65**	−0.08	0.001	0.14	−0.36	0.18
ICSR → SI-E	0.27	0.071	0.19	−0.03	0.71	0.62	0.071	0.12	**0.36**	**0.85**

p <0.05**, *p* <0.001***, SE = standard error, *R* = coefficient.
NB: The **boldfaced** elements represent a significant bootstrapped individual indirect effect because 0 does not occur within the lower and upper limit of the 95% confidence interval.

Paper References

Aguinis, H., & Henle, C. A. (2003). The search for universals in cross-cultural organizational behavior. In J. Greenberg (Ed.), *Organizational behavior: A management challenge* (2nd ed., pp. 373–411). Mahwah, NJ: Lawrence Erlbaum Associates.
Ashforth, B. E., & Mael, F. (1989). Social identity theory and the organization. *Academy of Management Review, 14*(1), 20.
Azmat, F., & Zutshi, A. (2012). Influence of home-country culture and regulatory environment on corporate social responsibility perceptions: The case of Sri Lankan immigrant entrepreneurs. *Thunderbird International Business Review, 54*(1), 15-27.

Brammer, S., Millington, A., & Rayton, B. (2007). The contribution of corporate social responsibility to organizational commitment. *International Journal of Human Resource Management, 18*(10), 1701–1719.

Hair, J. F., Black, W. C., Babin, B. J., & Anderson, R. E. (2010). *Multivariate data analysis: A global perspective.* Upper Saddle River, NJ: Pearson.

Hayes, A. F. (2009). Beyond Baron and Kenny: Statistical mediation analysis in the new millennium. *Communication Monographs, 76*(4), 408–420. doi:10.1080/03637750903310360

Hess, D., Rogovsky, N., & Dunfee, T. W. (2002b). The next wave of corporate community involvement: Corporate social initiatives. *California Management Review, 44*(2), 110–125.

Hofstede, G. H. (2001). *Culture's consequences: Comparing values, behaviors, institutions, and organizations across nations* (Vol. 2). Thousand Oaks, CA: SAGE Publications

Hofstede, G., & Bond, M. H. (1984). Hofstede's culture dimensions: An independent validation using Rokeach's value survey. *Journal of Cross-Cultural Psychology, 15*(4), 417–433. doi:10.1177/0022002184015004003

House, R., Javidan, M., Hanges, P., & Dorfman, P. (2002). Understanding cultures and implicit leadership theories across the globe: An introduction to project GLOBE. *Journal of World Business, 37*(1), 3–10. doi:10.1016/S1090-9516(01)00069-4

Jetten, J., Postmes, T., & McAuliffe, B. J. (2002). 'We're all individuals': Group norms of individualism and collectivism, levels of identification and identity threat. *European Journal of Social Psychology, 32*(2), 189–207. doi:10.1002/ejsp.65

Lee, J., & Lee, Y. (2015). The interactions of CSR, self-congruity and purchase intention among Chinese consumers. *Australasian Marketing Journal (AMJ), 23*(1), 19–26. doi:10.1016/j.ausmj.2015.01.003

Leung, A. S. M. (2008). Matching ethical work climate to in-role and extra-role behaviors in a collectivist work setting. *Journal of Business Ethics, 79*(1/2), 43–55. doi:10.1007/s10551-007-9392-6

Ma, R., Huang, Y.-C., & Shenkar, O. (2011). Social networks and opportunity recognition: A cultural comparison between Taiwan and the United States. *Strategic Management Journal, 32*(11), 1183–1205. doi:10.1002/smj.933

Maignan, I., & Ferrell, O. C. (2000). Measuring corporate citizenship in two countries: The case of the United States and France. *Journal of Business Ethics, 23*(3), 283–297.

MacKinnon, D. P., Lockwood, C. M., & Williams, J. (2004). Confidence limits for the indirect effect: Distribution of the product and resampling methods. *Multivariate Behavioral Research, 39*(1), 99–128.

Markus, H. R., & Kitayama, S. (1991). Culture and the self: Implications for cognition, emotion, and motivation. *Psychological Review, 98*(2), 224–253. doi:10.1037/0033-295X.98.2.224

Matten, D., & Moon, J. (2008). "Implicit" and "explicit" CSR: A conceptual framework for a comparative understanding of corporate social responsibility. *Academy of Management Review, 33*(2), 404–424.

Mowday, R. T., Porter, L. W., & Steers, R. M. (1982). *Employee-organization linkages: The psychology of commitment, absenteeism, and turnover.* New York, NY: Academic Press.

Munro, V. (2013b). Stakeholder understanding of corporate social responsibility (CSR) in emerging markets with a focus on Middle East, Africa (MEA) and Asia. *Journal of Global Policy and Governance, 2*(1), 59–77.

Munro, V., Arli, D., & Rundle-Thiele, S. (2016). CSR strategy at a crossroads: An example of a multinational corporation in a developing and developed society. In *Proceedings of the international association for business and society 27th annual meeting, Utah, USA.*

Munro, V. (2017). *Identification of CSR micro social initiatives within a developed and developing country context.* PhD thesis, Griffith University. Retrieved from https://www120.secure.griffith.edu.au/rch/items/5e1def2f-25a0-4c9b-aa72-8c4b8761cb80/1/. Embargoed till January 2021.

Peters, S., Miller, M., & Kusyk, S. (2011). How relevant is corporate governance and corporate social responsibility in emerging markets? *Corporate Governance, 11*(4), 429–445.

Peterson, D. K. (2004). The relationship between perceptions of corporate citizenship and organizational commitment. *Business & Society, 43*(3), 296–319.

Schwartz, S. H. (1994). Beyond individualism and collectivism: New cultural dimensions of values. In S. H. Schwartz, U. Kim, H. C. Triandis, C. Kagitcibasi, S.-C. Choi, & G. Yoon (Eds.), *Individualism and collectivism: Theory, method, and applications* (Vol. 18). Thousand Oaks, CA: Sage Publications.

Søndergaard, M. (1994). Hofstede's consequences: A study of reviews, citations and replications. *Organization Studies, 15*(3), 447–456. doi:10.1177/017084069401500307

Tajfel, H. (1978). *Differentiation between social groups: Studies in the social psychology of intergroup relations* (Vol. 14). London: Academic Press |for| European Association of Experimental Social Psychology.

Tajfel, H., & Turner, J. C. (1986). The social identity theory of intergroup behavior. In S. Worchel & W. G. Austin (Eds.), *Psychology of intergroup relations* (2nd ed., pp. 7–24). Chicago, IL: Nelson-Hall.

Triandis, H. C. (1972). *The analysis of subjective culture.* New York, NY: Wiley.

Triandis, H. C. (1995). *Individualism & collectivism.* Boulder, CO: Westview Press.

Triandis, H. C., Robert, B., Marcelo, J. V., Masaaki, A., & Lucca, N. (1988). Individualism and collectivism. *Journal of Personality and Social Psychology, 54*(2), 323–338.

Vogel, D. J. (2005). Is there a market for virtue? The business case for corporate social responsibility. *California Management Review, 47*(4), 19–45.

Wei, Y.-C., Egri, P. C., & Yeh-Yun Lin, C. (2014). Do corporate social responsibility practices yield different business benefits in eastern and western contexts? *Chinese Management Studies, 8*(4), 556–576. doi:10.1108/cms-05-2014-0091

Williams, J., & MacKinnon, D. P. (2008). Resampling and distribution of the product methods for testing indirect effects in complex models. *Structural Equation Modeling, 15*(1), 23–51.

Chapter 3

The Universal Sustainable Development Goals for Purpose and Change

Abstract

Since the 2015 introduction of the United Nations Global Goals, also referred to as the sustainable development goals (SDGs), we have witnessed a movement toward inclusion of goal-related initiatives listed under CSR strategy and in CSR sustainability reports. At the time of writing this chapter, the United Nations were presented a speech by young activist Greta Thunberg and many other activists commenced riots in major cities. All are pointing toward, what they perceive, as a lack of effort to solve issues related to climate warming. At the same time new research has revealed that targets for the SDGs are falling behind levels expected for 2030. There has also been concern for the potential of "SDG washing," reported in the academic literature. This would greatly decrease the credibility of the goals over time. For this reason, it is vitally important to measure the impact of initiatives introduced to fit each SDG category and label. This will also assist with funding SDG implementation at a much faster rate. This chapter commences with a brief introduction of the SDG framework and discusses the United Nations and OECD methodology and the development and implementation of key global goals. Various research reports are discussed alongside a tracking study on uptake of the SDGs, and the need for SDG metrics to create transparency and evaluation. The chapter ends with example case studies of CSR strategy implementing and measuring the SDGs, alongside a discussion of financial vehicles released to support further development. The chapter also makes suggestions for future research opportunities to assist SDG progression.

Introduction

Climate change escalation, the increasing global footprint, the decline of species, and the degrading of the world's ecosystems alongside many individuals still living below the poverty line with limited access to safe water, sanitation, safe

CSR for Purpose, Shared Value and Deep Transformation, 85–117 health and equal human rights, is the picture of current global circumstances. Add to this a lack of trust in big corporates, governments, and the media, as reported by Edelman Global Trust Barometer's (2018, 2019, 2020), and the concern continues to climb. It is hoped that the global movement toward innovation and collaboration under the United Nations sustainable development goals (SDGs) framework will help companies, governments, and organizations detract from this downward spiral and solve the accumulating systemic and wicked problems that exist. A scroll through the business internet and social media shows UN SDGs shaping local and global economies and driving business trends. Consultants from a variety of disciplines are also getting behind the lucrative business opportunity the SDGs provide. However, some issues continue to fall between the "cracks" and require academic focus and research. In addition, the young activist Greta Thunberg, mentioned above, and other climate activists are drawing attention to the lack of effort to solve issues related to climate warming and global emissions. New research also shows the SDGs are falling behind in their target to be resolved by 2030. This chapter identifies issues related to the SDGs and discusses the United Nations and OECD methodology and the development and implementation of key global goals.

Within this context, it's not new to say that governments and their international agencies have failed in their attempts to rid the planet of environmental issues, overdevelopment, and poverty. It's also not new that corporates and multinational companies are often blamed for not taking responsibility or playing a large enough part in finding solutions to fix societal social and environmental problems. What is new to this scenario, however, is the growing recognition that CSR activities can make a difference under the SDG framework. With a deadline of 2030 to reach targets under 17 goals, the world has in the last half decade seen a global shift in emphasis toward fulfilling these commitments, with many corporates reporting these SDGs in their CSR and/or sustainability reports, and also reporting their collaborations with governments, nongovernmental organizations (NGOs), and social enterprises. However, it appears there is much more to be done than first thought – as required by the member states of the 2030 Agenda for Sustainable Development – to get everyone on board and leave no one behind (UNDESA, 2018).

First and foremost, implementation of the SDGs has had some consequences. Concerns have arisen, such as the thought that SDGs may be used as PR or marketing vehicles, and come to pass as "green washing" or, in this case, "SDG washing" (Nieuwenkamp, 2017) or become just a set of norms, as they are not legalized or compulsory (Eccles, 2015). For this reason, encouraging "genuine" commitment and efficient and fair enforcement of the SDGs, alongside measurement mechanisms (Kim, 2018) that are easily accessible and standardized across nations and countries is necessary. Several tools to implement this are discussed within this chapter. Additional reports by the Ethical Corporation have revealed that a large majority of companies announced their engagement in SDGs, but less than 10% had measurable targets on their contribution to the SDGs (Ethical Corporation, 2018). This issue is discussed later this chapter alongside other reports such as the report by PwC and CSR Europe (2018), which outlines various risks and opportunities and recommends focusing on improving impact through collaboration to achieve targets by 2030.

The current chapter explains the objectives required to achieve integration and collaboration with SDGs in CSR strategy. Case study examples of SDG implementation and reporting are provided throughout alongside various products and funds tailored by impact investors and dedicated to support mitigation and adaptation effects. These topics are discussed in this chapter which also includes an update on measuring the SDGs alongside the difficulties in implementing them. The SDGs have also provided a context for the evolution of CSR strategy, as witnessed by inclusion of SDGs within CSR reporting. The SDG framework also provides a methodology to categorize CSR Social Initiatives (SIs), or social projects, to implement them and then measure them. Multinational enterprises (MNEs) benefit from this, as they are in an excellent position to implement CSR SIs and projects as part of the SDG framework and incorporate this into their CSR strategy in the many developed and developing country settings where they reside. This will allow MNEs to be key instigators of SDG implementation and become leaders in establishing collaboration across sectors, governments, and public and private entities.

Most readers will know of the SDGs, however, to provide greater depth with a CSR context; a brief history is provided here. The SDGs were first announced on September 25, 2015, when 150 world leaders adopted the *2030 Agenda for Sustainable Development*—to end poverty, protect the planet, and ensure prosperity for all—as part of the new sustainable development agenda (United Nations Development Programme, 2015). The full list of SDGs is discussed later this chapter. However, as broad categories, they are interrelated and cover a wide range of global challenges: *poverty, hunger, health, education, climate change, gender equality, water, sanitation, energy, the environment, and social justice.* It is proposed that achieving these goals could open up USD 12 trillion in market opportunities and create 380 million new jobs by 2030 (Business and Sustainable Development Commission [BSDC], Better Business, Better World report, 2017). With the top 1% of population growing richer each day and the majority of population growing poorer each day, global wealth generated in 2017 was documented at 82%, going to the wealthiest 1% of population (The Guardian, Inequality, 2018). In addition, Oxfam reported at the World Economic Forum in January 2018 that billionaires were now being created at a record rate of one every 2 days for the previous 12 months, while the bottom 50% of the world's population had seen no increase in wealth over the same time period (Elliott, 2018). While it is not yet 2030, the discrepancy on expectations for climate action and poverty levels continues, at the time of writing this book.

At the same time as these discrepancies are recognized, intangible business assets and business value can no longer be described in pure economic terms. When they are intangible and/or social, they require a different type of description or impact assessment. Furthermore, business models that allow for sustainable development with value creation at its core, will allow concepts of CSR and sustainability because value creation is the primary motivator for both (Wheeler, Colbert, & Freeman, 2003). Value creation in this context refers to a company achieving its goals to create value for all its employees, shareholders, customers, society, *stakeholders*, and the communities where they reside (Munro, 2013a). Added to this are new dimensions of competition for environmental and societal success (Iyigün, 2015) fueled by the requirements of the UN SDGs framework to be implemented by 2030.

A brief introduction to the SDGs provides an initial context for this chapter before moving on to more recent developments. The 17 SDGs now well-publicized through the business community and other mediums, provide a list of category labels to easily identify each problem, challenge or opportunity to address. However, there are a number of other concerns around the UN SDGs as a framework to drive change. Some say it's too ambitious and unrealistic to implement even a portion of the SDGs by the 2030 deadline. Others refer to it as the world's biggest "to do list."

The best way to implement the SDGs has been further assessed since their introduction. These reports and recommendations are discussed later this chapter. The first of these assessments came soon after the SDGs were introduced. The 2016 World Economic Forum Annual Meeting with many leaders from business, finance, civil society, and labor including the BSDC examination and delivery of the UN SDGs. This concluded in the "Better Business, Better World" report (January 2017), stating the urgency for the next 13 years to 2030, that all businesses be involved, with the well-known quote:

> "Business as usual is not an option: choosing to 'kick the can down the road' over the next four years will put impossible environmental and social strains on a stuttering global economy" (Better Business, Better World Report, Business and Sustainable Development Commission (2017), p. 7, cited in Munro, 2018).

The World Economic Forums continue to state that more rapid attention is required toward implementation of the UN SDGs by 2030, with a special focus on developing countries. Strategy with this type of inclusion is considered to be at the forefront of the solution to current global climatic change and escalating social problems such as poverty, hunger, and inequality (Munro, 2018, p. 138). Two years after the 2017 Better Business, World Report, the World Economic Forum met again in January 2019. In the interim, the UN Global Compact chief Lise Kingo spoke at the Ethical Corporation's premier European conference in June 2018, advising companies to take urgent action on the SDGs. In a phone interview with the Ethical Corporation publication, at the UN headquarters, Lise Kingo said:

> "...my message is one of urgency. We only have 4,500 days left (till 2030). It is the biggest transformation challenge the world has ever faced and it will take all stakeholders to pull it off: governments, the private sector, civil society as well as all of us as consumers. ... There is no plan B and it would be so embarrassing if we had to tell our children and grandchildren that we had this amazing plan with

17 very clear goals but we couldn't get our act together. I think
that would be unbearable." (Ethical Corporation publication,
2018).

The most recent report on the SDGs is discussed in Chapter 7, where it is
acknowledged that there has been a shift in perspectives on the SDGs between
2016 and 2019. Of the 1000 CEOs in 21 industries across 99 countries interviewed, 78% of CEOs saw opportunities to contribute to the Global Goals
through their core business in 2016, compared with 21% feeling in 2019 that
businesses are playing a critical role in contributing to the Global Goals
(UNGC-Accenture, 2019).

The SDG Context within a Corporate Framework

The push for corporates to be involved is now undeniable. The latest World
Economic Forum in January 2020 states the need for corporates to focus on *all*
their *stakeholders* and many sectors will need to undergo systemic change through
their entire supply chain. As part of the development of the SDGs across sectors,
a new blueprint for business is discussed, which includes transforming CSR to
reach the UN SDG deadline by 2030. An entire systems change is proposed, as
discussed in Chapter 6.

The ability for companies to implement the SDGs through corporate strategy
was first encouraged by the development of the OECD Guidelines. Before
introducing current difficulties in implementing the SDGs, a brief history is
provided here to explain the introduction of the SDGs and the various organizations involved. Firstly, the United Nations Global Compact (UNGC) was only
just set-up in 2000. At the time it was the world's largest initiative for corporate
sustainability and responsible business and provided a voluntary initiative to
support companies in implementing universal sustainability principles (United
Nations Global Compact. 2016). Its aim was to create an inclusive sustainable
economy and deliver lasting benefits to people, communities, and markets (United
Nations Global Compact, 2016, cited in Munro, 2018, p. 147). As part of this, the
UNGC supports companies to implement responsible business by aligning strategies and operations through 10 principles listed in Table 3.1.

Following the development of the 10 principles, the 8 Millennium Development Goals (MDGs) were drafted in 2000, followed by the 17 SDG in 2015. At
the time the SDGs were launched, the OECD Guidelines were the only existing
multilaterally agreed "corporate responsibility instrument" that governments had
committed to. The guidelines provide a list of government-backed recommendations on responsible business conduct and address all aspects of the corporate
or multinational corporate (MNC) or MNE in the private sector, including parent
companies, "subsidiaries," and/or local entities. The OECD also states they
express the "shared views and values of countries, including major emerging
economies, which are the sources and the recipients of a large majority of the
world's investment flows" (OECD, 2011, p. 1, cited in Munro, 2018, p. 149).

Table 3.1. The 10 principles of the United Nations Global Compact.

Principle 1: Businesses should support and respect the protection of internationally proclaimed human rights
Principle 2: Make sure that they are not complicit in human rights abuses
Principle 3: Businesses should uphold the freedom of association and the effective recognition of the right to collective bargaining
Principle 4: The elimination of all forms of forced and compulsory labour
Principle 5: The effective abolition of child labour
Principle 6: The elimination of discrimination in respect of employment and occupation
Principle 7: Businesses should support a precautionary approach to environmental challenges
Principle 8: Undertake initiatives to promote greater environmental responsibility
Principle 9: Encourage the development and diffusion of environmentally friendly technologies
Principle 10: Businesses should work against corruption in all its forms, including extortion and bribery

Source: United Nations Global Compact (2000) (also cited in Munro, 2018, if you need to add). The list is publicly available through United Nations Global Compact, 2000).

These guidelines for MNCs and MNEs relate to the "pillars" outlined by the UNGC framework and subsequent development of the UN SDGs. The "pillars" align corporate strategies and operations with the universal principles of human rights, labor, environment, and anticorruption (United Nations Sustainable Development Report, 2016 in; Munro, 2018, p. 149) and are expected to advance societal goals.

In this context, the 17 SDGs (labeled SDG 1 to SDG 17) were developed to encompass all social, environmental, and economic components (OECD, 2016, cited in Munro, 2018, p. 150) within this setting. A summary of these is shown in Table 3.2.

The 17 SDGs key themes are examined in case study examples later in this chapter and are listed below:

SDG 1: End Poverty
SDG 2: Zero Hunger
SDG 3: Good Health and Well-being
SDG 4: Quality Education
SDG 5: Gender Equality
SDG 6: Clean Water and Sanitation
SDG 7: Affordable and Clean Energy
SDG 8: Decent Work and Economic Growth
SDG 9: Industry Innovation and Infrastructure

SDG 10: Reduced Inequalities
SDG 11: Sustainable Cities and Communities
SDG 12: Responsible Consumption and Production
SDG 13: Climate Action
SDG 14: Life Below Water
SDG 15: Life on Land
SDG 16: Peace, Justice and Strong Institutions
SDG 17: Partnerships for the Goals

Source: United Nations Sustainable Development Goals (2016) (also cited in Munro, 2018).

Table 3.2. The 17 UN Sustainable Development Goals (SDGs).

The Sustainable Development Goals (SDGs 1–9)	The Sustainable Development Goals (SDGs 10–17)
1. End poverty in all its forms everywhere	10. Reduce inequality within and among countries
2. End hunger, achieve food security and improved nutrition and promote sustainable agriculture	11. Make cities and human settlements inclusive, safe, resilient and sustainable
3. Ensure healthy lives and promote well-being for all at all ages	12. Ensure sustainable consumption and production patterns
4. Ensure inclusive and equitable quality education and promote lifelong learning opportunities for all	13. Take urgent action to combat climate change and its impacts
5. Achieve gender equality and empower all women and girls	14. Conserve and sustainably use the oceans and marine resources
6. Ensure availability and sustainable management of water and sanitation for all	15. Protect, restore and promote sustainable use of terrestrial ecosystems
7. Ensure access to affordable, reliable, sustainable and modern energy for all	16. Promote peaceful and inclusive societies for sustainable development
8. Promote sustained, inclusive and sustainable economic growth, full and productive employment and decent work for all	17. Strengthen the means of implementation and revitalize the Global Partnership for Sustainable Development
9. Build resilient infrastructure, promote inclusive and sustainable industrialization and foster innovation	

Source: United Nations Sustainable Development Goals (2015) (also cited in Munro, 2018).

The academic literature reports a further division of the 17 goals. For example, Kim (2018) reports the division of the goals into three categories, which refer to key thematic areas closely connected to one another. The first category is the *extension of the Millennium Development Goals (MDGs)* mentioned previously. These are goals 1–7. The second category is *inclusiveness* (goals 8–10); and the third category is *sustainability and urbanization* (goals 11–17) (Kim, 2018).

Following the introduction of the SDGs in 2015, the World Economic Forum Annual Meeting (January 2016), incorporating the BSDC – comprised of a group of 35 CEOs and civil society leaders – launched the "Better Business, Better World" report (January 2017), which identified 60 key areas for investment. As stated previously, the report concluded that sustainable business models aligned to the SDGs could open new markets worth up to USD12 trillion and create up to 380 million new jobs by 2030. A more in-depth overview of this is reported in Munro (2018), Chapter 5 (in Hipsher (Ed.), *Examining the Private Sector's Role in Wealth Creation and Poverty Reduction*). The purpose of this chapter is to provide an update on current concerns and themes surrounding integration and collaboration.

Themes of Integration and Collaboration and Current Difficulties

Since the introduction of the SDGs in 2015, integration across sectors continues to be difficult. This was noted in previous approaches to sustainable development; however, the SDG system was developed to assist with this as it was acknowledged as a more integrated system than the original MDG framework (Le Blanc, 2015). The goals are now considered to be interconnected with the unanimous objective that no one is left behind (United Nations Sustainable Development Goals, 2015). As stated in the introduction of this book, this is expressed by the UNDESA (2018) in the following quote:

> "As we embark on this great collective journey, we pledge that no one will be left behind. Recognizing that the dignity of the human person is fundamental, we wish to see the goals and targets met for all nations and peoples and for all segments of society. And we will endeavour to reach the furthest behind first" (UNDESA, 2018).

The interconnection therefore exists between goals—as shown for example in the second category for *inclusiveness* (goal 8: Good jobs and economic growth, goal 9: Innovation and infrastructure, and goal 10: Reduced inequality). As reported by Kim (2018), the combination of these goals provides a more industry-related perspective than previous, and provides *inclusiveness* of jobs, infrastructure, industrialization, and distribution, which share the common objective of achieving socially inclusive sustainable development (Kim, 2018). The third category identified as *sustainability and urbanization,* is especially tough in developing nations (Kim, 2018).

This category also fits the request from the United Nations for an SDG focus particularly in emerging markets.

Research has reported a recognized movement toward a developing country focus. This has been propelled by the requirement that SDGs be adopted by corporates, not just in developed countries as under the MDGs, but now also in developing countries, and in particular the least developed countries (Munro, 2018). As mentioned elsewhere in this book, multinational corporations (MNCs) and MNEs are in a strong position to assist developing countries and their economies (McIntosh, 2015; Visser, 2016), by adopting SIs under the UN SDGs (and/or Global Goals) framework. They can do this by adapting their CSR strategy to fit these needs and the needs of the developing host country where the MNC/MNE resides (Munro, 2013b; in; Munro, 2018, p. 139).

This fits with the current escalating trend and perspectives of global corporates. There is also a growing and:

> "...evolving expectation that MNEs, as corporations in the private sector (in particular), are accountable for the economic and social consequences they impact between the interface of business, society, the environment and the nations or host countries they inhabit" (Munro, 2018, p. 141).

Other authors refer to the "complex and multifaceted relationships between business and society to account for the economic, social, and environmental impacts of business activity" (Jamali, Karam, & Blowfield, 2015, p. 1). This "interconnectedness" at the interface (of business and society) is central to discussions on CSR for MNE CSR initiatives (OECD, 2011). As reported in Munro (2018), large organizations such as MNEs can operate across interorganizational networks, allowing them to influence governments and societies in the host countries where they operate. The OECD Guideline for MNEs, mentioned previously, is therefore meant to provide guidance to MNEs at the interface of business and society, while they are operating in host environments (Munro, 2018, p. 142). Greta Thunberg the young climate activist, her followers, and other climate activists would disagree that the World Economic Forum (and its members) has assisted in protecting the interface between business and society or has done enough toward pushing rapid uptake of the SDGs, especially in the area of climate change. Recent and ongoing events suggest the need for heightened collaboration and integration at the interface of business and society.

Fitting with the theme of integration across sectors for the SDGs mentioned previously, there is also opportunity reported for collaboration directly across goals. Some of the goals themselves collaborate more strongly with others, for example, "the things you need to do to slow climate change are the same things you need to do to address poverty and inequality" (The Economist Intelligence Unit, 2017). Still, other scholars expect that some goals may clash due to the different interests of different sectors and the thought that some corporates may still attempt to maximize profit above all else (Tett, 2017). Kim (2018) also reports there is potential for a lack of integration across sectors and therefore also initiatives (i.e., economic, social, and environmental initiatives). The UN SDGs suggest specific goals in which each sector, including the business sector, should be strongly engaged (Kumar, Kumar, & Vivekadhish, 2016) alongside the realization that significant money and investment is also required. This again suggests the importance and strong need for support by the private sector (The Economist Intelligence Unit, 2017) and the need for greater engagement with this sector.

From the very beginning, the UN SDGs have been referred to as a global agenda (Munro, 2018), which has engaged and continues to involve intergovernmental discussion, civil organizations, citizens, scientists, academics, and the business sector (Kim, 2018; Kumar et al., 2016). This agenda has also added value to CSR strategy, highlighting both CSR and creating shared value (CSV) projects and case studies. Leading businesses have been quick to transform their CSR and sustainability strategies by placing their initiatives into SDG categories. Early adopters have been used as the "go-to" examples in the literature, such as Nestlé, Unilever, Allianz. This chapter provides some of the less reported examples of corporations aligning their CSR projects with the SDG framework. These case study examples are reported in the Appendix of this chapter.

Some proof of movement forward on the sustainable development agenda from the 2015 introduction of the SDGs is shown in the GlobalScan (2018) survey results (the SustainAbility Leaders Survey, 2018). As mentioned briefly in Chapter 6, the GlobeScan-SustainAbility Leaders Survey has tracked expert opinions on sustainable development leadership for the past 20 years. In 2018, the survey analyzed the perspectives of 729 qualified sustainability experts, who completed the online questionnaire from April 9th to May 15th, 2018. Respondents were from a variety of sectors (i.e., government 5%, corporate 36%, service and media 23%, academic and research 16%, NGO 15%) in 70 countries across 5 regions (i.e., North America 30%, Europe 37%, Asia-Pacific 20%, Africa 6%, Latin America 8%). Respondents were asked a number of questions, including the following: Which companies and NGOs do you believe are leading the sustainability agenda? What key factors set them apart? How well do leading companies perform against five leadership attributes—'Purpose,' Plan, Culture, Collaboration, and Advocacy?

The results from the GlobalScan survey reveal the impact of multisector partnerships and collaborations on the sustainable development agenda is perceived as steadily improving since 2015 (GlobalScan, 2018). Overall perceptions of the private sector contribution to sustainable development have also improved since 2016, during which time international finance institutions have seen a moderate increase in perceived favourability as well (GlobalScan, 2018). Worth noting is that the perceived impact of research and academic institutions declined between 2017 and 2018. This suggests that a boost in research is required by academic institutions in the area of collaboration on the sustainable development agenda, and provides an excellent opportunity for university curriculum development and future research to achieve greater impact.

CSR for Collaboration and Integration: Uniting through the SDGs

CSR *Europe*, the leading European business network for CSR, released a report in 2018, which also emphasizes the theme of collaboration for impact and maturity and integration of sustainability, through corporations implementing the SDGs:

> "Collaboration is vital to pursue the systemic changes needed in society and within business to achieve the *Sustainable Development Goals*. We believe, and there is a growing body of evidence, that sector and multi-stakeholder partnerships have the potential to raise the integration of sustainability on the agenda, which will lead to new business opportunities and enhanced competitiveness" (CSR Europe, 2018).

To determine the level of sustainability across many sectors, *CSR Europe* collaborated with PwC to survey 16 organizations from 11 different sectors. The key findings of their research are as follows:

- Maturity levels of sustainability vary across sectors
- Sectors perceive both risks and opportunities associated with the 17 SDGs
- A large gap exists between the board's vision and activities, particularly those focused on impact
- Four key ways organizations can increase SDG engagement—by improving education, enhancing collaboration, and communication more regularly on SDGs, plus information sharing on the SDGs.

Source: CSR Europe (2018).

The gap referred to in point 3 refers to the gap between good intentions and meaningful action. They found on average 72% of associations embed sustainability on a strategic level and 52% translate that commitment into policy work. However, just 35% put those policies into practice in the form of impact projects that could be measured. The report concluded that the current gap threatens the economic success of companies and the achievement of SDG targets, if these issues are not addressed quickly. However, the report confirms that *CSR Europe* members on the whole are adopting SDGs into their strategy (CSR Europe, 2018).

The issues regarding the range of SDGs in point 2 above refer to risks and opportunities across the 17 SDGs. Climate Action (SDG 13), Industry and Innovation (SDG 9), and Affordable and Clean Energy (SDG 7) are seen as most important both for risks and opportunities. No Poverty (SDG 1) is the top priority of associations and organizations (although it is deemed a fairly low risk). This is followed by Responsible Consumption and Production (SDG 12)—focusing on issues such as waste, sourcing, and supply chains. To understand the risks, opportunities, and priorities identified by organizations in

Table 3.3. Summary of Findings for the *CSR Europe* and PwC study.

Highest Risk	Biggest Opportunity	Most Prioritized
Climate Action (SDG 13), Affordable and Clean Energy (SDG 7), Life Below Water (SDG 14)	Industry and Innovation (SDG 9), Climate Action (SDG 13), Responsible Consumption and Production (SDG 12)	No Poverty (SDG 1), Responsible Consumption and Production (SDG 12), Climate Action (SDG 13)

Source: CSR Europe, 2018.

this survey further, the results are summarized into highest risk; biggest opportunity; and most prioritized. These are listed in Table 3.3.

Of interest, at the same time the SDGs were released by the United Nations in May 2015, *CSR Europe* released in June 2015, the *Enterprise 2020 Manifesto* for action by 2020 in response to current levels of unemployment, climate change, and demographic change in Europe. This is also mentioned in Chapter 5, with regard to the innovation components required.

The *Enterprise 2020 Manifesto* also became the CSR movement's response to the challenges set by the European Commission, requesting smart, sustainable, and inclusive growth (CSR Europe, 2015). In addition, three strategic priorities were identified:

- Make employability and inclusion a priority (across boards, management, and value chains)
- Encourage companies to engage as committed partners (with communities, cities, and regions) to implement new sustainable production, consumption, and livelihoods
- Place transparency and respect for human rights at the heart of business conduct

Source: CSR Europe, June 2015.

The progress of European businesses toward achieving the *Enterprise 2020 Manifesto's* priorities has been tracked over 5 years (from 2015 to 2020) via *CSR Europe's* interactive online Business Impact Maps which highlight hundreds of initiatives related to this across Europe (CSR Europe, 2015). They are also calling on governments and businesses across Europe to get on board and take action through their own initiatives. The report provides clear priorities and suggestions to achieve the Global Goals by 2030, with an emphasis also on *innovation and collaboration.* These themes should be examined in future research to examine the degree of uptake for corporates adopting SDGs as part of CSR strategy.

Concerns Regarding the SDGs

Since the announcement of the SDGs in 2015, progress has been made, although, as mentioned previously, this is not at the speed expected by many. There are plenty of business opportunities in addressing the SDGs; however, meeting the Global Goals by 2030 will require additional investment estimated at USD2.4 trillion each year (Sustainable Development Solutions Network, 2015). This requires contribution from the private sector and long-term planning (CSR Asia, 2018). It has been suggested that many are not planning enough in to the future for long-term investment as companies are accustomed to only planning for 3-year intervals (PwC, 2015). This is in line with the long-standing preference of investors to typically prefer short-term gains and liquidity (Business and Sustainable Development Commission, 2017; CSR Asia, 2018).

While the implementation deadline for the SDG goals is set for 2030, various conversations and research have reported there will be difficulty in delivering on this deadline (for example, see Tett's article in the *Financial Times*, Tett, 2017). There have also been a number of critics and concerns on efficient implementation and businesses' actual genuine commitment to the SDGs (Kim, 2018). One of these concerns is that while the SDG is a global agenda with global-level targets, some considerations are necessary to redefine the strategy and report at a national level (Kumar et al., 2016). Addressing highly complicated social issues is also an uncertain task, as often the issues (including systemic wicked problems and challenges) are often ambiguous and so are the solutions. This requires layers of depth in *multistakeholder* partnerships and policy integration across nations and sectors (Le Blanc, 2015; Kim, 2018). Like CSR strategy, interpretation and outcome of the SDGs may also vary across countries (Munro, 2018). With the introduction of the "collaborative" multilayered component of the SDGs, this is further complicated as it involves new ways of communicating with government—and about new processes and ideas. There is also the inclusion of new actors, and new actions arising from growing sustainability issues (Tett, 2017). This then requires complex follow-up and review systems (Eccles, 2015; Kim, 2018) and a standardized method of reporting.

As mentioned in the introduction to this chapter, there are concerns that the SDGs may come to pass as "green washing" or "SDG washing" (Nieuwenkamp, 2017) and/or become just a set of norms, as they are not legalized or compulsory (Eccles, 2015), suggesting that adoption of SDGs is dependent on voluntary commitment (Kim, 2018). A similar argument has been posited for uptake of CSR discretionary activities. If the exercise or task is voluntary, the level of reporting tends to reflect this, leaving the impact unknown. Supporting this idea is a report by the Ethical Corporation, which (as previously mentioned) revealed a large majority of companies announced their engagement in SDGs, but less than 10% had measurable targets on their contribution to the SDGs (Ethical Corporation, 2018).

This means researchers and business commentators not only have concerns on the failure of measuring SDG uptake and their impact – there are also concerns regarding the use of SDGs as a public relations and marketing vehicle, suggesting the risk of "SDGs washing" (Ethical Corporation, 2018; Kim, 2018). If allowed to continue, this "washing" will decrease the credibility of the goals over time. It is suggested that maintaining the credibility of the goals requires the encouragement of "genuine" commitment from organizations, alongside the development of efficient and fair enforcement of the SDGs and the development of measurement mechanisms (Kim, 2018). Measurement mechanisms also need to be easily accessible and standardized across nations and countries. All these areas require further research and are considered emerging research opportunities for scholars in this area. In particular, future examination of SDG implementation and measurement across MNCs/MNEs from various sectors in both the developed and developing countries where they reside, is critical to achieving further progress in measuring SDG uptake and understanding methods of successful SDG implementation.

Measuring the SDGs: A Research Example

An example of research leading the way in developing measurement tools is provided by Trucost. They studied 13 corporates already generating real value from business strategies aligned with the SDGs, utilizing an SDG Evaluation Tool. They found the corporations studied were already generating $233bn in business revenues in 2017 from SDG uptake, which was, equivalent to 87% of their total revenues (Trucost News, 2018a). The report also revealed the challenges, including the need for a solution on measurement. In November 2018, Trucost reported that 193 countries, including 9,000 companies, and investors with more than USD 4 trillion in assets have pledged their support to the UN SDGs. These same companies also reported a challenge in the transition to SDG-aligned business strategies and capital allocation, including some of the issues discussed in preceding sections of this chapter.

For SDG implementation and standardized measurement to progress, Truscott found a set of SDG metrics to provide transparency. They worked with multiple companies and an advisory panel of investment professionals, interest group representatives, and academics to create a tool to identify SDG-aligned business value and prioritize risks and opportunities to inform sustainable growth strategies (Trucost News, 2018b). They developed a tool referred to as the Trucost SDG Evaluation Tool, to measure performance on the SDGs across the value chain. The tool is also able to determine which SDGs are most relevant to an organization's business operations, supply chains, and products, and therefore prioritize investment in SDGs in areas where it matters most (Trucost News, 2018b).

The results of the Trucost study mentioned above reports new ways to think about social and environmental issues, and it is an important consideration for future academic research. One example of the importance of tools such as this is the ability to report on greenhouse gas emissions alongside these SDG themes. Although companies have been reporting on greenhouse gas emissions in CSR and GRI sustainability reports for many years, the SDG 13 Climate Action goal highlights the importance of implementing and reporting climate adaptation, which is less commonly disclosed by companies (Trucost News, 2018b). The type of evaluative reporting suggested by Truscot allows for this, and could therefore assist in speeding up the global movement toward overall climate action through reporting. Testing this assumption further is an important consideration for future research.

The Trucost SDG Evaluation report also made several recommendations which are relevant themes for future research:

- Regional considerations: suggests market participants need to assess SDGs with a regional local lens
- Supply chain risks: to provide fast and efficient ways to identify materiality items
- Sales in developing markets: to create more positive contribution to the SDGs by accelerating sales where the need is greatest

Source: Truscot (2018b).

As stated, these recommendations and findings provide an opportunity and direction for future research on the SDGs. In particular, the difficulty in supply chain material and measurement issues related to this is a complex issue. This measurement tool may provide a faster and more efficient method to determine significant parts of an organization's ecosystem and as a result ensure the correct adoption of SDGs through the supply chain. In addition, as the developing and emerging markets is a primary focus for the development of SDGs (United Nations, 2015), the focus on sales and marketing in these markets as a result of SDG implementation could be measured using this type of tool and provide information on how to accelerate these markets more quickly. While a regional focus is suggested above, an additional opportunity for future research is to test this tool (and other available measurement tools) further to determine a standardized measure across different sized companies (MNEs and SMEs) and across different countries in local, regional, and global contexts.

Corporates and Investors: Measuring Impact of the SDGs

The concern surrounding "SDG washing" as mentioned previously makes measuring the impact of the SDGs extremely important for corporates and investors to pursue. The Global Goals challenge corporates, enterprises, and investors to understand and manage all their effects on the communities where they reside. This also includes the effects that will enable and determine progress toward the SDGs. It is suggested that the Global Goals will also provide a common ground for previously siloed activities (Impact Management Project, 2018). Measuring this activity is relevant alongside ESG risk management, which many companies already assess.

Overall, it is hoped the SDG framework will provide a method to achieve a shared set of targets and indicators, where businesses and investors can differentiate their roles, based on their social and environmental goals (Impact Management

Project, 2018). The aim of the Impact Management Project network, for example, is to create an impact-based measurement and management approach so that organizations can make a comparison of their total effects on people and planet and compare this across organizations (Impact Management Project, 2018). The network is a collaboration of organizations, many involved in current CSR and sustainability reporting and impact investing. Network members include the United Nations Development Program (UNDP), the Global Reporting Initiative (GRI), the Global Impact Investing Network (GIIN), the Principles for Responsible Investment (PRI), the International Finance Corporation (IFC), the Global Steering Group for Impact Investment (GSG), Social Value International (SVI), the Organization for Economic Co-operation and Development (OECD), and the World Benchmarking Alliance (WBA). It is hoped that their collaboration as a network will facilitate consensus on the definition of impact and join together many different perspectives and terminology to measure impact throughout the supply chain.

In addition, it is expected that a set of tools and measurements that measure the impact of what works and what does not work, will allow organizations to work more rapidly toward achieving the SDGs by 2030. Future academic research should therefore assist in developing an impact-based measurement system and determine a management approach to standardize measures across SDG-related research projects. This provides an excellent research opportunity to examine organizational differences in impact and examine this across an organization's supply chain to measure and standardize their progress across the different countries that they operate within.

Impact Investing to Address the UN SDGs

As discussed above, it is now well acknowledged that progressing the SDGs by the 2030 deadline will require not only support by corporates but also significant investment by foundations, funders, government, and philanthropy, including private capital markets. Various products and funds have been tailored by impact investors to specifically address the SDGs. Examples of these are listed in Table 3.4.

A few months after the announcement of the SDGs, the conclusion of COP 21 (the 21st meeting of the Conference of the Parties) in December 2015 adopted the final wording of the Paris Agreement. This put forward the climate mitigation and adaptation plan which included targets to reduce emissions and provide strategies for adaptation and increased resilience in vulnerable regions. Suggestions were also made on how to finance these goals (Global Impact Investing Report, 2018). The Global Impact Investing report (2018) assessed the outcomes of financing in 2017 and found reduction target progress had stalled. Vehicles to support mitigation and adaptation efforts were then launched. These range from small-scale investments in clean energy innovation, conservation, and smallholder agriculture to large-scale investments in infrastructure and green bond issuances (Global Impact Investing Report, 2018). Examples of these are provided in Table 3.5.

Table 3.4. New products launched to target particular SDGs.

The UBS Global Impact Fund. A public equity fund that targets SDGs 1–3, 6–7, 11, and 13 by investing in sustainable companies providing innovative products or services to meet environmental or social challenges, including climate change, air pollution, water and sanitation, health, food security, and poverty alleviation. The team engages with investee companies to measure positive impact and minimize ESG risks and sets targets aligned with the SDGs, measuring outputs, outcomes, and impacts of their products and services.	***Mirova Land Degradation Neutrality Fund.*** Aims to raise USD 300 million to target SDG15 (Life on Land). The fund invests in sustainable agriculture, forestry, and related sectors, including green infrastructure and ecotourism in emerging markets, and has developed an Environmental and Social Management System (ESMS) to mitigate risks and measure the positive impact generated toward SDG target 15.3 (land degradation neutrality).
Blue like an Orange Sustainable Capital Fund. A private debt fund aiming to raise USD 1 billion targeting toward SDGs 1–4, 6–9, and 11 through investments into small- and medium-sized enterprises in sectors such as renewable energy, sustainable infrastructure, healthcare, education, financial services, and agribusiness.	***Financial Definitions*** *Public equity = publicly traded stocks or shares.* *Private debt = bonds or loans placed to a select group of investors rather than being syndicated broadly.* *ESG risk = risk derived from noncompliance with environmental, social, or governance criteria.*

Source: Adapted from Global Impact Investing Network, 2018.

Measuring uptake of these financial vehicles provides an excellent opportunity for future research to determine the success of these projects and document the number of organizations supported by impact investing. It also provides an opportunity to further improve the measurement of the SDGs to determine actual impact.

The Appendix of this chapter includes a selection of case study examples and projects related to SDG inclusion in corporate strategy. Analysis and measurement of these projects is a much needed and large potential area for future academic and commercial research. Further information regarding this area of research is also included in the Appendix of this chapter.

Table 3.5. Vehicles Launched to Support Mitigation and Adaptation Efforts.

The Breakthrough Energy Ventures Fund raised USD 1 billion to invest in clean energy technologies and reduce emissions. *The Breakthrough Energy Coalition* includes individual investors, corporations (that produce/consume large amounts of energy), and financial institutions

The Caribbean Climate-Smart Coalition—a public–private coalition aiming to catalyze USD 8 billion to scale renewable energy and build low-carbon infrastructure in the Caribbean region. The coalition also established an accelerator to develop projects and businesses (with USD 6–10 million budget). Funding received from Inter-American Development Bank, World Bank and Caribbean Development Bank, and private investors and companies

Unilever and the Government of Norway – announced new fund to raise USD 400 million to invest in businesses that combine high-productivity agriculture with smallholder farming and forest conservation. The fund will leverage public and private investment to enhance resilience on climate change in vulnerable regions.

Livelihoods Carbon Fund—aims to raise USD 125 million from private companies for ecosystem restoration, agroforestry, and energy projects in Africa, Asia, and Latin America. The fund will produce cash flows by financing projects to generate carbon credits and returns on investment will be paid to the investors in carbon credits

Climate Investor One—a blended fund developed by the Global Innovation Lab for "end-to-end" financing of renewable energy infrastructure projects in emerging economies. Has attracted capital from donors and investors, including DFI (development finance institutions as specialized development banks supporting private sector development in developing countries) and institutional investors

Financial Definitions
Blended finance = a strategy that combines capital with different levels of risk in order to catalyze risk-adjusted market-rate-seeking capital into impact investments
Public equity = publicly traded stocks or shares
Private equity = a private investment into a company or fund in the form of an equity stake (not publicly traded stock)

Source: Adapted from Global Impact Investing Network, 2018.

Conclusion

A scroll through the business internet and related social media sites show the United Nations SDGs are, or appear to be, shaping local and global economies and driving business trends. As mentioned previously, consultants from a variety of disciplines are also getting behind the lucrative business opportunity the SDGs provide. The role of assisting corporates on deciding which SDGs to select, by working out those that are "material" to their current and/or future strategy, is one of the larger consulting opportunities. This is also an emerging trend and opportunity for future academic research. The methodology to select SDGs can be implemented through a materiality assessment (a common procedure in sustainability reports) to determine the particular SDGs to fit *stakeholders* needs and map this on to each unique business case. Standardized tools have been developed by the Global Impact Investing Network and Trucost, for example, which are discussed as examples in this chapter to provide standardized measurements. However, the findings of these studies need to be replicated in future academic research to provide rigor in testing these tools in different contexts.

Since the announcement of the United Nations SDGs in 2015, many corporates have been reporting their CSR and sustainability activities, initiatives, and projects alongside SDG reporting, and many coalitions and collaborations have been set-up to take on board the most difficult social and environmental challenges. However, as mentioned earlier in this chapter, researchers and authors not only have concerns on the failure of measuring SDG uptake and impact but also have concerns regarding the use of SDGs as a public relations and marketing vehicle (Nieuwenkamp, 2017), suggesting the risk of "SDG washing" (Ethical Corporation, 2018; Kim, 2018), which will decrease the credibility of the SDG goals over time. For this reason, encouraging "genuine" commitment and providing efficient and fair enforcement of the SDGs is necessary, alongside measurement mechanisms (Kim, 2018) that are easily accessible and can be standardized across different nations and countries. This is an emerging research opportunity requiring future research. In particular, the opportunity to analyze SDG implementation and measurement across MNEs from various sectors in the developed and developing countries where MNEs reside would be extremely beneficial. The Appendix of this chapter highlights a number of case study examples of corporations mapping strategy on to the SDGs. It is hoped that future research can identify new examples of corporations combining their social projects to align with the SDG framework.

As commentators have mentioned, the SDGs are a very large "to do list." As reported above, there is also extensive opportunity for future research. For example, the *Journal of International Business Studies* (special issue, 2019) includes not just the need for more interdisciplinary approaches to academic research on SDGs but also action research in which SDG implementation experience can be shared on a case-by-case basis. This chapter has attempted to share case studies of SDGs, but much more needs to be done to examine "live" action-based research examples of implementation of SDG projects (i.e., in-field experimentation) and determine the level of "SDG washing" that may also be present in reporting these activities.

By way of concluding, it is worth noting that the report by PwC and *CSR Europe* (2018) recommends focusing on improving impact through collaboration to achieve targets by 2030. Knowledge on successful case studies utilizing collaboration is mentioned throughout this chapter. However, what is key to the future of SDG uptake is measuring the impact of initiatives aligned to SDGs, and sharing successful case study examples of corporates, governments and multi-level collaborations implementing the global goals. Future research should therefore focus on these types of case studies in the academic literature to provide businesses models to assist future cross-sector collaborations.

Regardless of what level of progress SDG implementation has reached at present, the UN's launch of the SDGs appears to have kick-started a global movement to address the pressing issues and social and environmental challenges that the world is facing today. The achievement of these goals is dependent on the commitment from world leaders and businesses to build a more sustainable, safer, and prosperous planet for all. Corporates are in an excellent position to lead the way on the campaign for a better world by including SDGs as part of their business and CSR strategy. At the conception of the 17 SDGs in 2015, a gathering of 150 leaders witnessed Unilever Chief Executive Paul Polman as the only corporate who took part in drafting the document. He was perceived as the strongest early adopter among corporates for incorporating the SDGs. The Nikkei Asian Review (2017) reported him stating that the goals are the seeds of business opportunities and the role of business is "to solve societal problems." This further supports the theme that tackling the SDGs provides "enormous economic opportunities." Corporations have come a long way since then, with the release of the new *Statement on the Purpose of a Corporation* by the Business Roundtable (August 2019), signed by 181 CEOs of major corporations to make a commitment to lead their companies for the benefit of *all stakeholders*—customers, employees, suppliers, and communities—outlining the new "modern standard for corporate responsibility" (Business Roundtable, 2019).

As mentioned in the introduction of this book, the SDGs have placed *stakeholders* and societal problems in the spotlight, where business is no longer there to just create profits (Friedman, 1970). However, there is much more to be done. UN Global Compact chief Lise Kingo interviewed in June 2018 by the Ethical Corporation stated the SDG targets provide good clarity to companies:

> " [But] the challenge is to go to scale. We need to involve many more companies. We need to have many more partnerships that take all the good projects and programmes and implement them on a big scale" (Ethical Corporation, 2018).

The opportunities for corporates in emerging economies are immense (Munro, 2018) and these can now be matched to the environmental and social challenges of the region, as outlined by the SDG framework. The final challenge is to take these projects and initiatives to scale. The Global Sustainability Leaders Survey

(2018) by the team at GlobeScan, confirms some MNEs are able to act as leaders in their industry or field, and show how to make a genuine lasting and sustainable difference. Many are adopting the SDGs as part of their CSR strategy and have integrated these initiatives throughout their company. However, the GlobeScan team reports that there is still much more to do with only a handful of companies adopting the deep sustainability integration that is required. Many more need to get on board:

> "… global sustainability cannot be achieved by a tiny number of leaders, it requires determination and ambition from the thousands of global companies yet to embrace the sustainable development agenda. When this mass of companies engages, transforming their business models to deliver more value to society in addition to shareholders, the balance will tip" Global SustainAbility Leaders Survey, GlobeScan (2018).

Similar sentiments were reported from the GlobeScan 2018 study. In addition, the Edelman Trust Barometer (2019) states that the trust to do what is right has moved to the employer. As previously mentioned in Chapter 2, it is more vital than ever that employers select CSR initiatives and strategy aligned with saving the planet environmentally and socially and incorporating the social 'business-for-purpose' movement, alongside the inclusion of SDGs as part of CSR strategy. Going forward, full implementation of the 17 SDGs (or a collaboration of them) is required. Many argue that a new economic ecosystem is required to do this, as we usher in the new era of Globalization 4.0. This is discussed further in the following chapters.

The introductory chapter of this book mentions that many corporates are attempting to make the transition to adoption of at least some of the SDGs into their CSR strategy and by creating SIs and social projects under SDG categories. But there is much more to be done to reach 2030 targets. Some of the SDG case study examples reported in the Appendix are projects utilizing a CSV methodology (Porter and Kramer, 2011), and a few companies are working within an integrated value creation (IVC) structure (Visser, 2014). The following two chapters will examine these respectively.

References

Ayala Corporation. (2017a). Commitment to sustainability. Retrieved from http://www.ayala.com.ph/commitment-sustainability

Ayala Corporation. (2017b). Integrated report. Retrieved from http://www.ayala.com.ph/sites/default/files/pdfs/Ayala%20Corp%202017%20IR_lowres.pdf

BASF Global. (2018). Starting ventures. Retrieved from https://www.basf.com/en/company/sustainability/employees-and-society/societal-commitment/starting-ventures.html

Business and Sustainable Development Commission. (2017). Better business, better world report. Retrieved from http://report.businesscommission.org/uploads/Executive-Summary.pdf

Business Roundtable. (2019). *Business roundtable redefines the purpose of a corporation to promote 'an economy that serves all Americans'*. Retrieved from https://www.businessroundtable.org/business-roundtable-redefines-the-purpose-of-a-corporation-to-promote-an-economy-that-serves-all-americans

CSR Asia. (2018). The business opportunities in addressing the Sustainable Development Goals. Retrieved from http://csr-asia.com/newsletter-the-business-opportunities-in-addressing-the-sustainable-development-goals

CSR Europe. (2015). Enterprise 2020 manifesto: The future for Europe we need. Retrieved from https://www.csreurope.org/enterprise-2020-manifesto

CSR Europe. (2018). Collaboration for impact: Maturity and integration of sustainability in European sector associations. Retrieved from https://www.csreurope.org/collaboration-impact-maturity-and-integration-sustainability-european-sector-associations

Eccles, B. (2015, October). UN sustainable development goals: Good for business. *Forbes*.

Edelman. (2018). 2018 Edelman Trust Barometer reveals record-breaking drop in trust in the U.S. Retrieved from https://www.edelman.com/news-awards/2018-edelman-trust-barometer-reveals-record-breaking-drop-trust-in-the-us

Edelman. (2019). 2019 Edelman Trust Barometer. Retrieved from https://www.edelman.com/trust-barometer

Edelman. (2020). *2020 Edelman Trust Barometer*. Retrieved from https://www.edelman.com/trustbarometer

Elliott, L. (2018). *Inequality gap widens as 42 people hold same wealth as 3.7bn poorest*. The Guardian, January 22. Retrieved from https://www.theguardian.com/inequality/2018/jan/22/inequality-gap-widens-as-42-people-hold-same-wealth-as-37bn-poorest

Ethical Corporation. (2018). Risk of 'SDG wash' as 56% of companies fail to measure contribution to SDGs. Retrieved from http://www.ethicalcorp.com/risk-sdg-wash-56-companies-fail-measure-contribution-sdgs

Friedman, M. (1970). The social responsibility of business is to increase its profits. *The New York Times Magazine*, *32–33*, 122–126.

Global Impact Investing Network. (2018). Annual impact investor survey 2018. Retrieved from https://thegiin.org/research/publication/annualsurvey2018

GlobeScan. (2018). The 2018 globeScan-sustainAbility leaders survey. Retrieved from https://globescan.com/wp-content/uploads/2018/06/GlobeScan-SustainAbility-Leaders-Survey-2018-Report.pdf

Hindustan Unilever Limited. (2017). Unilever sustainable living plan. Retrieved from https://www.hul.co.in/Images/uslp-india-progress-report-2017-21may2018_tcm1255-522773_en.pdf

Impact Management Project. (2018). Retrieved from https://impactmanagementproject.com

Iyigün, N. Ö. (2015). What could entrepreneurship do for sustainable development? A corporate social responsibility-based approach. *Procedia - Social and Behavioral Sciences*, *195*(2015), 1226–1231. doi:10.1016/j.sbspro.2015.06.253

Jamali, D., Karam, C., & Blowfield, M. (2015). *Development-oriented corporate social responsibility: Multinational corporations and the global context* (Vol. 1). Sheffield: Greenleaf Publishing.

Kim, R. C. (2018). Can Creating Shared Value (CSV) and the United Nations Sustainable Development Goals (UN SDGs) collaborate for a better world? Insights from East Asia. *Sustainability, 10*(11), 4128. doi:10.3390/su10114128

Kumar, S., Kumar, N., & Vivekadhish, S. (2016). Millennium Development Goals (MDGs) to Sustainable Development Goals (SDGs): Addressing unfinished agenda and strengthening sustainable development and partnership. *Indian Journal of Community Medicine, 41*(1), 1–4. doi:10.4103/0970-0218.170955

Le Blanc, D. (2015). Towards integration at last? The sustainable development goals as a network of targets. *Sustainable Development, 23*(3), 176–187.

McIntosh, M. (2015). *Thinking the twenty-first century: Ideas for the new political economy.* Sheffield: Greenleaf Publishing.

Munro, V. (2013a). Stakeholder understanding of corporate social responsibility (CSR) in emerging markets with a focus on Middle East, Africa (MEA) and Asia. *Journal of Global Policy and Governance, 2*(1), 59–77. doi:10.1007/s40320-013-0026-3

Munro, V. (2013b). Stakeholder preferences for particular corporate social responsibility (CSR) activities and social initiatives (SIs): CSR initiatives to assist corporate strategy in emerging and frontier markets. *The Journal of Corporate Citizenship,* (51), 72–105. Retrieved from http://search.proquest.com.libraryproxy.griffith.edu.au/docview/1467970925?accountid=14543

Munro, V. (2018). Changing the boundaries of expectations: MNE uptake of universal principles and global goals. In S. A. Hipsher (Ed.), *Examining the private Sector's role in wealth creation and poverty reduction.* Hershey, PA: IGI Global.

Nieuwenkamp, R. (2017). Ever heard of SDG washing? The urgency of SDG due diligence. *OECD Development Matters.* Retrieved from https://oecd-development-matters.org/2017/09/25/ever-heard-of-sdg-washing-the-urgency-of-sdg-due-diligence/

Nikkei Asian Review. (2017). Unilever CEO values sustainable-development opportunities in Asia. *Nikkei Asian Review.* October 15. Retrieved from https://asia.nikkei.com/Business/Unilever-CEO-values-sustainable-development-opportunities-in-Asia

OECD. (2011). OECD guidelines and SDGs. Retrieved from http://oecdinsights.org/wp-content/uploads/2015/09/MNE-Guidelines-SDGs1.pdf

OECD. (2016). *About the OECD.* Retrieved from https://www.oecd.org/about/

Porter, M. E., & Kramer, M. R. (2011). Creating shared value. *Harvard Business Review, 89*(1/2), 62–77.

PwC. (2015). *Make it your business: Engaging with the sustainable development goals.* Retrieved from https://www.pwc.com/gx/en/sustainability/SDG/SDG%20Research_FINAL.pdf

Sustainable Development Solutions Network. (2015). Investment needs to achieve the sustainable development goals. Retrieved from http://unsdsn.org/wp-content/uploads/2015/09/151112-SDG-Financing-Needs.pdf

Tett, G. (2017). The UN has started to talk business. *Financial Times.* September 22. Retrieved from https://www.ft.com/content/11b19afc-9d97-11e7-9a86-4d5a475ba4c5

The Economist Intelligence Unit. (2017). Meeting the SDGs: A global movement gains momentum. Retrieved from https://perspectives.eiu.com/sites/default/files/Meeting%20the%20SDGs_A%20global%20movement%20gains%20momentum.pdf

Trucost. (2018a). Trucost identifies $233 billion SDG-aligned revenues in inaugural SDG evaluation. Retrieved from https://www.trucost.com/trucost-news/trucost-identifies-233-billion-sdg-aligned-revenues-in-inaugural-sdg-evaluation/

Trucost. (2018b). The Trucost SDG evaluation tool. Retrieved from https://www.trucost.com/corporate-advisory/sdg-evaluation-tool/

Trucost ESG Analysis, & S & P Global. (2018). Discovering business value in the United Nations sustainable development goals (SDGs): Insights from the inaugural application of the trucost SDG evaluation tool. Retrieved from https://www.trucost.com/publication/discovering-business-value-in-the-untied-nations-sustainable-development-goals-sdgs/

UNDESA. (2018). Leaving no one behind. Retrieved from https://www.un.org/development/desa/en/news/sustainable/leaving-no-one-behind.html

UNGC-Accenture. (2019). *UNGC-Accenture strategy CEO study on sustainability 2019*. Retrieved from https://www.accenture.com/_acnmedia/PDF-109/Accenture-UNGC-CEO-Study-Infographic.pdf

United Nations. (2015). The millennium development goals report 2015. Retrieved from http://www.un.org/millenniumgoals/2015_MDG_Report/pdf/MDG%202015%20rev%20(July%201).pdf

United Nations Development Programme. (2015). World leaders adopt sustainable development goals. Retrieved from http://www.undp.org/content/undp/en/home/presscenter/pressreleases/2015/09/24/undp-welcomes-adoption-of-sustainable-development-goals-by-world-leaders.html

United Nations Global Compact. (2000). Who we are. Retrieved from https://www.unglobalcompact.org/what-is-gc

United Nations Global Compact. (2016). Who we are. Retrieved from https://www.unglobalcompact.org/what-is-gc

United Nations Sustainable Development Goals. (2015). Sustainable development goals: 17 goals to transform our world. Retrieved from http://www.un.org/sustainabledevelopment/sustainable-development-goals/

United Nations Sustainable Development Report. (2016). *Global sustainable development report 2016*. Department of Economic and Social Affairs, New York. Retrieved from https://sustainabledevelopment.un.org/globalsdreport/2016

Visser, W. (2014). Eco-innovation: Going beyond creating technology for technology's sake. *The Guardian*, December 4, 1–2.

Visser, W. (2016). The future of CSR: Towards transformative CSR, or CSR 2.0. In A. Örtenblad (Ed.), *Research handbook on corporate social responsibility in context* (pp. 339). Cheltenham: Edward Elgar Publishing.

Wheeler, D., Colbert, B., & Freeman, R. E. (2003). Focusing on value: Reconciling corporate social responsibility, sustainability and a stakeholder approach in a network world. *Journal of General Management, 28*(3), 1–28.

Appendix

Corporate Case Study Examples: Incorporating SDGs into Strategy

This appendix provides a selection of case study examples and projects related to SDG inclusion in corporate strategy. Analysis and measurement of these projects is a much needed and large potential area for future academic and commercial research.

Unilever SDG Case Study

Since its origins in the late 19th century, Unilever has continued to address social issues, starting with the company's original product, Sunlight soap, in the then developing country of Britain. The Unilever soap example in India is probably one of the most well-known examples, and this project continued to function and operate under the CSR banner for many years. In addition to being listed as a CSR example, it is also listed in the literature as a creating shared value (CSV) example and an integrated value creation (IVC) example and is therefore briefly mentioned in other chapters in this book relating to these topic areas.

To illustrate the SDGs in the Unilever case study example, an example of the *Unilever Sustainable Living Plan* (USLP) is reported here from the Unilever subsidiary *Hindustan Unilever* (HUL) in India, titled the *Unilever Sustainable Living Plan – HUL Summary of Progress, 2017.* Firstly, the organization has three key goals in relation to the SDGs outline 1. Improving health and well-being; 2. Reducing environmental impact in manufacturing; 3. Enhancing livelihoods.

The three goals are then supported by targets grouped across nine pillars which span their social, economic and environmental performance across the value chain, of which there are six key initiatives as listed below. The UN Sustainable Development Goals (SDGs) are a part of each initiative as listed below:

Unilever Sustainable Living Plan *Hindustan Unilever* (HUL)—Key Initiatives

(1) **Washing Initiative**
- Reached over 140 million people through the Water, Sanitation and Hygiene (WASH) initiative driving clean habits through Lifebuoy handwashing behavior change, Pureit safe drinking water, and access to improved sanitation through the Domex Toilet Academy *SDGs: SDG 6 Clean Water and Sanitation; SDG 3 Good Health.*

(2) **Water Conservation and Crop Yield**
- Water conservation: More than 450 billion liters of water has been created through improved supply and demand management.
- Crop yield: Additional agriculture production of over 650,000 tonnes has been generated.
- Livelihoods: More than 5 million days of employment created through water conservation and increased agriculture production. *SDGs: SDG 6 Clean Water and Sanitation.*

(Continued)

(3) **Reduce, Recycle, Reuse Packaging**
   - Commits to 100% of plastic packaging as reusable, recyclable, or compostable by 2025. Innovations in packaging led to reduced plastic use in 2017, resulting in reduced waste. A saving of 1300 tonnes of paper across categories and 95 tonnes of glass through material usage optimization in 2017.
   - 80% recycled PET blister packs for personal care brands. Launch of Surf Excel Matic Liquid in a refill packaging pouch.
   SDGs: SDG 12 Responsible Consumption and Production.

(4) **Improving Nutrition and Hygiene for Smallholder Farmers and Families**
   - Working through tea supply chains to improve diet and hygiene through the *Seeds of Prosperity* program, a partnership between Unilever, the Global Alliance for Improved Nutrition (GAIN), and the Sustainable Trade Initiative (IDH). Have impacted over 34,000 workers, smallhold farmers, and families.
   SDGs: SDG 3 Good Health; SDG 2 No Hunger.

(5) **Prabhat Initiatives**
   - "Prabhat' contributes to the development of local communities around key sites including manufacturing locations.
   - Key areas are enhancing livelihoods, water conservation, and health and hygiene in over 30 locations across India, directly benefitting over 1.7 million people.
   SDGs: SDG 3 Good Health; SDG 6 Clean Water and Sanitation; SDG 8 Good Jobs and Economic Growth.

(6) **Rainwater Saving Initiative**
   - Launched Rin detergent bar that helps save up to two buckets of water in every wash cycle. It's called 'smart foam' technology which cuts foam after cleaning during the rinse stage. Product innovations help achieve Unilever's target to halve the water associated with the consumer use of their products by 2020.
   SDGs: SDG 6 Clean Water and Sanitation.

Source: Adapted extracts from the Hindustan Unilever Limited, 2017 Report: A report by Unilever Indian subsidiary Hindustan Unilever (HUL), titled the *Unilever Sustainable Living Plan – HUL Summary of Progress, 2017*, Hindustan Unilever Limited, 2017.

Ayala Group SDG Case Study

An early adopter of SDGs into their business strategy, even before the launch of the SDGs, is the *Ayala Corporation Group* from the Philippines. *Ayala* were already working on implementing SDGs into their CSR and sustainability strategy as shown in their 2014 Sustainability report (CSR Asia, 2018) before the launch of the SDGs in mid-2015. *Ayala* developed a *360 degree Sustainability Framework* by studying their impacts on the environment, society, and economy and identified external factors that affect their businesses. From this they developed management strategies to help mitigate risks and take advantage of emerging opportunities. In doing so, they give a comprehensive view of the material aspects, indicators, and metrics that are relevant to their business plans and regularly assess their performance on these parameters via an internal reporting processes (Ayala Corporation, Sustainability Commitment, 2017a).

Their 2017 Integrated Report is entirely themed on moving into the future and provides a shared value approach, as discussed further in Chapter 4. Their aim is:

> To transform our businesses and harness disruptive innovation, so we can create more shared value. The faster we keep moving, the sooner we can generate more opportunities, reach other markets, and help improve lives (Ayala Corporation Integrated Report, 2017). *Source:* Trucost ESG Analysis and S&P Global, 2018.

In order to understand their SDG reporting content below, it is important to understand the *Ayala Corporation* is one of the largest and most diversified business groups in the Philippines, covering real estate, banking, telecommunications, water, power, industrial technologies, infrastructure, healthcare, and education. The report also lists that their foundation focuses on education, youth leadership, sustainable livelihood, and the promotion of arts and culture.

The recent *Ayala Corporation* Integrated Report (2017b) lists their contribution under each of the 17 SDGs as follows:

SDG 1: No Poverty
- Provided P44.5 mil of microfinance loans for self-employed micro-entrepreneurs
- Distributed P422.5 million in community investments for poverty alleviation and social welfare projects in livelihood, education, and healthcare among others

SDG 2: Zero Hunger
- Provided P156 billion worth of agribusiness loans to support agriculture and food security

SDG 10: Reduced Inequalities
- Provides equal opportunities and fosters nondiscrimination in the workplace

SDG 11: Sustainable Cities and Communities
- Muntinlupa-Cavite Expressway served 29,000 vehicles per day, generating savings of P519 million in fuel consumption and man-hours
- Developed a total of 25 master planned estates that are resilient, pedestrian-friendly,

(Continued)

SDG 3: Good Health and Well-being
- Provided affordable primary care services to more than 65,000 unique patients through its 21 community-based clinics
- 41.7 mil sales transactions, 32.8 mil of which were generic medicine sales, through its 750 drugstores nationwide

SDG 4: Quality Education
- Provides affordable quality secondary education to over 16,000 students
- Provided ICT education facilities to 11 public schools, benefitting 10,896 students nationwide
- Produced 647 college graduates

SDG 5: Gender Equality
- Male 1:female 1.33 ratio for the Ayala group

SDG 6: Clean Water and Sanitation
- Delivered 570 million cubic meters of water to over 1 million connections in its service areas
- Treated 56.4 million cubic meters of used water from more than 147,000 sewer connections in its service areas

SDG 7: Affordable and Clean Energy
- Generated 6,552.1 GWh of power
- Renewable energy generation assets generated 410.3 GWh of power

SDG 8: Decent Work and Economic Growth
- Spent P173.5 billion in capital expenditures
- Generated a total of 139,074 jobs

public-transport connected, and eco-efficient
- Light Rail Manila Corporation served 157 million passengers in LRT 1 with 99.39% train punctuality
- Ayala Malls provide space for bus terminals to encourage commuters to use public transportation

SDG 12: Responsible Consumption and Production
- Diverted 98% and 9% of waste from landfill, respectively
- Hauled 216,816 kg of e-waste
- Manila Water generates 1.3kWh of electricity per day from 0.67 cubic meters of septage through its waste to energy facility

SDG 13: Climate Action
- Maintains 450 hectares of carbon forest and planted 3498 seedlings
- Renewable energy assets avoided 196,224 tonnes of CO_2 emissions

SDG 14: Life Below Water
- Removed 9087 tonnes of organic pollutants from used water
- Planted 2000 mangrove propagules
- Protects nine threatened aquatic animals

(Continued)

SDG 9: Industry, Innovation and Infrastructure
- With over 37,000 base stations, served 63.4 million customers and enabled exchange of 600 petabytes of information
- Manufactured more than 31 million units of automotive, connectivity, and smart energy technology components

SDG 15: Life on Land
- Protects five threatened plants and 20 threatened land animals
- North Luzon Renewables' biodiversity study yielded 29–60 bird species, 14–21 of which are endemic
- Planted 15,800 seedlings in 79 hectares of land and 1700 trees in 4.3 hectares of land

SDG 16: Peace, Justice and Strong Institutions
- Continue to uphold good governance and respects human rights

SDG 17: Partnerships for the goals
- Disbursed P201.8 billion worth of loans for sustainable development projects in food and agriculture, sustainable energy, education, nutrition, and other sectors
- Sustained its partnership with the UN Global Compact Network Philippines

Source: Adapted from Ayala Corporation, Integrated Report, 2017b, p. 16–17.

BASF SDG Case Study

BASF also provides an example of incorporating SDGs into their international development and social project reporting. Many of these initiatives commenced in 2018, with their impact yet to be listed and incorporated in the BASF overall Value-to-Society measure.

Below is an example list of BASF projects related to the SDGs:

West Bengal ecovio® Plus Project (India): community engagement in rural agricultural communities with organics, recycling sustainable agriculture, Women's Self-Help Groups, and improved urban amenity for the community at large.
Achievement: Improving urban amenity by diverting food waste from the streets and regenerating healthy soils. **SDGs: 3 and 11.**

BASF Lighting (China): developed an innovative, energy-efficient LED product that converts blue light into natural warm white light to protect school children from long-term exposure to blue light. Effect on school children will be monitored and evaluated.
Achievement: Reduction of school children's myopia by lowering the risk of long-term exposure to blue light. **SDGs: 3, 4, and 12.**

Sustainable Entrepreneurs (Ghana and Nigeria): introduced an innovative technology for smallholder farm management of soybean and groundnuts. Development of a spray service provider program to train and certify providers, in responsible use, equipped with BASF's personal protective equipment and knapsack sprayers.
Achievement: Smallholder trainings result in more sustainable crop management and higher yields. **SDGs: 1, 2 and 17.**

Better Environment Better Life (China): co-developing a cleaning solution. Producing an environmental-friendly product while helping low-income residents to gain the working skills for professional application.
Achievement: Improve low-income residents' life with an innovative business model. **SDGs: 1, 6 and 8.**

Novasil Flour Fortification (2016, Kenya, Tanzania): an aflatoxin-binding natural clay developed by BASF to prevent aflatoxin absorption in the body. Aflatoxin is carcinogenic and occurs in many agricultural products. Novasil can be incorporated into fortified flour in developing countries to prevent sickness.
Achievement: Training of an increasing number of mills each year. Design of a clinical study to provide evidence of the positive impacts. **SDGs: 2, 3, and 12.**

Award: BASF is recognized by the Global Compact Network Canada for its outstanding efforts to advance action toward the SDGs receiving an SDG award in the large organization category (BASF News, September 2017).

Source: Adapted from, BASF 2018, Starting Ventures.

Other Examples of SDG Uptake Include the Following Brief Case Study Examples:

Case 1—HP Inc. SDG Case Study

HP Inc. creates printers, PCs, mobile devices, solutions, and services and refers to technology for a better life. Their SDG Approach is reflected in their Sustainable Impact strategy, which is reinventing everything from how they run their operations to how they conduct business (with their partners, suppliers, and customers) to how they design, deliver, and recover their products. They state they are committed to making a positive and enduring impact by protecting the planet, supporting their people, and strengthening the communities where they live, work, and do business (Trucost ESG Analysis and S&P Global, 2018). Their CSR strategy is aligned to the SDGs. An example of this is shown below:

SDG 12: Consumption and Production	SDG 9: Industry, Innovation & Infrastructure	SDG 13: Climate Action
Driving progress toward a more efficient, circular, and low-carbon economy	Investing in disruptive technologies, such as 3D printing that will help drive a more sustainable Fourth Industrial Revolution	Reducing GHG emissions in operations in support of Climate Action
SDG 10: Reduced Inequalities		**SDG 12: Responsible Consumption and Production**
Promoting social and economic inclusion for their workers and those in their supply chain through policies, programs, and partnerships	**SDG 4: Quality Education** Building technology-based education solutions for millions around the world, including women and girls, and underrepresented and marginalized groups	An overall commitment to lessening their impact on the planet across their value chain
		SDG 10: Reduced Inequalities Creating an inclusive workplace where all workers are treated with respect and dignity
		SDG 11: Sustainable Cities and Communities Making a difference in communities around the world

Case 2—S&P Global SDG Case Study

S&P Global is a leading provider of transparent and independent ratings, benchmarks, analytics, and data for capital and commodity markets worldwide. S&P Global refer to their CSR strategy in relation to their mission statement, and refer to their CSR as more than just philanthropy. In addition, their CSR strategy is related to the SDGs with an emphasis on *bridging the skills gap and creating a sustainable future.*

Their initiatives include the following:

- Bridging global skills gap by helping people develop STEM and digital skills
- Skilled employees donate time/expertise to mentor next-generation leaders
- Development of a key partner that supports and inspires students from diverse backgrounds to be science and technology leaders and innovators
- Partnering with Upwardly Global to help skilled immigrants and refugees overcome employment barriers in the United States; East London Business Alliance (ELBA), which places disadvantaged people into employment; Lead India 2020 focuses on training and leadership development for youth; and American Corporate Partners (ACP) helps military veterans succeed in the civilian workforce.
- Promoting a Sustainable Future by reducing environmental impacts of operations by using site-based environmental management systems (EMS) to identify impacts, establish performance targets, and collect, monitor, and report environmental data, LEED® Certified™ buildings, and ISO 14001 EMS certified offices
- Reduced paper use by 48% and energy use by 18%, and increased waste diversion from landfill to 78%
- Provide ESG tools and solutions to promote sustainable markets (e.g., S&P Global Ratings offers Green Evaluations; S&P Global Market Intelligence; S&P Dow Jones Indices including the Dow Jones Sustainability Indices; S&P Global Platts covering GHG emissions, renewables, and energy outlooks)
- ESG data and analysis delivering ESG intelligence to the global marketplace
- Creating an inclusive economy through expanding opportunities for the underserved; support for women; supporting partners that provide financial tools to meet their needs; and sharing collective knowledge and experience through employee-led mentorships
- Tackling challenges women face in developing their businesses with skills and insight, and addressing lack of access to capital
- Partnering with MicroMentor, a growing online community of entrepreneurs and volunteer mentors, to match their employees' skills and talents to support budding women entrepreneurs
- Employee roundtables, mock interviews, and mentoring to successfully connect companies with skilled STEM job seekers

Source: Adapted from Trucost ESG Analysis and S&P Global (2018).

Case 3—Walgreens Boots Alliance SDG Case Study

Walgreens Boots Alliance is reported as the first global pharmacy that is health and well-being led and the largest retail pharmacy, health, and daily living destination across the United States and Europe in 25 countries, with more than 415,000 employees and 18,500 stores in 11 countries. It also has one of the largest global pharmaceutical wholesale and distribution networks, with more than 390 distribution centers delivering to more than 230,000 pharmacies, doctors, health centers, and hospitals each year in more than 20 countries. It is also one of the world's largest purchasers of prescription drugs and many other health and well-being products (Trucost ESG Analysis and S&P Global, 2018, p. 45–46). They also map their initiatives on to the following SDG framework:

***Walgreens Boots Alliance* CSR and SDG Approach:**
- Their overall CSR strategy and 12 CSR goals work to achieve the SDGs
- Key success that benefits Good Health and Well-being (SDG 3), ensuring healthy lives and promoting well-being for all at all ages
- *Walgreens (US)* has expanded its efforts to help combat the opioid epidemic
- Globally, they have delivered life-saving vaccines and life-changing vitamins impacting millions of lives around the world, especially children and pregnant women in at-risk populations
- They have raised millions of dollars for cancer research and implemented specialized training for pharmacists

Have driven large-scale initiatives which positively impact the environment, benefiting Climate Action (SDG 13):
- Have reduced their carbon footprint through energy-efficiency projects in retail pharmacies and support offices
- Fuel-efficiency programs for their wholesale delivery fleets
- Innovative Energy Care program educates employees about energy waste

Key learnings from their SDG evaluation: to address all 17 of the SDGs and to prioritize and narrow their focus on high-priority SDGs where they have the greatest impact and can measure progress

Source: Adapted from Trucost ESG Analysis and S&P Global (2018).

Walgreens Boots Alliance then merge these goals into their CSR strategy, stating their:

"… overall Corporate Social Responsibility (CSR) strategy and (our) 12 CSR goals work to achieve the SDGs" (Trucost ESG Analysis and S&P Global, 2018, p. 46).

Chapter 4

Creating Shared Value for Social Initiatives and Shared Purpose

Abstract

A full and adequate *Systematic Quantitative Literature Research Analysis* of the academic literature and research on creating shared value (CSV) is long overdue. This chapter commences this process by introducing some of the academic literature currently on CSV and examining the strengths and weaknesses of this literature, while identifying gaps for future research. The chapter builds on current academic literature to include writing and research from the business community in an attempt to make this chapter both topical and accessible to anyone interested in CSV, including practitioners interested in implementing these types of projects as direct CSV projects or as part of already existing CSR strategy. It is expected that the inclusion of this type of business literature will add value to academic research going forward. The Appendix brings the chapter together by presenting examples of a variety of CSV case studies to provide ideas for future project implementation and opportunities for future research in both implementation and measurement.

Introduction

Shared value also known as creating shared value (henceforth CSV or shared value) is a concept originating from Porter and Kramer (2011) and is increasingly discussed in the academic literature and in particular the academic 'management' literature. The authors define CSV as the *"Policies and operating practices that enhance the competitiveness of a company while simultaneously advancing the economic and social conditions in the communities in which it operates"* (Porter & Kramer, 2011, p. 66).

The concept resonates with many, as it includes a methodology with the view to 'scale up' and therefore potentially assist at greater levels, impacting millions of people and the environment. The CSV framework is of great interest as it allows organizations, multinational corporations (MNCs) and enterprises (MNEs) to work toward the concept of addressing social problems. It can, however, also be

CSR for Purpose, Shared Value and Deep Transformation, 119–159
Copyright © 2020 Emerald Publishing Limited
All rights of reproduction in any form reserved
doi:10.1108/978-1-80043-035-820200007

quite daunting for companies who not only see so many opportunities but also face constraints as an organization, especially where large-scale reinvention of their operations may be required. As part of this, there is a growing body of literature discussing the strengths and weaknesses of CSV, how CSV contrasts and overlaps with CSR, the integration of CSR and CSV, and how CSV can be part of CSR strategy. These issues are discussed later in this chapter.

The chapter opens with an examination of the academic research published on CSV. This review discusses a selection of research case study examples in-depth and raises several issues such as a methodology for examining the three pillars, a CSR case study developing into a CSV model, and a CSV project that worked in one developing country rural region but not another. Case studies in the academic literature review include *Glaxo Smith Kline (GSK)* as a new model for pharmaceutical companies; *Bangchak Petroleum Public Company Limited* in Thailand; *Nestlé* in East Java; and the integration of CSV in the CSR *European Commission* definition (2011). Also discussed is Mühlbacher and Böbel's (2018) example of the complex conditions necessary for successful shared value strategy implementation, alongside Pfitzer, Bockstette, and Stamp (2013) examples of successful commonalities across companies who have been able to create scalable models. The chapter then ends with a number of academics discussing the strengths and weakness of the CSV model, which provides several fruitful ideas for numerous new research avenues in the area of CSV. A unique aspect of this chapter is the discussion of overlaps between case studies labeled CSR as well as CSV and integrated value creation (IVC), as mentioned for Intel below, who are also studied as CSR case studies.

The Appendix provides additional cases study examples of CSV from the Shared Value Initiative Platform; the Australian Department of Foreign Affairs and Trade (DFAT) Business Partnerships Platform (BPP), the Shared Value 2018 Awards in India, and the Australian Shared Value Awards 2018. Examples of the five mutually reinforcing elements across CSV models are also included, plus example case studies of CSV measurement and long-term growth strategy for measuring shared value. The chapter also outlines the challenges in measuring shared value and the need for much more research on how to measure impact going forward.

By way of introduction, the 2011 Harvard Business Review (HBR) article, *"Creating Shared Value"* by Porter and Kramer (2011), first coined and defined CSV. The article has been cited 7828 times according to Google Scholar (as of March 15, 2019). At the time of writing their 2011 article, Porter and Kramer listed the organizations already implementing CSV. They were listed as GE, Wal-Mart, Nestlé, Johnson & Johnson, and Unilever and illustrate the dimensions of CSV by providing examples of their outcomes. Since the original HBR article, Pfitzer et al. (2013) conducted a study examining over 30 companies CSV. Nestlé is the only company included in the new list from the previous Porter and Kramer (2011) list. From their research, they selected seven companies who have created scalable models to deliver both social benefits and business value:

- **Dow Chemical**—removed 600 million kg of trans fats and saturated fats from the US diet and created a major business with its Nexera sunflower and canola seeds

- **Nestlé**—helped millions of malnourished families in India and other countries by providing inexpensive micronutrient-reinforced spices, which are a fast-growing, profitable business
- **Novartis**—provided essential medicines and health services to 42 million people in 33,000 rural villages in India through a social business model that became profitable after 31 months
- **Mars**—catalyzed a cross-sector coalition to transform farms and surrounding communities in Ivory Coast with the aim of avoiding looming cocoa shortages
- **Intel**—trained more than 10 million teachers in the use of technology to improve educational outcomes, turning education into a profitable business for the company
- **Becton Dickinson**—protected millions of health workers by creating needleless injection systems, which are now a $2 billion business for BD, accounting for 25% of the company's revenue
- **Vodafone**—extended mobile banking services to 14 million people in East Africa through M-Pesa, one of the company's most important offerings

Source: Adapted extract from Pfitzer et al., 2013.

Intel is positioned in the new 2013 list; however, they were already practising these initiatives under their CSR strategy in 2010 (Munro, 2013a, 2013b). As discussed previously, this is one of the many overlaps between CSR and CSV. The potential overlap between the two terms and the strengths and weaknesses of CSV are discussed further, later this chapter. Some of the case studies listed above are also discussed in more detail later this chapter followed by an examination of the key components of a successful model for CSV.

Before commencing a literature review of the academic literature, it is important to acknowledge that accurate CSV examples are described as the "simultaneous advancing of economic and social conditions" as described by Porter and Kramer (2011). It is also important to mention the three pillars. Porter and Kramer (2011) explain the CSV approach is not about sharing the value already created by firms nor is it a redistribution approach. Instead, it is about expanding the total pool of economic and social value through a three-pillar approach:

(1) reconceiving profits and markets
(2) redefining productivity in the value chain
(3) building supportive industry clusters at the company's locations.

These pillars are covered in the various sections identifying CSV examples throughout this chapter, plus in the academic literature section below.

Shared Value Case Studies in the Academic Literature

As mentioned in the introduction to this chapter, a full and adequate *Systematic Quantitative Literature Research Analysis* of the academic literature and research on CSV is long overdue. From an academic perspective, it is acknowledged that the shared value business model has been less studied at depth within the research literature. In particular, what is required is a thorough examination on the three levels or pillars of CSV, mapped on to various solutions for societal problems. Although finding one paper attempting this analysis, there is a significant gap in the literature for this detailed level or pillar reporting and this is therefore an excellent opportunity for future research. In order to understand the magnitude of these possibilities, several shared value case studies are included below from the sprinkling of case studies available in existing pure academic literature, as opposed to business writings, social media, and blog sites, of which there are a growing number.

The first academic paper listed in this section provides a mapping on to the three levels of CSV and gives an indication of the possibilities for this type of research. However, I first provide a case study from the Shared Value Initiatives Platform (2018), which better illustrates the three levels or pillars of CSV. First, some background regarding the organization is covered to provide an understanding of their CSV partnership and strategy. *CJ CheilJedang* is a food production company requiring ongoing agricultural products. It partnered with Korea International Cooperation Agency (KOICA) to tackle endemic poverty in a region of Vietnam by integrating rural Vietnamese farmers into their supply chain. To do this they developed a *shared value strategy and partnership*, improving their manufacturing and distribution while also enhancing the life and capabilities of local Vietnamese farmers. As a result, their province (Ninh Thuan) also became a successful and sustainable agricultural community, through increased wealth and also the development of infrastructure, technology, and skills. At the same time, *CJ CheilJedang* also benefits with ongoing and high-quality raw food ingredients for their retail business (Shared Value Initiative, 2018). Mapping these achievements on to the CSV framework and three pillars listed previously illustrates how this unique public–private collaboration developed.

The three pillars of shared value development for *CJ CheilJedang*:

---

(1) **Redefining productivity in the value chain**—*CJ CheilJedang* provided the latest farming techniques and practices and redesigned the agricultural water system (infrastructure) in the province. Through technical assistance, model farms, and research facilities, local farmers receive timely information, and with an assured steady market, the farmers receive a fair price, improving the local environment and the company's value chain.

(2) **Improving the local operating environment**—in addition to the above, many tactics were used to reinforce Vietnamese farming by increasing profits and strengthening farmer's skills. This also reinforced the capabilities of the community by supporting farmer unions, providing microcredit, and by renovating educational facilities and remodeling town facilities.

(3) **Advancing partnerships and responsible business leadership**—a global network of partnerships organized by *CJ CheilJedang* connects the company with KOICA, the Vietnamese Central Government, the Ninh Thuan Provincial Government, and Syngenta (a Swiss global agribusiness). These relationships also enhanced *CJ CheilJedang's* business knowledge and integration.

Source: Extract adapted from the Shared Value Initiative, 2018.

Returning to the academic literature, a paper by Kherchi and Fellague (2015) explains the business model of *Glaxo Smith Kline (GSK)* as a new model for pharmaceutical companies to create social and economic value through shared value. They do this by reporting the three pillars of CSV mentioned above. To do this, Kherchi and Fellague (2015) include in their article the tables by Porter (2014), which best illustrate for each category the level or activity. Table 4.1 refers to the first level of the CSV model: reconceiving products.

Table 4.1. Reconceiving Products and Markets.

Area of Activity	Approaches	Company
Tailored product offerings to meet local market conditions	Product portfolio selection Tiered pricing Adapted packaging to reduce unit cost or improve safety	GSK set prices for its patented products in the least developed countries at a maximum of 25% of the price in the United Kingdom and France GSK repackaged its Ventolin asthma medication from a 200-dose prefilled inhaler at $5 each to packs of two to three doses retailing for just a few cents

Source: cited in Kherchi & Fellague, 2015, p. 23 from Porter, 2014, FSG, p. 22.

Table 4.1 above shows how GSK have adopted tiered or discounted pricing for poor consumers and redeveloping existing product lines to meet the needs of these new markets (Kherchi & Fellague, 2015). The second level of the CSV model, redefining productivity in the value chain, is shown in Table 4.2.

Table 4.2 shows how GSK learn to deliver reconceived products to new markets, including investments to boost value chain productivity which will become more common. In addition, innovative partnerships are emerging in their model to share the risks and reduce the costs of R&D, such as ViiV Healthcare (Kherchi & Fellague, 2015). The third level of the CSV model, enabling local cluster development, is shown in Table 4.3.

Table 4.2. Redefining Productivity in the Value Chain.

Area of Activity	Approaches	Company
Collaborative and homegrown R&D to reduce cost and risk Locally adapted sales and distribution to penetrate new markets and better meet patient needs	Investment in new or existing local research institutions and collaborative approaches to reduce cost and share development risk Sales force reconfiguration New distribution approaches	GSK created a new, jointly owned company, ViiV Healthcare, that combines compounds owned by both firms to create a viable pipeline for new HIV medicines GSK is working with its distributors to share the risk of switching to a higher volume model to ensure that price reductions are passed on to patients

Source: cited in Kherchi & Fellague, 2015, p. 23 from Porter, 2014: FSG, p. 23.

Table 4.3. Enabling Local Cluster Development.

Area of Activity	Approaches	Company
Behavior change campaigns to increase demand for pharmaceuticals products	*Social marketing* to increase health-seeking behavior by patients, and patient education about disease management	Partnership with Population Services International

Source: cited in Kherchi & Fellague, 2015, p. 23 from Porter, 2014: FSG, p. 24.

Table 4.3 shows how GSK invest in health care clusters within low- and middle-income countries to improve patient awareness and demand, and health systems, within a policy and regulatory environment. This not only bolsters their own ability to reach new markets but also provides value to society that goes beyond the immediate benefit of their medicines (Kherchi & Fellague, 2015). From an interdisciplinary perspective, *social marketing* is an approach used in local cluster development to increase health-seeking behaviors by patients. An interesting area for future research would be to conduct an additional *Systematic Quantitative Literature Research Analysis* on CSV models and papers which include *social marketing* within CSV themes, as a means of achieving local cluster development. This would determine the best way to enhance cluster development using a *social marketing* methodology, while also measuring the impact and change from the campaign, to determine the success of the CSV project, and therefore allow for greater inclusion of *social marketing* methodologies.

Academic research such as that provided in the paper by Kherchi and Fellague (2015) provides an excellent overall methodology to test the three levels which are central to the CSV approach. Their paper also provides ways to measure social value and business value separately, and also the overlap of value between the two, and provides an excellent example of how to incorporate shared value measurement into future research.

Another academic paper to provide a case study for CSV is *Bangchak Petroleum Public Company Limited* in Thailand, established in 1984 as a state enterprise. The authors explain *Bangchak's* CSV through explaining their CSR approach. They describe it as a good corporate citizen, fully committed to creating value to society, referring to a CSR in-process and out-process, which is:

> "...designed and executed at all levels from local communities, communities surrounding the refinery and the nation. All work activities promote stability and strengthen preventive capability toward better, sustainable economy, society, environment, and energy security for Thais" (Nittapaipapon & Atchattabhan, 2016, p. 56).

The study's objective was to classify the critical factors required for implementation and propose business and social conditions required to adopt an inclusive business model for CSV.

To do this, *Bangchak's* added the following to their CSR processes:

(1) Initiated a 'Green Partnership Award'—a gas service station's good deeds are promoted through the 'Green Society' with a focus on the CSR in-process, ISO 26000 CSR International for consumer stewardship, environmental stewardship, community and social stewardship, and employee stewardship by serving customers, the environment, society, and communities as well as employees and business partners

(2) Staged sales promotional campaigns—by picking community goods to distribute income, launch new markets, and create jobs for local areas to strengthen community economies. Three items were promoted (sending THB 16 million back to communities): (1) fruit from the three southernmost provinces; (2) organic tea products; and (3) organic rice made by farmers which created jobs and income for communities.

(3) A membership card for connecting people and community service station projects—it was launched to stage sales promotional campaigns and customer relationship activities suiting each local area. This way, sales volumes will be raised, strengthening community service stations while supporting community economies.

Source: Extract adapted from Nittapaipapon and Atchattabhan (2016, p. 59).

This paper therefore reveals that much of the CSV program is an extension of already existing CSR projects plus the addition of some new projects. *Bangchak's* way of doing CSV is referred to as their 'CSR in-process' and 'out-process' (Nittapaipapon & Atchattabhan, 2016). This allows them to operate the business while supporting and making its community economically healthier. The idea of the community service station is also to provide opportunities to the agricultural sector by upgrading farmers' business competitiveness while also strengthening community economic growth. This is the cluster component of CSV; however, it is not clear exactly how this was achieved and if the initiative created both social and economic value back to the business and if this impact was measured.

The mistake this research paper makes is to include a case study which is not yet distinctly CSV, but label it as such prematurely. Future collaborations, however, are planned for the company, in cooperation with the Ministry of Agriculture, the Ministry of Energy, and the Bank for Agriculture and Agricultural Cooperatives, to convert abandoned orange farms into palm plantations for orange farmers, which then will provide new sources of income and promote the use of alternative energy (Nittapaipapon & Atchattabhan, 2016). Hence, more direct examples of CSV are in the pipeline. The concept of this case study is however interesting and provides opportunities for future research, and alerts to the importance of measuring shared value wherever possible, to determine if economic and social relationships are successful or are indeed a proper shared value relationship.

While there is a limited number of papers strongly focused on exact CSV examples in the academic literature, there is also a gap in the literature with regard to organizational conditions necessary for successful implementation of shared value strategies. In an attempt to fill this gap, Mühlbacher and Böbel (2018) examined examples of empirical evidence in the literature of successful shared value strategies combined with an examination of *stakeholder management*, CSR, and positive social change strategies.

Mühlbacher and Böbel (2018) propose five complex conditions in their paper, which they see as necessary for successful shared value strategy implementation. These conditions include shared value-oriented entrepreneurial vision; shared value-oriented innovation; strategic alignment; networking capabilities; and impact monitoring. The findings of their research suggest that to implement these shared value strategies successfully, managers of business functions should make coordinated sense of the *purpose* of their company, whereby managers need to align their strategic focus on the solutions to problems relevant to the business domain of the company. The study also confirmed that to be competitive, companies need to possess *innovation* processes that allow quick identification of relevant *stakeholder* problems and opportunities for new products, services, and processes alongside ongoing impact monitoring. Furthermore, Mühlbacher and Böbel (2018) found that successful implementation of shared value strategies is near impossible without highly developed *networking* capabilities with a wide range of relevant *stakeholders* and *co-creating* and *sharing value* with those *stakeholders* which requires transparent communications and developing the skills of *stakeholders* through training and encouragement. These areas are discussed further under Innovation in Chapter 5 and from an integrated value perspective in Chapter 6.

Another example of an academic paper on CSV is by Kaplan, Serafeim, and Tugendhat (2018) who argue that companies have tried to upgrade their traditional CSR programs to shared value strategies. This is indeed the case for the *Bangchak* example above. To determine this result, Kaplan et al. (2018) interviewed 30 chief sustainability officers to understand why CSR and sustainability initiatives often fail to upgrade to CSV and/or scale up successfully. Key problems identified were poor integration with the company's core business; difficulty engaging with multiple actors in local communities; and a lack of relevant measures to evaluate benefits for the company and the target population. Furthermore, they state the problem is not in the execution of shared value projects but in the limited 'scale' for projects selected.

The researchers concluded that there needs to be a new ecosystem level replacing inefficient supply chains. By examining the experiences of several companies, the authors provide three principles to achieve scale:

- Search for systemic, multisector opportunities
- Mobilize complimentary partners
- Obtain seed and scale up financing

Source: Kaplan et al., 2018.

A potential fourth principle, suggested by Kaplan et al. (2018), is to implement a new measurement and governance system to monitor progress and keep key players aligned in a new ecosystem. With the 'new ecosystem' now a contemporary theme, the principles suggested by Kaplan et al. (2018) need to be replicated and examined in future research, by studying actual case study examples, rather than the perspectives of chief sustainability officers, as the research methodology of Kaplan et al. (2018) implements.

A paper by Voltan, Hervieux, and Mills (2017) attempts to study the broad array of *stakeholders* and answer the call to researchers to study a range of concepts and various models in developing countries. To do this, Voltan et al. (2017) focus on CSV as a win-win proposition. In their 2017 article in *Business Ethics (A European Review)*, they examine the concept of CSV in non-Western 'developing' countries and Western 'developed' country contexts. They conducted a critical discourse analysis of 66 articles to identify how CSV is being cited by authors.

Their findings reveal that Western perspectives tended to be more supportive of CSV, but they also refer to the need to "recognize the increasing complexity of the business-society nexus and *stakeholder* engagement" (Voltan et al., 2017, p. 347) in creating CSV projects. They suggest the CSV framework requires further development to maintain "credibility and applicability," especially in non-Western countries. In addition, their research suggests more CSV projects need to be set-up and studied in Eastern and developing countries to determine greater knowledge of CSV in these developing countries. This they state would greatly enhance the credibility of the CSV framework. This study however needs to be replicated in future research and provides an excellent opportunity to assess this in emerging and developing Eastern countries.

An Academic Perspective of a Pioneering CSV Example: Nestlé

In a single in-depth research study, Prafitri (2017) examined Nestlé Indonesia's CSV initiatives in a dairy farming case study example in East Java to determine if CSV will create a win-win solution for both the company and society. The Nestlé case study's key CSV initiative involves providing financial and technical support to farmers to increase milk quality. Nestlé argued that the increase in milk quality would automatically increase farmers' income because Nestlé offered a higher price for better quality milk, which in turn improves the quality of life in these communities (Prafitri, 2017, p. iii). However, Prafitri found that while the CSV initiatives created economic value for the company, this did not automatically improve social conditions for dairy farmers in related communities. Hence, Prafitri (2017) points out that in her study, the micro-economic lens to address social issues limited the effectiveness of CSV as a win-win solution through the CSV lens. In this case, the CSV lens (that will only be created if the CSV initiatives create economic value for both the business and society) did not emerge from this example.

Prafitri (2017) therefore concluded, that in her study, CSV does not reshape capitalism as promised by Porter and Kramer (2011); rather, it brings a neoclassical logic to the discourse of CSR (Prafitri, 2017, p. 164) (i.e., a firm's economic obligation being the main 'purpose' of business in neoclassical theory). From this she concluded that CSV does not advance CSR theory. Rather, it repackages neoliberal logic as a new rational discourse of CSR (Prafitri, 2017, p. iii).

To support her findings, Prafitri (2017) argues that reinventing capitalism is not only about connecting social problems. It also requires moral capabilities and for these to be suitable and acceptable to the social context beyond economic discourse (Beschorner, 2014 cited in Prafitri, 2017, p. 164). This would mean, for example, that the dairy farmers will not go elsewhere to sell their milk for a better price and Nestlé would not buy their milk from a cheaper source beyond the farmers supported by their business model. In the Nestlé Indonesia example, CSV initiatives were provided to increase the milk quality for Nestlé Indonesia as the main buyer of the product. Better milk quality leads to high-quality raw material for the company. The company's initiatives successfully changed dairy farmers' attitudes to this. However, the study found that in the case of Nestlé Indonesia once the CSV initiatives no longer created economic value for the company, the company discontinued the initiative.

The study by Prafitri (2017) has some limitations, however. It only utilizes one case study and in only one developing country. The researcher also points to the unusual context of extreme poverty in some areas, mixed with political difficulties across many levels in Indonesia, alongside its earlier history of Dutch exploitation of Indonesian farmers. The study would need to be replicated in other developing countries where Nestlé has similar dairy farm case study examples and across different sectors and therefore types of CSV projects.

It is therefore pertinent that additional research is conducted before a definitive conclusion is made from this study, as there are many other successful CSV stories such as Unilever and Intel whose social projects have been listed as part of CSR strategy for many years and more recently as their CSV strategy by CSV proponents. This is an excellent opportunity to study these case study examples more deeply and measure their impact in future academic research.

Research Outlining the Integration of CSR and CSV

Porter and Kramer state that CSV has the potential to lead to "the next major transformation of business thinking" (2011, p. 64). In contrast, Visser (2011) talks about 'integrated value' where shared value is only a part of the overall value. This suggests 'integration' of terms for both CSV and CSR play a part in a larger system. Integrated value is discussed further in Chapter 6. In this section, we examine the integration of CSR and CSV.

The new definition of CSR from the European Commission (EU) announced in October 2011, also focuses on integration. As previously mentioned in Chapter 5, their new definition for CSR is further extended in the box below. Of interest it also reflects aspects of CSV. Two bullet points in the broader definition for CSR integrate CSV into the definition and process, as shown below. This is the only time they mention CSV in their 16-page report on their renewed strategy and new definition for CSR:

To fully meet their *corporate social responsibility (CSR)*, enterprises should have in place a process to integrate social, environmental, ethical, human rights and consumer concerns into their business operations and core strategy in close collaboration with their *stakeholders,* with the aim of: ... *maximising the creation of shared value for their owners/shareholders and for their other stakeholders and society at large...to maximise the creation of shared value, enterprises are encouraged to adopt a long-term, strategic approach to CSR, and to explore the opportunities for developing innovative products, services and business models that contribute to societal wellbeing and lead to higher quality and more productive jobs.*
Source: Extract from the European Commission, 2011

The EU report discusses CSV, as a part of CSR, suggesting that there is room to use both terms under the umbrella of CSR strategy and that one term is not always seen to be replacing the other. The report also mentions the term *integrate.* This acknowledgment could lead to the inclusion of interesting research related to the IVC approach of Visser (2012) discussed in Chapter 6. As the EU report discusses CSV, not only alongside CSR but also as a part of CSR, it is also important to consider the integration of CSR and CSV in research. The authors, Voltan et al. (2017) (discussed in the next section), accommodate this in their research paper examining the win-win proposition of CSV across Western and non-Western contexts.

Further supporting the integration of both terms, CSR and CSV in the literature, is the study of Voltan et al. (2017) on CSV. As previously mentioned, this study quotes extracts from different CSR papers in the academic literature. The Munro (2013a) paper they quote examines aspects of CSR in the Middle East and Africa. Voltan et al. (2017) describe the paper as an empirical study illustrating different preferences for Social Initiates (SIs) across *stakeholders* for specific regions, suggesting SIs under the CSR umbrella can also be implemented with a CSV methodology. In this regard, multinational enterprises (MNEs) can "strategically pursue avenues for shared value models of CSR" (Porter & Kramer, 2011, p. 352). To further prove the integration of CSR and shared value (CSV), the CSR Initiatives Munro (2013a) paper discussing Porter and Kramer's CSV is quoted by Voltan et al. (2017):

> "What's more, some of the leading management and marketing academics agree that companies should advance their social benefits to improve public perception, public credibility and image (Porter & Kramer, 2011). The perspective of stakeholders and an understanding of their needs, is therefore of utmost importance." (Munro, 2013a, p. 75, cited in Voltan et al., 2017, p. 356).

In their CSV-based paper, Voltan et al. (2017) also quote the Munro (2013a) article again as an example of an area to be considered in future research, particularly in developing countries. The Munro (2013a) article also quotes Porter and Kramer from a CSV perspective in relation to the integration of CSR activities with CSV:

> "Bronn and Vrioni (2001) and Porter and Kramer (2006) agree that integration of CSR activity and SIs strengthens the firm's long-term competitiveness and image… whereby CSR is embedded in overall strategy beyond profit maximisation and includes long-term business survival alongside meeting societal needs and expectations (Balmer and Greysdner, 2006)" (Munro, 2013a, p. 76).

Voltan et al. (2017) also discuss the dominant perspective of CSV as a form of '*strategic CSR*' providing tangible benefits to firms. To further this theme, they include several quotes from research integrating CSR and CSV. George, McGahan, & Prabhu (2012), for example, states that "at its core, the Porter and Kramer (2011) approach retains the conceptualization of the corporation as primarily chartered to generate returns on invested capital" (p. 17). This quotation illustrates the instrumental nature of CSV, and that the value created is measured based on its capacity to generate wealth. Voltan et al. (2017) also select a quote from Karam and Jamali (2017) to reiterate the point of utilizing shared value models of CSR alongside CSV within management scholarship where:

> "… attempts to build the business case for CSR predominate. These discussions more often than not expound instrumental

logics in support of the idea that corporations are an instrument for wealth creation (Garriga & Mele, 2004) or can strategically pursue avenues for shared value models of CSR (Porter & Kramer, 2011, p. 468)" (Voltan et al., 2017, p. 352).

As previously mentioned, Porter and Kramer state CSV has the potential to lead to "the next major transformation of business thinking" (2011, p. 64). This is an emerging opportunity for future research to study CSV and to also determine its integration with CSR and its use in developing countries. To present a balance in the literature, there are also several criticisms of CSV, which are covered later this chapter.

Commonalities of CSV across Successful Organizations

To determine the success of integrating CSV into corporate strategy, the research paper previously mentioned by Pfitzer et al. (2013) examines over 30 companies. As mentioned previously, they list seven companies from their study who have created scalable models to deliver both social benefits and business value. These are listed in the introduction to this chapter. Individual examination of each of these companies is beyond the scope of the current chapter; however, their research allows us to understand more about CSV implementation through commonality of what is successful. Pfitzer et al. (2013), for example, found particular elements in the organizations that assisted them to create scalable models to deliver both social benefits and business value (Pfitzer et al., 2013). These *commonalities* across organizations studied include five mutually reinforcing elements which also provide opportunities for future academic research as a measure of success and impact across case study examples.

The five commonality examples for future research include:

1. *Embedding a social purpose involves organizations reinforcing and embedding their social purpose through their organization's culture to unleash the best in employees and help mobilize external partners with similar goals (Pfitzer et al., 2013).* It would be interesting to quantify this with measurement in future research. Examples of companies embedding 'social purpose' are provided in the Appendix of this chapter.
2. *Defining a social need helps organizations gain insight into the needs they wish to address by conducting research into underlying social conditions and how best to change them.* This is an area of research that could be conducted academically to make rigorous comparisons in different countries relative to different industries and is an important consideration for future research. The paper in Chapter 2 is an example of research that asks employees as internal *stakeholders* (who are also 80%–98% from the country of origin where the MNE resides) to specify what needs to be addressed and what may be required in situations where their relatives and family may be affected directly or indirectly by the problem (Munro, 2017). For systemic wicked problems it is better to ask *stakeholders* and officials

(Continued)

directly involved in the problem or issues. This type of market level research will help develop a business case to identify execution capabilities internally and externally and anticipate resourcing requirement (Pfitzer et al., 2013). Future academic research could examine the findings further at a multilayered level to determine differences across problem types and the longitudinal experience across various sectors. The Appendix for this chapter provides example(s) of companies embedding 'social purpose.'

3. *Measuring shared value is necessary to monitor progress and be scalable. The steps are the following:*
   (i) *Estimate the business and social value*
   (ii) *Establish intermediate measures and track progress*
   (iii) *Assess the shared value produced.*

Source: Extract adapted from Pfitzer et al., 2013.

The Appendix for this chapter provides further explanation of the three-step process with an example from Coca-Cola. Pfitzer et al. (2013) discusses this example using the Coca-Cola measures of Coletivo in Brazil with two goals: to increase employability of low-income youths and young adults; and to increase sales by strengthening distribution channels and awareness. If the individual measures had changed over time for the youth through the training program rather than examining only increased sales, other measurement methodologies could be considered such as social return on investment (SROI) as an impact measurement assessment. The addition to CSV measurement of measuring social impact, using the *Theory of Change* through SROI methodology, is an opportunity for future research, in measuring changes that occur through CSV.

4. *Creating the optimal innovation structure by creating a semiautonomous unit in the organization. This provides a shield for the new innovative initiative during the development phase, until it satisfies the company's normal financial requirements and procedures (Pfitzer et al., 2013).* Of interest, the authors suggest obtaining philanthropic or government funding to test the waters for the innovation and shield until it finds a viable business model that can be integrated into the established business. As discussed below, this is also a methodology which is being increasingly incorporated into CSR strategy.

Source: Extract from Pfitzer et al., 2013.

As discussed in point 4, Pfitzer et al. (2013) recommend financing independent entrepreneurs to tackle the challenge or problem first for the company to learn from and/or partner with an existing social enterprise that has a solution already to a problem. Chapter 5 on Innovation (in the following chapter) suggests that this can also be done under the umbrella of an existing CSR strategy. Testing which method (e.g., CSV or CSR strategy incorporation) works best to create an optimal innovation structure (for a new product or initiative) is an excellent opportunity for future research.

---

5. *Co-creating with external stakeholders was also found to be effective enlisting a wide range of stakeholders: governments, foundations, universities, NGOs, and other companies to co-create with and understand their social needs.* Successful companies also funded *stakeholder* research and sought leaders as consultants, hiring people with experience in both the business and social sectors to lead the program.
Source: Extract from Pfitzer et al., 2013.

Pfitzer et al. (2013) also found in their study that successful companies learnt to leverage off others' capabilities. They provide Nestlé as an example, who discovered that the Drishtee Foundation assisting in rural regions of India already had a distribution system in place for supplying remote retail shops in a region most affected by micronutrient deficiencies. They therefore engaged Drishtee to help distribute their product (Masala-ae-Magic spices). This is discussed further in the case study examples in the Appendix of this chapter. Similarly, in a rural area of India, Novartis noted a lack of finance meant pharmacists and doctors could not purchase diagnostic medicine and equipment. Novartis therefore partnered with a local microfinance enterprise who had the capability to assist at that level.

In summary, it is clear from this research that a deeply held *social purpose* is important for *co-creation*, as it helps form trusted relationships. In fact, the five key ingredients (and commonalities) discovered by Pfitzer et al. (2013) discussed above, were found to be all mutually reinforcing. These ingredients may also be dependent on a company's culture, context, and strategy. The suggestion that an organization's culture, context, and strategy are responsible for creating an environment to foster these key ingredients provides an excellent opportunity for future research.

At the time of writing this chapter, an academic literature review in *EBSCOhost* revealed limited coverage of these issues. The managerial implications from this type of research would undoubtedly enhance managerial training and foster social innovators in organizations. To determine that these five ingredients exist in companies across different regions and industries that are successful in implementing CSV projects, would also be valuable for rigorous academic research to determine and consider identified commonalities further. This in particular is relevant to the academic literature for MNEs setting up their subsidiary companies in new and emerging markets. There is a need to determine innovative structures that work and to also estimate how much of this function can or is still implemented through the CSR department and CSR strategy of companies in developing regions. An advantage of this approach is that it will also provide a framework for measuring CSV.

Measuring Shared Value: Through Research and Case Studies

Being able to measure the impact of social models such as the CSV model and its indirect and direct effects is relevant to both ongoing academic research and also financial investors in the field. Nittapaipapon and Atchattabhan (2016), for example, identify indirect company benefits as "brand positioning, customer loyalty, and employee motivation" and refer to "external social benefits" as "community benefits such as jobs, knowledge, environmental responsibility, and health" (Nittapaipapon and Atchattabhan, 2016, p. 57). However, shared value business models in developing markets imply high start-up costs (Nittapaipapon and Atchattabhan, 2016) meaning that profits may take some time, but they are essential to the concept of CSV. CSV therefore requires a long-term perspective and a form of measurement to make it attractive to investors.

Progress therefore needs to be measured on social objectives, including the degree to which social performance improves economic value for the business over time. Previous CSR and sustainability reporting has measured financial, social, and environmental measures separately or in a separate integrated report, a reporting area still in its infancy (Adams, 2014). Examples of popular CSR rankings include Transparency International, Anti-Corruption Indices, RepTrak 1,000, Fortune 100 Best companies to work for, Social Progress Index, and GRI Benchmark (Laudal, 2018). The Forbes Top 10 list uses the MSCI ESG STAT to measure CSR behavior. The findings of the research by Bendoraitienė and Gaigalienė (2015) revealed that systems vary considerably, according to the scope, 'purpose,' and concepts of CSR employed. To have similar ratings, rankings, and indexes for CSV is an excellent opportunity for future research going forward. Some of the difficulties with this are discussed below.

One of the difficulties is that the area of measuring CSV is still developing. Laudal (2018) sites a gap in the academic literature for the topic of measuring shared value, stating there are limited attempts to measure CSV at the corporate level in the academic literature. The one example available for measuring CSV by Porter et al. (2012) is stated by Laudal as nonempirical, with the empirical section only providing the experience of five case studies, but with no measurement methodology, comparison matrix, or comparative analysis. To date, the criticism is that this does not enable us to use a standardized or general model to track the development of CSV or compare CSV across firms (Grindle, Smith, Longo, and Murray, 2014; Laudal, 2018). Porter, Stern, and Loria (2013) presented the *Social Progress Index*; however, it is noted that it was developed to compare countries not corporations (Laudal, 2018) and is therefore not relevant to measuring CSV per se. One way to approach this gap in the literature is to measure the three pillars of shared value across corporations and industries. These pillars, as previously listed, expand the company's pool of available economic and social value through shared value but need to be measured. Different company performances for these pillars are not compared in the academic literature to validate them. This therefore provides a significant opportunity for future research.

Since the aim of CSV is to capture the entirety of a business strategy, not just predefined impacts, measurements of CSV impacts are differently reported in the traditional literature on CSR measurement. This makes benchmarking and measuring CSV quite extensive and has as a result been criticized, as there is thought to be no rigorous quantitative or qualitative data across companies to confirm this notion (Laudal, 2018).

As mentioned above, Porter et al. (2012) propose an approach to measuring CSV where the focus lies on the intersection between business and social value creation. This is explained through the analysis of case studies. Nittapaipapon and Atchattabhan (2016) explain that companies can measure their compliance with social environmental and governance (ESG) and still demonstrate positive impact and CSR measures. However, to measure CSV, the company must first identify its social issues to target, make the business case, then track progress, and measure results using 'insight' to unlock new value (Porter et al., 2012). It is important that social and business results are measured relative to costs and that the CSV measures be distinguished from other reports. Unfortunately examining this specific area of CSV is beyond the scope of this current book; however, this is touched on briefly here to determine the emerging and future research potential and direction for measuring impact of CSV.

With the future in mind, Porter et al. (2012) are asking companies to lock shared value measurement into their strategies and make it a repeatable and integrated process. The authors provide several examples of companies that have attempted to do this. In order for the assessment to be of value, the authors report the need to measure the direct link between social needs and improving business and assess the value creation by tracking social and business results relative to costs. This is an extensive process and not surprisingly companies have reported a number of challenges in doing this. Some of the more successful case studies, however, are reported by Porter et al. (2012) and listed in brief below.

Across the three levels or pillars of shared value, Earlier written as Nestlé provides a 'cluster development' example for measurement in rural communities. The Prafitri (2017) research example discussed earlier is of a Nestlé case study example in Java, Indonesia. This Nestlé measurement example, however, is from Rajasthan, India, and is an example of a successful CSV case study often used in the business and academic literature. The supply of milk in India, and in particular Rajasthan, is discussed in the context of increasing the productivity of cattle. In this example, Nestlé assures purchase of milk at a certain price and provides established collection and chilling centers, agricultural advice, veterinary services, and other essential infrastructure (Porter et al., 2012). When Porter et al., (2012) wrote their article on *Measuring Shared Value*, Nestlé had worked with 8,000 framers in Rajasthan, monitoring their progress with regular visits and tracking indicators such as herd size, cattle health, and volume of milk sourced. The reliable income from higher volumes of milk has significantly helped these farmers and their communities by improving the lives of farmers and Nestlé has a better and more reliable source of raw material for their products.

Further measurement examples for Coca-Cola and Intel are listed in the Appendix of this chapter. The company examples provided here and in the Appendix for measuring CSV did well to find ways to measure their impact, but as mentioned above companies and researchers have identified a number of difficulties with implementing CSV measurement (e.g., Grindle et al., 2014; Laudal, 2018). Porter et al. (2012) agree that there are a number of challenges in measuring shared value and clearly outline these in their *Measuring Shared Value* paper. These are listed below to suggest ways to tackle more directly the problems in CSV measurement and find ways to examine and develop these measures in future research.

Challenges in Measuring Shared Value

Challenge 1—A wide range of social issues need to be addressed and measured.

- *This refers to the fact that companies can be overwhelmed by the range of potential social impacts for their activities and what can be realistically tracked and analyzed.* However, employing social impact assessment specialists can help organizations identify and prioritize key agendas by engaging third-party research firms to complete assessments.

Challenge 2—Measuring social outcomes for large populations.

- *A product that reaches millions of customers or an issue that effects the population as a whole, for example, is hard to measure. Extrapolation on a large scale based on evidence of smaller scale impacts is sometimes made and targeted studies may be used. Selecting measurable outcomes is a key as it is for social impact assessments and the theory of change.* An example of this is selecting the right social proxies to determine a social return on investment (SROI). Testing this with current shared value measurement themes would be an excellent opportunity for future research when researchers are unable to determine exact economic or social value. A comparison of different measurements types should be examined in future research.

Challenge 3—Business value accrues on a different timeline than social value.

- *This challenge acknowledges that in measurement assessments, business results and social results have different timelines which can mean it may be better to focus on short-term outcomes in the early stages of a social project.*

Challenge 4—Measuring business value for cluster investment.

- *This challenge refers to the fact that impact in the communities or cluster where businesses operate is difficult to measure and may require tracking proxy indicators for business value.* The proxy issue is similar to what is written for challenge 2 above, unless the overall amount of the issues produced in the community can be measured.

Challenge 5—Determining a company's attribution when strategies and activities require the efforts of many partners.

- *This challenge suggests rather than focusing on attributing social results solely to company actions, the focus should be on how company actions contribute to social progress as social and environmental outcomes cannot be determined by one organization or one influence.*

Challenge 6—Management desires an aggregation of social impact.

- *This refers to the fact that different social dimensions cannot be aggregated together (e.g., health and education outcomes are not additive).* Programs, however, can be compared and is an opportunity for future research.

Source: Extract adapted from Porter et al., 2012.

The authors are honest in stating that the tools to measure the concept of CSV in practice are still in early development, and hence, a framework that measures the interaction between business and social results will be one of the most important developments for CSV practice. This will assist shared value methodology to become more established and encourage scalable solutions to the world's most difficult problems. This provides an excellent opportunity for future research alongside finding ways to tackle the challenges of measuring CSV.

Criticisms of Shared Value

There is much excitement from the shared value initiative and its platforms in different parts of the world, with excellent potential in emerging markets and the developing country context. In order to provide a balanced account, this section provides an examination of the strengths and weaknesses of CSV proposed in the academic literature. From an academic perspective, it is difficult to discuss the literature in relation to a concept without revealing its critics, proponents, and its strengths and weaknesses. Many of the strengths are mentioned at the end of this section, following a discussion of some of the proposed weaknesses.

Firstly, the CSV framework has been criticized by academic scholars as repacking or overlapping already existing concepts. Voltan et al. (2017) cite Dembek, Singh, and Bhakoo (2016) as an example. They focus on the confusion "surrounding both views on how shared value relates to different concepts and theories, and the views on how it differs from them as a distinct concept" (p. 240). Crane, Palazzo, Spence, and Matten (2014) refer to the claim made by Porter and Kramer in their 2011 article that CSV has triggered substantial change in the behavior of firms. They argue that this claim needs to be backed by evidence, but add that this is probably not feasible because *"there is no realistic way to distinguish a CSV initiative from, say, a strategic CSR initiative, except for its label"* (Crane et al., 2014, p. 153). This is certainly an area for important future research as is working out a system to measure shared value and/or CSV.

One of the major criticisms of CSV, however, is that it resembles many already existing concepts such as blended value (Emerson, 2000), conscious capitalism (Mackey, 2011), bottom of the pyramid (Prahalad, 2012), and *stakeholder theory* (Freeman, 1984), among others. Strand and Freeman (2015) agree and present *stakeholder theory* as the original logic for CSV (cited in Voltan et al., 2017, p. 350). These and additional concepts are included in the next section in reference to Porter and Kramer's response to Crane et al. (2014) criticisms. As part of this critique, Crane et al. (2014, p. 130) referred to CSV as a "seductive proposition" gathering widespread attention. In this vein, Voltan et al. (2017) also refer to the associations and near-celebrity status of Kramer and Porter. Other researchers and scholars have referred to publishing in the *Harvard Business Review* as the pull, referring to the concept as representing mainstream thought. Beschorner (2014), for example, refers to the aspect of having mass appeal to management practitioners and also research scholars, which is also very positive.

Additional criticisms have stated a lack of guidance for how to overcome social-economic trade-offs (and/or tensions). This is perhaps hard to know unless you have implemented in-depth CSV projects and been involved at the micro level of a CSV project and seen it in action, fully functioning and operating. A similar view can be put forward for the criticism, stating a lack of evidence that the concept considers the complexity of value chain activities and impacts, when in fact it is proposed that CSV attempts to address system-level problems with organization-level changes (Crane et al., 2014).

Feedback from various CSR research scholars (e.g., Carroll & Brown, 2018) and various CSR email bloggers (e.g., academic and prolific email blogger, David Chandler) indicate that the CSV model is simple to understand, and this is why it has had so much appeal. However, it is this simplicity that some authors criticize, as it is seen to "ignore the complex nature of the relationship between business and society" (Voltan et al., 2017, p. 350). Similar to the argument regarding simplicity, Dembek et al. (2016) described CSV as "vague," and although advancing the win-win discussion, it is seen by some scholars as "a narrow conceptualization of social value and (an) avoidance of potential tensions between business and society" (Aakhus & Bzdak, 2012, cited in Voltan et al., 2017, p. 350). Similar to this, Crane et al. (2014) argue that CSV over-simplifies complex relations and is naïve about assumptions made pertaining to regulatory compliance and the *tensions* (or lack thereof) between social and economic goals and the potential trade-offs between the two goals as a result. Other researchers have criticized CSV for not dealing with additional components of traditional CSR, such as the legal, ethical, and governance issues which are an integral part of CSR alongside the social, discretionary, and/or philanthropic components. Voltan et al. (2017) illustrate this point by quoting Aakhus and Bzdak (2012), who disagree with Porter and Kramer's "umbrella framework" suggesting the focus on finding "social value sweet spots leads to blind spots about what societies value" by not addressing "harmful business activities" (p. 237). They also quote, Dembek et al. (2016), that although "CSV may contribute to raising incomes in poor communities, it is unlikely to solve the problem of poverty" (p.350).

Professor of IVC, Wayne Visser (2015), states that while he is generally a fan of CSV, he believes that rather than replacing CSR, CSV has cleverly changed "the language of social responsibility into the language of value creation" which is better understood by business leaders (p. 126). He also questions how different CSV is from CSR (Visser, 2015). In addition, Visser reports that CSV is an evolution of Porter and Kramer's thinking, as in 2002 they wrote about 'the competitive advantage of corporate philanthropy' (Porter and Kramer, 2002) which was then referred to in 2006 as 'strategic CSR' (Porter and Kramer, 2006). Hence, Visser therefore comments that CSV is their third move into the field of social responsibility, but also states the CSV concept as "not going far enough" (Visser, 2015, p. 127).

Visser (2015) further comments that there is nothing new about CSV, stating it echoes the work of Prahalad and Hart (2002) on the 'bottom of the pyramid' and supports 'inclusive business' by IFC. Prahalad and Hart (2002), for example, discuss MNE investment lifting:

> "...billions of people out of poverty and desperation, averting social decay, political chaos, terrorism and environmental meltdown that is certain to continue if the gap between rich and poor countries continues to widen" (p. 2).

The 'bottom of the pyramid' (BOP) concept also refers to the issue of scalability like CSV, but refers to the MNEs need to reevaluate "their understanding of scale, from a 'bigger is better' ideal to an ideal of highly distributed small-scale operations married to world-scale capabilities" (p. 2). The authors report that this will also require a new level of efficiency and ways of measuring financial success.

Again, this discussion returns to the pillars or three key levels of CSV. In this way CSV provides a methodology or a way to implement projects. Also, it must be noted that since Prahalad and Hart's much quoted article, in 2002, the United Nations sustainable development goals (SDGs) were introduced in 2015 and Social Impact Assessment in business markets has taken off as a way to measure both social and financial success.

Overall, these criticisms seem harsh given the intent of the CSV methodology and/or model. Their significance therefore needs to be assessed further in future research contrasting CSV with other models and examining CSV case studies at the impact measurement level.

Linking CSV to Other Concepts: The Key Criticism

One of the most criticized aspects of CSV is the originality of the idea. Critics proclaim it is not original. Porter and Kramer respond by saying they acknowledge the following "important contributions" in this broad area:

(1) Jed Emerson's blended value (Emerson, 2000)
(2) Stuart Hart's mutual benefit (Hart, 1997)
(3) Prahalad and Hart's bottom of the pyramid (Hart & Prahalad, 2002)

(4) John Elkington's work on sustainability and the triple bottom line (Elkington, 1998)
(5) Andrew Savitz and Karl Weber's work on sustainability and the triple bottom line (Savitz and Weber, 2006)
(6) David Schwerin's and John Mackey's work on conscious capitalism (Mackey and Sisodia, 2013; Schwerin, 1998)
Source: Porter and Kramer, 2011.

In the letter of response, Porter and Kramer respond to the particular criticism of originality. Their key mantra is that "related work does not mean that the concepts are the same" (Crane et al., 2014, p. 149). They respond to the criticism of likeness to the above concepts as follows:

> "Jed Emerson emphasizes the need to blend the social, environmental, and economic value created by both for-profit and nonprofit enterprises, so that enterprises and capital markets can maximize the sum of all forms of value created. CSV, however, is about solving societal problems in order to create economic value, not about blending or balancing different types of value. Stuart Hart's framework for sustainable value creation includes pollution prevention, clean tech, bottom of the pyramid, and product stewardship, all of which overlap but are not the same as the levels of CSV. Prahalad and Hart's path-breaking work on selling to the bottom of the pyramid can also be an aspect of CSV, however, as Hart and Kash Rangin have separately written, BOP products and services only create sustainable value when they benefit the communities they serve, and not all BOP initiatives do so. A similar point about the overlap with CSV can be made about sustainability, which has been defined in many ways ranging from a focus on environmental improvements that reduce costs or improve products and create shared value, to a broad call for the protection of future generations through systemic changes that would distort capitalism and undermine competitiveness" (Quote by Michael E. Porter and Mark R. Kramer', cited in Crane et al., 2014, p. 149).

Strengths of CSV

While the previous section and the Crane et al. (2014) article quoted earlier focus on the weaknesses they foresee in CSV, the authors also refer to its many strengths. Crane et al. (2014), for example, mention that the "concept (of CSV) has met with considerable success" (p.132) and note that it is an "idea developed for and with senior leaders in large corporations and therefore has succeeded in gaining a substantial and positive practitioner audience" (p.132), attracting many large companies such as Nestlé, Coca-Cola, and Unilever, to name a few. Again, Crane et al. (2014) claim the concept achieved this through its success with the

Harvard Business Review (HBR) audience. However, at the same time, the CSV concept was released by other media including *The New York Times, The Economist, The Guardian, Forbes,* and the *Huffington Post.* According to Crane et al. (2014) it was also discussed at *Davos* and is compulsory reading for a variety of MBA and executive courses and won the *2011 McKinsey Award* for best HBR article. There is reference made to the authors closeness to the HBR faculty, but it has also had the ability to attract other media. Typically, academics with concepts to release are often busy solely chasing A-level academic journal submissions as required by their tenure, which are often read by a different group or audience that does not always include the C-Suite directors and business decision-makers of the HBR readership.

Related to this audience readership is the success of CSV in framing CSR activities in appealing managerial language which is as the authors note is "particularly important for advancing social causes inside companies" (Crane et al., 2014). A further positive note is that the CSV concept "invites corporations to perceive these problems as real opportunities and serious strategic targets for genuine business decisions" (Crane et al., 2014, p. 132). In the same vein, Crane et al. (2014) mention a key strength of CSV is its ability to elevate social goals to the strategic level required for business and explain their strategic relevance. They also noted the role of government when looking at the social initiatives of corporate companies. Porter and Kramer have explained this as the "role for state actors" in constructing "regulations that enhance shared value, set goals, and stimulate innovation" (Porter & Kramer, 2011, p. 64). Evidence of success in involving governments is a program which involves the Australian DFAT set-up of a BPP platform. The DFAT BPP was introduced to Australia and is mentioned in the conclusion of this chapter, with examples of projects in the Appendix of this chapter.

In summary, the largest compliment to CSV of all is the one that states that the CSV framework has the ability to unify the unconnected ongoing debates for separate terms, such as "CSR, non-market strategy, conscious capitalism, social entrepreneurship, social innovation, and the bottom of the pyramid." By providing this holistic view, CSV also offers some kind of potential promise for "more integrated thinking about the intersection of business and social progress"(Crane et al., 2014, p. 134).

By placing CSV at a broader system level (i.e., amongst the problems of a capitalist system), Porter and Kramer bring to the debate a more conceptual level to the "caring" or "conscious capitalism" themes (Crane et al., 2014; O'Toole & Vogel, 2011). These themes are discussed in more detail in Chapter 1.

In reference to the boxed quote above, many critics in general are adamant that CSV does not replace CSR (and other terms) but is complimentary to CSR (Carroll & Brown, 2018). Porter and Kramer suggest that CSR is superseded by

CSV with the core argument that the CSR definition is separate from profit maximization; however, Crane et al. (2014) argue that this ignores several decades of research exploring the business case for CSR. When examining the business case for CSV, however, the direct profit made in the rethinking of a product or the direct profit of rethinking, the cluster development for a product or service is made obvious. This becomes apparent when you also look at the three pillars in the development of a CSV project or model.

A final strength of the CSV model is the elements of inclusive business that it incorporates.

In this light, the IFC reports the need for large corporates to instigate 'inclusive business' and 'change.' IFC say todays rising business leaders "... understand that people living in low-income communities are value-conscious consumers seeking out goods and services that can improve their lives." Global businesses increasingly see interesting new supply and distribution opportunities in emerging and newly emerging economies. This correlates with positive growth with models that offer goods, services, and job opportunities to low-income communities, all of which are examples of 'inclusive business' models' (IFC, 2018).

Hence, with their 'inclusive business' investments, IFC tend to not only focus on poverty but also refer to a 'shared' prosperity. They talk about creating transformational solutions to development challenges through partnerships with business, government, and civil society to accelerate inclusive business around the world. Shared value also appears to be a vehicle to do this through the core business of the corporate designing opportunities throughout the value chain with partnerships across the three pillars, especially the third pillar listed here. As mentioned previously, the three pillars referred to are (1) reconceiving profits and markets; (2) redefining productivity in the value chain; and (3) building supportive industry clusters at the company's locations (Porter and Kramer, 2011).

Further aspect of CSV reminiscent of the inclusive business model is the emphasis on challenges and solutions through the value chain from product development and distribution through to marketing sales and customer service. The IFC research identified five lessons or solutions through these shared and inclusive strategies to spark innovation:

(1) Plan for scale for financial sustainability and long-term impact
(2) Minimize delivery cost through technology and lean staffing
(3) Invest in capacity building and training to enhance knowledge and skills
(4) Raise awareness and educate BOP customers
(5) Develop smart partnerships with tangible benefits for both parties. Therefore win-win partnerships are more likely to endure.

Source: IFC, 2018

Innovation is discussed in the following chapter, Chapter 5. As a final note for this section, CSV singles out the core strategy of the company and the social problems it can have an impact on, directly through its existing business lines (or creating new products and business lines) based on the three pillars of shared value mentioned above. As stated previously this is an attractive feature of CSV, as it provides a methodology to do this. Future research needs to determine the success of these different types of related business models, i.e., BOP, inclusive business, blended value, mutual benefit, to name a few, and examine the many case studies that utilize these models. Future research should focus on measuring the social impact of available case study examples in the various locations where the corporate and organization resides to determine the benefits and contribution these projects make to both business and society in those locations.

Conclusion

Some of the most current academic papers released on CSV acknowledge that the number of publications on CSV strategies has begun to increase in numbers, but it is still early days for this topic area in the academic literature. There is also a gap in the literature, with regard to the organizational conditions necessary for the successful implementation of shared value strategies (Mühlbacher & Böbel, 2018). As part of the available literature for this area, some researchers comment that CSV is oversimplified, allowing general business managers and the business community to understand it more quickly and easily. The concept also resonates with many, as it includes a methodology with the view to "scale up" and therefore potentially assist at greater levels, impacting millions of people with the equivalent impact in the environmental context.

This chapter has attempted to explain the potential ability for CSV methodology to embed a 'social purpose' throughout the organization; to define a social need to fit this purpose based on social need and co-creation with external *stakeholders*; and to implement the project, followed by measuring shared value as an end result. An explanation on the three pillars of CSV is illustrated in case study examples in this chapter. A summary of the academic research examining this methodology and reviewing these pillars is also given, alongside inclusive growth models and potential funding for these projects. Examining directly how each organization has followed the three tiers of the CSV model provides an excellent opportunity for future academic research.

As mentioned earlier, the Australian DFAT has put together the BPP, to promote the development of CSV projects in the countries they support by partnering with NGOs from these selected countries and Australian corporates within these countries. Some corporates will choose to develop these partnership projects as part of their CSR strategies or under their CSR umbrella of activities. The Appendix of this chapter includes several project examples from the DFAT/ BPP program.

More academic critique needs to be gathered on the strengths and weaknesses of CSV projects contrasted with other similar projects. This is therefore an emerging and interesting area of research with plenty of opportunities for future research at an academic and business level, including measurement of the social, environmental, and business impact of these projects. As stated in the beginning of this chapter, what would be helpful is a full and adequate *Systematic Quantitative Literature Research Analysis* of the available literature on CSV and how it compares to CSR. Future academic research should examine this and consider the strengths and weaknesses of the CSV concept with a focus on measuring impact.

Following the CSR versus CSV debate briefly mentioned in this chapter, Porter and Kramer admit there are blends and overlaps of CSV with other areas, but it is the methodology that they provide to achieve CSV projects that is inspirational, backed by a process to implement these projects at scale, as part of CSR or CSV strategy. The methodology involved in implementing CSV also has the potential to develop a system of standardized measurement to measure impact at scale, providing an excellent opportunity for future academic research.

This chapter has reported numerous examples of corporates that have taken CSV projects on board, and others who have done so under their CSR strategy. However, some scholars argue that shared value or CSV projects are more integrated into the fabric of the company than CSR projects, arguing that CSV tends to have more of a top-down approach led by CEOs and C-suite executives. Hence, CSV is often quoted as being more central to the organization. It has also been argued in the literature that CSR must be made more central to the organization and that the corporate or organization must implement Social Initiatives (SIs) or social projects that are core to their business (Munro, 2013a, 2013b) and be relevant to internal and external *stakeholders* where they 'identify' with these SIs or social projects and therefore become more 'engaged' with them (Munro, 2017). The model shown for the research paper in Chapter 2 could be utilized to examine identification and engagement by *stakeholders* involved in CSV projects, and this is proposed for future research in this chapter and Chapter 2.

CSR guru Archie Carroll argues that "the idea of creating shared value is an integral part of modern-day CSR" (Carroll, 2015, p. 95). In contrast, other researchers have argued that companies have tried to upgrade their traditional CSR programs to a CSV strategy "designed to deliver positive economic returns while improving the quality of life in low-income, distressed communities" (Kaplan et al., 2018, p. 4) but with limited impact on producing transformational change. They provide examples of CocoaAction alliance in Cote d'Ivoire and Ghana and also Syngenta's Good Growth Plan in Indonesia and Nicaragua only helping a small number of farmers with limited impact on company sales in return.

The rightful place for CSV may therefore possibly be alongside the evolving current vision for CSR, where action oriented Social Initiatives (SIs) and social projects are being developed. The SIs or larger social projects as discussed in chapter 2, have involved employees in corporate volunteering, assisting by utilizing their core skills and implementing projects relative to their core business (Munro, 2013a, 2013b). CSV can provide the tools and the methodology to implement projects where the emphasis can be on the monetary benefit returned to the company, rather than what is volunteered. These types of projects involving new products and jobs for locals in the community, in relation to the projects, and collaboration with officials to organise projects at this level, take a lot of energy, time, and skill to set-up, but in the end provides incredible value for all involved. The success of these projects needs to be examined in future research to determine the credibility of this notion and the direction for both fields: practical application and academic scholarship.

Much of the CSV aim and ambition sounds similar to aspects of CSR's aims and ambitions. It therefore may be suggested that CSV can exist alongside CSR, with CSR providing guidance on the ethical and legal components of CSR (Carroll, 1974) and CSV aiding on the implementation side of CSR Social Initiatives (SI) or social projects.

Many of the CSV case study examples mentioned in the Appendix of this chapter are inspirational, multileveled, and extremely interesting. However, future research should be devoted toward examining their strengths and weaknesses and measuring their impact to society and the communities directly surrounding these projects. In addition, further case studies need to be examined with respect to CSV related SDG impact, as only Arup noticeably includes this as part of their case study.

Porter and Kramer have provided tools and a methodology to implement projects, whether they be under the umbrella of CSR as a social project or developed as a shared value project with the three pillars of CSV as the driving force. Although more research is required, of interest is the statement that:

> " ...using the profit motive and the tools of corporate strategy to address societal problems, a practice that is growing rapidly in part motivated by the shared value concept can contribute greatly both to the redemption of business and to a better world" (Crane et al., 2014, p. 150).

Hence, rather than worrying about the fact that CSV may or not be 'original' or a 'reinvention' or a 'repackage' of past methodologies, theories, terms or strategies – as many of its critics portray – the focus should instead be on the tools and methodology it potentially provides to social projects and to corporate strategy.

References

Aakhus, M., & Bzdak, M. (2012). Revisiting the role of "shared value" in the business-society relationship. *Business & Professional Ethics Journal, 31*(2), 231–246. doi: 10.5840/bpej201231211

Adams, C. (2014). What is integrated reporting? And how do you do it? Retrieved from https://drcaroladams.net/what-is-integrated-reporting-and- how-do-you-do-it/

Arup News. (2018a). Arup in top 10 for CSR for the sixth time. Retrieved from https://www.arup.com/news-and-events/arup-in-top-10-for-csr-for-the-sixth-time? query=CSR

Arup News. (2018b). Arup tops 2018 shared value awards. Retrieved from https:// www.arup.com/news-and-events/arup-wins-2018-shared-value-award

AXA. (2019). AXA home page. Retrieved from https://www.axa.com/en/

Balmer, J. M. T., & Greyser, S. A. (2006). Corporate marketing – Integrating corporate identity, corporate branding, corporate communications, corporate image and corporate reputation. *European Journal of Marketing, 40*(7–8), 730–741. doi:10.1108/03090560610669964

Bendoraitienė, E., & Gaigalienė, A. (2015). Analysis of CSR measurement criteria of social ratings system. *Applied Economics: Systematic Research, 9*(1), 61–75. doi: 10.7220/aesr.2335.8742.2015.9.1.4

Beschorner, T. (2014). Creating shared value: The one-trick pony approach—A comment on Michael Porter and Mark Kramer. *Business Ethics Journal Review, 1*(17), 106–112.

Bronn, P. S., & Vrioni, A. B. (2001). Corporate social responsibility and cause-related marketing: An overview. *International Journal of Advertising, 20*(2), 207–222.

Carroll, A. B. (1974). Corporate social responsibility: Its managerial impact and implications. *Journal of Business Research, 2*(1), 75–88. doi:10.1016/S0148-2963(74)80008-1

Carroll, A. B. (2015). Corporate social responsibility. *Organizational Dynamics, 44*(2), 87–96. doi:10.1016/j.orgdyn.2015.02.002

Carroll, A. B., & Brown, J. A. (2018). Corporate social responsibility: A review of current concepts, research and issues. In J. Weber & D. Wasleleski (Eds.), *Corporate social responsibility* (pp. 39–69). Bingley: Emerald Publishing Co.

Crane, A., Palazzo, G., Spence, L. J., & Matten, D. (2014). Contesting the value of "creating shared value". *California Management Review, 56*(2), 130–153. doi: 10.1525/cmr.2014.56.2.130

Dembek, K., Singh, P., & Bhakoo, V. (2016). Literature review of shared value: A theoretical concept or a management buzzword? *Journal of Business Ethics, 137*(2), 231–267.

DFAT. (2018a). Mobile banking for the poor in Vietnam. Retrieved from https://dfat.gov.au/aid/who-we-work-with/private-sector-partnerships/bpp/Pages/mobile-banking-for-the-poor-in-vietnam.aspx

DFAT. (2018b). Improving child nutrition in Indonesia. Retrieved from https://dfat.gov.au/aid/who-we-work-with/private-sector-partnerships/bpp/Pages/improving-child-nutrition-in-indonesia.aspx

DFAT. (2018c). Improving access to global cotton markets for farmers in Pakistan. Retrieved from https://dfat.gov.au/aid/who-we-work-with/private-sector-partnerships/bpp/Pages/improving-access-to-global-cotton-markets-for-farmers-in-pakistan.aspx

DFAT. (2018d). Job information and recruitment service in Cambodia. Retrieved from https://dfat.gov.au/aid/who-we-work-with/private-sector-partnerships/bpp/Pages/cambodia-job-information-recruitment-service.aspx

Elkington, J. (1998). Cannibals with forks: The triple bottom line of 21st century business. *Environmental Quality Management, 8*(1), 37–51.

Emerson, J. (2000). *The nature of returns: A social capital markets inquiry into elements of investment and the blended value proposition* (Vol. 1). Boston, MA: Division of Research, Harvard Business School.

European Commission. (2011). A renewed EU strategy 2011–14 for corporate social responsibility. Communication from the commission to the European parliament, the council, the European economic and social committee and the committee of the regions. Retrieved from https://eur-lex.europa.eu/legal-content/EN/TXT/?uri=CELEX%3A52011DC0681

Freeman, R. E. (1984). *Strategic management: A stakeholder approach.* Boston, MA: Pitman.

Garriga, E., & Melé, D. (2004). Corporate social responsibility theories: Mapping the territory. *Journal of Business Ethics, 53*(1/2), 51–71. doi:10.1023/B:BUSI.0000039399.90587.34

George, G., McGahan, A. M., & Prabhu, J. (2012). Innovation for inclusive growth: Toward a theoretical framework and a research agenda. *Journal of Management Studies, 49*(4), 661–683.

Grindle, A. K., Smith, D., Longo, M. P., & Murray, M. (2014). Shared value in Chile: Increasing private sector competitiveness by solving social problems. Retrieved from https://www.issuelab.org/resource/shared-value-in-chile-increasing-private-sector-competitiveness-by-solving-social-problems.html

Hart, S. (1997). Beyond greening: Strategies for a sustainable world. *Harvard Business Review, 75*(1), 66–76.

Hart, S. & Prahalad, C. K. (2002). The fortune at the bottom of the pyramid. *Strategy + Business, 26*, 54–67.

Hart, S. L., & Milstein, M. B. (1999). Global sustainability and the creative destruction of industries. *Sloan Management Review, 41*(1), 23–33.

IFC. (2018). *Built for change: Inclusive business solutions for the base of the pyramid.* Retrieved from https://www.ifc.org/wps/wcm/connect/topics_ext_content/ifc_external_corporate_site/inclusive + business/resources/publications/built + for + change + inclusive + business + solutions + for + the + base + of + the + pyramid

Kaplan, R. S., Serafeim, G., & Tugendhat, E. (2018). Inclusive growth: Profitable strategies for tackling poverty and inequality. *Harvard Business Review, 96*(1), 126–133.

Karam, C. M., & Jamali, D. (2017). A cross-cultural and Feminist perspective on CSR in developing countries: Uncovering latent power dynamics. *Journal of Business Ethics, 142*(3), 461–477. doi:10.1007/s10551-015-2737-7

Kherchi, I., & Fellague, M (2015). Creating shared value as a new business model for pharmaceutical companies: Glaxo Smith Kline (GSK) model. *Algerian Review of Economic Development, 2*(3), 17–29.

Laudal, T. (2018). Measuring shared value in multinational corporations. *Social Responsibility Journal, 14*(4), 917–933. doi:10.1108/srj-08-2017-0169

Lion. (2018). Sociability & living well. Retrieved from http://lionco.com/sociability-living-well

Mackey, J. (2011). What conscious capitalism really is: A response to James O'Toole and David Vogel's "two and a half cheers for conscious capitalism". *California Management Review, 53*(3), 83–90. doi:10.1525/cmr.2011.53.3.83

Mackey, J., & Sisodia, R. (2013). *Conscious capitalism: Liberating the heroic spirit of business.* Cambridge, MA: Harvard Business School Press.

Mahindra Insurance. (2018). Who we are? Retrieved from https://www.mahindrainsurance.com/

Mühlbacher, H., & Böbel, I. (2018). From zero-sum to win-win - organisational conditions for successful shared value strategy implementation. *European Management Journal.* Retrieved from https://www.sciencedirect.com/science/article/pii/S0263237318301221 doi:10.1016/j.emj.2018.10.007

Munro, V. (2013a). Stakeholder preferences for particular corporate social responsibility (CSR) activities and social initiatives (SIs): CSR initiatives to assist corporate strategy in emerging and Frontier markets. *The Journal of Corporate Citizenship, September 2013*(51), 72–105.

Munro, V. (2013b). Stakeholder understanding of corporate social responsibility (CSR) in emerging markets with a focus on Middle East, Africa (MEA) and Asia. *Journal of Global Policy and Governance, 2*(1), 59–77. doi:10.1007/s40320-013-0026-3

Munro, V. (2017). *Identification of CSR micro social initiatives within a developed and developing country context.* PhD Thesis, Griffith University. Retrieved from https://www120.secure.griffith.edu.au/rch/items/5e1def2f-25a0-4c9b-aa72-8c4b8761cb80/1/

Nittapaipapon, N., & Atchattabhan, T. (2016). Creating shared value embedded an inclusive business model: A case study. *Asian Journal of Business Management, 4*(2), 56–64.

O'Toole, J., & Vogel, D. (2011). Two and a half cheers for conscious capitalism. *California Management Review, 53*(3), 60–76.

Pfitzer, M., Bockstette, V., & Stamp, M. (2013). Innovating for shared value. *Harvard Business Review, 91*(9), 3–9.

Porter, M. (2014). *Competing by saving lives: How pharmaceutical and medical device companies create shared value in global health.* Retrieved from https://www.fsg.org/publications/competing-saving-lives-0

Porter, M. E., Hills, G., Pfitzer, M., Patscheke, S., & Hawkins, E. (2012). *Measuring shared value: How to unlock value by linking social and business results.* Boston, MA: FSG.

Porter, M. E., & Kramer, M. R. (2002). The competitive advantage of corporate philanthropy. *Harvard Business Review, 80*(12), 56-69. Retrieved from http://libraryproxy.griffith.edu.au/login?url=http://search.ebscohost.com/login.aspx?direct=true&db=bth&AN=8587406&site=ehost-live&scope=site

Porter, M. E., & Kramer, M. R. (2011). The big idea: Creating shared value. *Harvard Business Review, 89*(1–2), 1–17. Retrieved from http://www.nuovavista.com/SharedValuePorterHarvardBusinessReview.PDF

Porter, M. E., & Kramer, M. R. (2006). Strategy and society: The link between competitive advantage and corporate social responsibility. *Harvard Business Review, 84*(12), 78–92.

Porter, M., Stern, S., & Loria, R. (2013). *Social Progress Index 2013.* Social Progress Imperative. Washington, DC. Retrieved from: https://www2.deloitte.com/content/dam/Deloitte/se/Images/promo_images/artiklar/Global_Social_Progress_Index_2013.pdf

Prafitri, R. (2017). Creating shared value (CSV) in East Java, Indonesia: A critical analysis of CSV impacts on dairy farming communities. PhD Thesis, Murdock University. Retrieved from http://researchrepository.murdoch.edu.au/id/eprint/42583

Prahalad, C. (2012). Bottom of the pyramid as a source of breakthrough innovations. *Journal of Product Innovation Management, 29*(1), 6–12. doi:10.1111/j.1540-5885.2011.00874.x

Savitz, A., & Weber, K. (2006). *The triple bottom line: How today's best-run companies are achieving economic, social, and environmental success—And how you can too.* San Francisco, CA: Jossey-Bass.

Schwerin, D. (1998). *Conscious capitalism: Principles for prosperity.* Boston, MA: Butterworth-Heinemann.

Shared Value Initiative. (2018). CJ CheilJedang: Sustainable agricultural development in rural Vietnam. Retrieved from https://www.sharedvalue.org/resources/cj-cheiljedang-sustainable-agricultural-development-rural-vietnam

Shared Value Project. (2017). New case studies from world vision. Retrieved from https://sharedvalue.org.au/new-case-studies-world-vision/

Shared Value Project. (2018a). 2018 shared value awards winners. Retrieved from https://sharedvalue.org.au/awards/2018-winners/

Shared Value Project. (2018b). Carnival Australia, YuMi tourism partners - 2018 shared value awards. Retrieved from https://sharedvalue.org.au/profiles/carnival-australia-yumi-tourism-partners/

Strand, R., & Freeman, R. E. (2015). Scandinavian cooperative advantage: The theory and practice of stakeholder engagement in Scandinavia. *Journal of Business Ethics, 127*(1), 65–85. doi:10.1007/s10551-013-1953-2

Visser, W. (2011). *The age of responsibility: CSR 2.0 and the new DNA of business.* London: Wiley.

Visser, W. (2012). *CSR 2.0: Reinventing corporate social responsibility for the 21st century.* Management eXchange, May 13. Retrieved from https://www.managementexchange.com/hack/csr-20-reinventing-corporate-social-responsibility-21st-century

Visser, W. (2015). *Sustainable frontiers: Unlocking change through business, leadership and innovation.* Sheffield: Greenleaf Publishing.

Visser, W., & Kymal, C. (2015). Integrated value creation (IVC): Beyond corporate social responsibility (CSR) and creating shared value (CSV). *Journal of International Business Ethics, 8*(1), 1–14.

Voltan, A., Hervieux, C., & Mills, A. (2017). Examining the win-win proposition of shared value across contexts: Implications for future application. *Business Ethics: A European Review, 26*(4), 347–368. doi:10.1111/beer.12159

Case Study Appendix

Case Study Appendix I

Case Study: Shared Value Initiative Platform

The Shared Value Initiative was created out of Porter and Kramer's (2011) framework, to act as a collaborative platform for initiatives in a region or country to achieve goals via scalable and replicable solutions and discuss different shared value relationships. A case study example illustrating the strength of the shared value partnerships platform is provided below:

To address poverty faced by Cambodian farmers, **World Vision** partnered with iDE (an NGO that activates entrepreneurs) and Lors Thmey (a social enterprise helping rural households). The project considered issues regarding economic value and cost savings with private sector engagement and the potential to scale up the project with Lors Thmey, by connecting local farmers to agricultural markets and equipping them with technical skills and new growing techniques to produce higher crop yields. Lors Thmey then contracted the farmers to purchase their crops to then on-sell to premium markets. The *Farm Business Advisor Model* at the center of the project is a group of micro entrepreneurs working for Lors Thmey to improve farmers' livelihoods. World Vision then supports Lors Thmey to recruit and train more local entrepreneurs to become part of the *Farm Business Advisor Model* (Shared Value Project, 2017).

This role can also be played by a corporate whose core business is farming and or agriculture and produce, whereby the corporate supports the social enterprise as part of its CSR strategy or shared value strategy. An example of this is Korean-based *CJ CheilJedang* project in Vietnam, explained earlier this chapter.

Case Study Appendix II

Case Studies: The Australian Shared Value Awards (2018)

Award 1: CEO Damien Mu from AXA Australia won the award for 2018

The *Shared Value Awards Australia 2018* are selected from the Shared Value Initiatives platform listed above. A sample of winners of the awards is provided below:

Shared Value Champion. A glance at the AIA website at the time they won the award shows AIA separate out their shared value from their CSR and ESG components. They have listed CSR only as philanthropy. By philanthropy they document employee volunteering one day a year with three partner organizations: Ardoch Youth Foundation, United Way, and OzHarvest. No measurement is suggested, and it is not obvious if it is one day a year or more per employee, and if it is for all three partner organizations. However, there is plenty of measurement for ESG (Shared Value Project, 2018a). The ESG component (typically listed for CSR strategy) covers business risks and responsible business practices. Under this they include energy consumption and greenhouse gas emissions; installation of motion sensors to reduce lighting energy costs; and office paper recycling.

Health and wellness of employees is also included under the ESG component. They state that through education and engagement they highlight health, fitness, and general well-being issues and encourage their team to think proactively about their well-being. They also offer the following to all employees: *AIA Vitality and fitness device*, Women@Work, Occupational Health and Safety, Fire Up Fitness (bootcamp), Massages, Annual health checks, and flu shots (AXA, 2019).

AXA state their shared value covers creating measurable economic benefits by identifying and addressing social issues that intersect with their business. Under the shared value component, they state as a life insurer they have looked at ways to proactively improve the lives of people who suffer or are at risk of suffering these problems, while also improving their competitiveness as a business. The social issues they have chosen for shared value innovation include mental health and obesity, which they help through giving customers a free *AIA Vitality health and wellness program* (AXA, 2019).

The AIA Vitality Health and Wellness Program Case Study for AXA includes:

---

(1) AIA Vitality: is a health and wellness program that helps members get healthier by giving them the knowledge, tools, and motivation to improve their health. They state millions of people around the world are already living healthier, more fulfilling lives with this program *(This global measure is the impact listed for their initiative)*.

(2) AIA Rehabilitation: involves rehabilitation for claimants to support their return to work after serious illness or injury. AXA state they have been active in the worker rehabilitation space for a long time, particularly in regard to mental illness, which is estimated to cost industry over \$150 million dollars a year in claims and which currently affects around one in five Australians every year *(Again this overall industry figure is the measure of impact they provide for their initiative)*.

Source: Adapted from AXA (2019).

AXA make their case by stating their research shows 'work' is good for your health (i.e., it gives confidence and purpose). Hence, they state they help employees by providing a return to work though rehab. They list their impact by stating 88 million days are lost to the Australia economy due to absenteeism, at a cost of \$27.5 billion per annum in sick leave costs and lost productivity, commenting this is not only a cost to society but also to them as an insurer.

In summary, AXA covers environmental and employment CSR issues under their ESG component. Under CSR they cover their assistance in volunteering for charities/NGOs which they call philanthropy, and under 'shared value' they cover their assistance with two social issues involving rehabilitation using their own products (and using general population numbers for impact measures) (AXA, 2019).

Award 2: Arup won the 2018 leading corporate organization award for shared value. Arup is quoted as a global leader in engineering and construction (2018a) and acknowledged for its significant role in helping urban and rural communities tackle challenges in society relating to cities, water, energy, and transport. Although Arup is in 34 countries, they won this as an Australian award (Shared Value Project, 2018a).

The Shared Value Project (2018a) explains that from the start, Arup created shared value for society while making a profit for its people and kept this at the forefront of their decision-making. In 2017, Arup also made it into the Top 10 firms for CSR–in the *Annual Review of the State of CSR in Australia and New Zealand* – for the sixth time. The top two goals addressed by companies was noted as Gender Equality, Good Health and Well-being, and the most challenging goals were noted as Climate Action and Gender Equality (Arup News, 2018a). Hence, there is some overlap of terminology here between CSR and CSV.

While the exact shared value projects for Arup are not immediately clear from a quick glance at their website, on receiving the award, Arup acknowledge their key initiatives briefly in a press release:

"Alongside our project work for clients, Arup invests in research and innovation, community engagement for humanitarian and charitable causes and provides specialist services to humanitarian organisations to reduce suffering and improve the lives of those in need" (Arup News, 2018b).

Much of this also sounds like earlier definitions of CSR. In addition, an earlier press release noted their work toward the sustainable development goals (SDGs):

"We are also embedding the United Nations' Sustainable Development Goals into our business planning and procurement while collaborating with leaders of social and economic transformation including the World Economic Forum, The C40 Cities Climate Leadership group, the Rockefeller Foundation and the Ellen Macarthur Foundation" (Arup News, 2018b).

SDGs are often embedded in CSR strategy as well as CSV strategy. Arup is also included in Chapter 3 as an SDG case study.

Award 3: Lion was runner up to Arup. Lion is a founding member of the Shared Value Initiative and has spoken at several of their conferences. A food and beverage company, Lion's core products are beer (aiming for below full strength), and include: "nutrient enriched yoghurts and juices and reformulated product choices (with lower sugar, fat, and salt)." Their key thrust is to be innovative with products and their 'purpose' is listed on their website as "to enrich our world every day by championing sociability and helping people to live well" (Lion, 2018).

At the time of winning this award, they did not list shared value (or CSV) as a term on their website. Their shared value examples, however, are listed under the menu tab Sociability and Living Well:

- Supporting Better Choices—we believe the reach of our brands means we can play a direct role in improving the food and beverage choices of Australians and New Zealanders. Through better-for-you innovation and broadening our product options, we aim to do just that.
- Get the Facts on Alcohol—the real prize in tackling alcohol misuse is a whole-of-community effort to champion positive social behavior and consumption, while ensuring people have the information they need to make good choices when they are drinking.
- Get the Facts on Dairy and Drinks—dairy, juice, and plantmilks (such as soy) provide a wide variety of essential nutrients, vitamins, and minerals for all ages and all stages of life, helping you maintain a healthy, balanced diet.
- Tips for Living Well—equip yourself for living well—learn how to read food labels, how our products stack up against school canteen criteria for your kids and discover a range of tools to help you better manage your diet and weight.

Source: Extracts from Lion (2018).

Award 4: The winner of a *'shared value project by an organization'* is a collaboration with the YuMi Tourism Project (Carnival Australia), in partnership with the NGO, The Difference Incubator, and Department of Foreign Affairs and Trade (DFAT). This is included in the DFAT section at the end of this Appendix.

Award 5: In contrast, to the Australian Awards, the *Shared Value 2018 India Awards* **prize** (the GNFC Porter Prize for Creating Shared Value) was won by Mahindra Insurance and Mahindra & Mahindra (Farm Equipment Sector). Jaideep Devare, MD, Mahindra Insurance, and Atindriya Bose, CEO, Mahindra & Mahindra, received the award on behalf of their companies for their outstanding performance and ability *"to recognize high impact as an organization that created economic success by redefining markets, products, way of doing business, creating collaborative efforts and in turn creating societal and economic progress"* (Mahindra Insurance, 2018). These are also listed as pillars of their CSR strategy.

To receive this award, Mahindra Insurance was evaluated on the following:

(1) Social problems addressed
(2) Geographical reach and societal activities
(3) Investment in community development
(4) Linkage between a social problem and the company's strategy
Source: Mahindra Insurance (2018)

Shared value is not listed on their website; however, there is a large section on CSR with their current CSR report listing many of these initiatives, as follows:

Thrust areas:

*   *Education—promoting education and enhancing vocation skills among children, women, elderly, and the differently abled*
*   *Health—eradicating hunger, poverty, malnutrition, promoting preventive health care, sanitation, and making available safe drinking water.*
*   *Environment—ensuring environmental sustainability, ecological balance, protection of flora and fauna, animal welfare, agro forestry, conservation of natural resources, and maintaining quality of soil, air, and water.*

Others:

*   *Promoting gender equality, empowering women, setting up homes/hostels for women and orphans, setting up old age homes, day care centers and facilities for senior citizens, and measures for reducing inequalities faced by the socially and economically disadvantaged.*
*   *Protection of national heritage, art, and culture including restoration of buildings and sites of historical importance and works of art; setting up public libraries; promotion of traditional arts and handicrafts.*

(Continued)

- *Measures for the benefit of armed forces veterans, war widows, and their dependents.*
- *Training to promote rural, nationally recognized, and Paralympic and Olympic sports.*
- *Contribution to the Prime Minister's National Relief Fund or any other central government fund for socio-economic development, relief and welfare of scheduled castes, minorities, and women.*
- *Contribution to technology located within academic institutions approved by the central government*
- *Rural development projects.*

Source: Extract adapted from the Mahindra Insurance (2018).

In summary, there are noticeable regional issues not just with CSR definition and strategy (as mentioned in Chapter 1) but also with CSV objectives and terminology varying across countries and regions. Examining if these differences exist across countries and regions for CSV as they appear to for CSR strategy, would provide an excellent opportunity for future research and provide knowledge on how to set-up these projects in the many different settings provided in emerging markets and developing countries.

The Australian Shared Value Awards (2019) had similar corporate organizations winning again, such as AIA as a lead winner and IAG as highly commended. Anne Sherry was voted Shared Value Champion (as part of the Carnival Australia's YuMi Tourism Project), followed by Shared Value Trailblazer, the CEO of Good Shepherd Microfinance and NGO Intrepid Group, also often quoted in CSV materials. A few newcomers were mentioned in the SME and cross-border section. The 2018 Award examples listed above therefore provide a good cross section of case study awards currently available for CSV.

Case Study Appendix III

Case Studies: DFAT and the Business Partnerships Platform (BPP)

As mentioned in the conclusion of this chapter the Australian Department of Foreign Affairs and Trade (DFAT) has put together a Business Partnerships Platform (BPP) platform to promote the development of CSV projects in selected countries (including various countries in Asia), and by partnering with NGOs from those countries and Australian corporates. Some of these companies or corporates will choose to develop these partnership projects (or CSV projects) as part of their CSR strategies or under their CSR umbrella of activities. A few DFAT/BPP partnerships are listed below which are listed as case studies on the DFAT website and linked through the reference list for this chapter.

(1) **Mobile banking for the poor in Vietnam** is a partnership which brings together: The Asia Foundation (TAF), Vietnam Bank for Social Policies (VBSP), and MasterCard to provide the first mobile banking platform for low-income populations in Vietnam. The example illustrates funding by private sector contribution with a corresponding DFAT contribution. The partnership and project create shared value (CSV) by driving down the cost of banking for low-income populations while also providing access to more diversified services, such as SMS banking. The partnership enabled MasterCard to reconceive their products and the financial markets to utilize their intellectual property and technical services while also integrating the Vietnam Bank for a social policy software system to enable financial inclusion for the poor
(*Source:* DFAT, 2018a).

(2) **Improving child nutrition in Indonesia** involves a partnership between Global Alliance for Improved Nutrition (GAIN) to provide services alongside a private sector funding contribution with a corresponding DFAT contribution. The partnership and project creates shared value (CSV) by encouraging midwives to provide more frequent and timely nutrition counseling to mothers alongside creating greater access to micronutrient powders. This initiative fills the current gap of essential nutrients needed for young children in vulnerable households. In addition, the sales of these powders will generate an income for a social franchise of 900 midwives
(*Source:* DFAT, 2018b).

(3) **Improving access to global cotton markets for farmers in Pakistan** involves a partnership that will support the training of approximately 200,000 farmers in Pakistan to become part of the Better Cotton Initiative (BCI) and access the global growers market for sustainably produced cotton. Cotton Australia is providing their expertise with their recent accreditation under the BCI. The partnership is supported by a private sector funding contribution matched by a DFAT contribution. The partnership and project created shared value (CSV) by supporting the training of farmers so they can become BCI accredited and therefore opening up extensive opportunity for farmers in Pakistan to engage in safer, more sustainable farming operations while also obtaining access to a growing market for sustainably produced cotton
(*Source:* DFAT, 2018c).

(4) **Job information and recruitment service (Krawma) in Cambodia** is a partnership which develops Cambodia's first for-profit job listing and recruitment platform providing low-skilled workers (women in particular), with information and links to employment opportunities and job

information for job-seekers and employers. This raises Krawma's position to market leader in job listings. In addition, The Asia Foundation's (TAF) program addresses gender and women's economic empowerment issues, fulfilling the DFAT/BPP's aim to actively promote initiatives that drive women's economic empowerment, and provides a private sector funding contribution matched with a corresponding DFAT contribution. The partnership and project creates shared value (CSV) by enabling Krawma to move into a new market space, increasing their number of clients and sales of job listings. Up to 200 factories and 300,000 low-income households will potentially have access to this service. The service will provide better access to job opportunities for low-skilled low-income workers, particularly women, and also better assist employers
(*Source:* DFAT, 2018d).

(5) **The winner of a *'shared value project by an organization'*** (at the *Shared Value Awards Australia 2018* referred to above) is the collaboration with Carnival Australia's YuMi Tourism Project, delivered in partnership with The Difference Incubator, NGO, and Department of Foreign Affairs and Trade (DFAT). This is an example of how projects can be embedded within CSR strategy and/or CSV strategy, where the corporate supports the NGO to develop a service or concept in a selected developing country, where they operate, which the government department (e.g., DFAT) is also interested in, and therefore also contributes funding toward. This project improves the livelihoods of the community members who set-up new businesses in the developing country, and in return the tourists and guests traveling to this destination on Carnival ships have a special experience while visiting the community and visiting their business activities
(*Source:* Shared Value Project, 2018b).

Measuring the impact of these projects and the lessons learned from implementing them is an emerging opportunity for future research.

Case Study Appendix IV

Case Studies of CSV Measurement

In Brazil, **Coca-Cola** assisted skill development among 'low-income youth' as a key social challenge. They used their own value chain to incorporate the Coletivo initiative in partnership with local NGOs to train local youth in retailing, business development, and entrepreneurship. They tracked progress by measuring the following each month. This included numbers of youth involved in training, retailers involved, and performance of retailers over time. They then measured youth job placement, youth self-esteem, company sales and brand connections. About 30% of youth trained immediately received their first job and 10% set-up their own business with microcredit from the company. This led to significant changes to 'low-income youth' in these communities by dramatically improving their lives through skills training and employment. This also meant better retail performance and brand connection for retailers in these communities, while also improving sales for Coca-Cola overall.

Source: Adapted from Porter, Hills, Pfitzer, Patscheke, & Hawkins (2012).

As a global manufacturer of computer hard drives, **Intel**, used their technology for education transformation. Across the three levels of shared value, **Intel** provides a 'reconceiving product and markets' example:

Recognizing that many students in the world are without computers and teachers often lack the ability to integrate technology into the classroom, **Intel** launched their education transformation strategy to help close the gap while also growing business opportunities for the global information and communications technology (ICT) ecosystem. This involved supporting governments to improve their education systems, provide advocacy for policy reform and leadership, curriculum assessment, professional development of teachers, deployment of ICT, and research and evaluation support. This in turn provided business opportunities for the entire ICT ecosystem, increased computer sales, and helped improve the future workforce (Porter et al., 2012). Among numerous innovations, they also researched how student and teachers interact to develop a worldwide teacher professional development program.

Measurement was gathered from many parts of the value chain including technology effectiveness from product development; teacher engagement with the program; and student performance with the program (and having their own computer). Also measured was the quality of lesson plans and levels of integration of ICT in education. As a result, Intel were able to measure technology effectiveness in the classroom to inform further product innovation while also improving school education and curriculum.

Source: Adapted from Porter et al. (2012)

As can be seen from the above example, the insights created by this type of measurement led to further product development, growth of the global education technology market, and increased market share for **Intel**, through increased product sales.

Case Studies of Long-term growth strategy and measuring Shared Value

Global Health Care Company **Novo Nordisk** provides an example of a long-term growth strategy and demonstrates measuring shared value for their long-term growth strategy in China. Commencing over two decades ago, with the aim to improve diabetes, **Novo Nordisk** invested in physician training, patient education, and local production (Porter et al., 2012). By increasing the diagnosis of diabetes, they not only helped diabetes sufferers but also increased their insulin product sales. To measure their success, they were able to track progress of the number of physicians trained and patients educated. Knowing the numbers and what works meant they were able to then strategically scale up and take the project to other parts of China. Like **Intel**, they were able to add additional shared value from analysing their research results, which ultimately refined their physician training and location of such. **Novo Nordisk** were then able to put numbers to their data to measure performance over a decade in China. The results were therefore able to estimate 80% improvement in total patient years and a 40%–63% increase in Chinese market share for **Novo Nordisk**.
Source: Adapted from Porter et al. (2012).

As stated earlier in this chapter, the methodology for measuring CSV is still developing. Laudal (2018) sites a gap in the academic literature for the topic of measuring shared value, stating there are very few attempts to measure CSV at the corporate level in the literature. The one example available for measuring shared value by Porter et al. (2012) was stated by Laudal as non-empirical, with the empirical section only providing the experience of five case studies, but with no measurement methodology, comparison matrix, or comparative analysis. This is an excellent opportunity for future research.

Case Study References

Arup News. (2018a). Arup in Top 10 for CSR for the sixth time. Retrieved from https://www.arup.com/news-and-events/arup-in-top-10-for-csr-for-the-sixth-time?query=CSR
Arup News. (2018b). Arup tops 2018 shared value awards. Retrieved from https://www.arup.com/news-and-events/arup-wins-2018-shared-value-award
AXA. (2019). AXA home page. Retrieved from https://www.axa.com/en/
DFAT. (2018a). Mobile banking for the poor in Vietnam. Retrieved from https://dfat.gov.au/aid/who-we-work-with/private-sector-partnerships/bpp/Pages/mobile-banking-for-the-poor-in-vietnam.aspx
DFAT. (2018b). Improving child nutrition in Indonesia. Retrieved from https://dfat.gov.au/aid/who-we-work-with/private-sector-partnerships/bpp/Pages/improving-child-nutrition-in-indonesia.aspx

DFAT. (2018c). Improving access to global cotton markets for farmers in Pakistan. Retrieved from https://dfat.gov.au/aid/who-we-work-with/private-sector-partnerships/bpp/Pages/improving-access-to-global-cotton-markets-for-farmers-in-pakistan.aspx

DFAT. (2018d). Job information and recruitment service in Cambodia. Retrieved from https://dfat.gov.au/aid/who-we-work-with/private-sector-partnerships/bpp/Pages/cambodia-job-information-recruitment-service.aspx

Lion. (2018). Sociability & living well. Retrieved from http://lionco.com/sociability-living-well

Mahindra Insurance. (2018). Who we are? Retrieved from https://www.mahindrainsurance.com/

Pfitzer, M., Bockstette, V., & Stamp, M. (2013). Innovating for shared value. *Harvard Business Review, 91*(9), 3–9.

Porter, M. E., Hills, G., Pfitzer, M., Patscheke, S., & Hawkins, E. (2012). *Measuring shared value: How to unlock value by linking social and business results.* Boston, MA: FSG. Retrieved from http://www.fsg.org/Portals/0/Uploads/Documents/PDF/Measuring_Shared_Value.pdf

Shared Value Project. (2017). New case studies from world vision. Retrieved from https://sharedvalue.org.au/new-case-studies-world-vision/

Shared Value Project. (2018a). 2018 shared value awards winners. Retrieved from https://sharedvalue.org.au/awards/2018-winners/

Shared Value Project. (2018b). Carnival Australia, YuMi tourism partners - 2018 shared value awards. Retrieved from https://sharedvalue.org.au/profiles/carnival-australia-yumi-tourism-partners/

Chapter 5

Innovation, Entrepreneurship, and Solving Wicked Challenges through CSR and CSV

Abstract

The Fourth Industrial Revolution has escalated innovation to new heights unseen, creating an evolution of innovation and corporate social responsibility (CSR), and as a result, a more *Innovative CSR*. With this evolution comes also the evolution of the 'Preneur' from social entrepreneur to corporate social entrepreneur and corporate social intrapreneur. It is therefore important to acknowledge that social entrepreneurship is not just for the social sector, or start-up entrepreneur – corporations can also be social entrepreneurs. This chapter establishes an understanding of this possibility alongside solving wicked problems and challenges, and how to provide collaborative networks and co-creation experiences to assist others on this journey. More importantly, the chapter discusses how corporates can assist millennials (and Generation Z) by funding and incubating their innovative or social enterprise idea under the umbrella of CSR strategy, until it is ready to be released to the world. The chapter is supported by academic literature and business publications with suggestions for future research opportunities.

Introduction

Corporate Social Responsibility (CSR) without considering innovation is no longer viable (Grayson et al., 2008; Kim, Brodhag, & Mebratu, 2014). Innovation is now well acknowledged as the sustainable engine for a firm's growth and survival and is fundamental to the latest definition of CSR announced by the European Commission, as referred to later in this chapter. Innovation also lies at the heart of social entrepreneurship. "Social enterprise and social entrepreneurship – as a business-inspired approach to solving social problems – has exploded across the United States and the world in the last decade" (Ganz, Kay, & Spicer, 2018, p. 59). It has fixed itself within a wide number of disciplines, from economic development and urban planning to health and education policy. Since Harvard

CSR for Purpose, Shared Value and Deep Transformation, 161–201
Copyright © 2020 Emerald Publishing Limited
All rights of reproduction in any form reserved
doi:10.1108/978-1-80043-035-820200008

Business School established their first *Social Enterprise Initiative* over 25 year ago, this type of course has embedded itself in many of the elite universities in the US and helped turn social enterprise into an industry, funded by $1.6 billion in foundation grants (Ganz et al., 2018).

The CSR discipline has long identified its need for inclusion of social entrepreneurship into CSR SIs and CSR strategy:

> "Corporate thinking needs to incorporate 'social entrepreneurship' (Nagler, 2012) and manifest social initiatives as individual activities for corporate citizenship and societal improvement Khan & Lund-Thomsen (2011). It also needs to emphasise the creation of a 'social mission with a business engine' (Sabeti, 2011), by creating and assisting social enterprises and NGOs, and do all this in a sustainable way, within balanced guidelines for selecting socially responsible initiatives within CSR strategies." (Munro, 2013a, pp. 97 and 98)

Clarification of the need to integrate social entrepreneurship with CSR activities has come from past research examining the perspective of employees, as local citizens in developing and developing countries and communities. The research study below, for example, confirmed that *stakeholders* from numerous countries and cultures are ready for the inclusion of innovation in CSR:

> "They (stakeholders) welcome the transition to 'social entrepreneurship' and 'socially oriented corporate missions,' which assist social enterprises, NGOs and activities within communities. The study also confirms that the traditions and experiences of particular nationalities and cultures .... and will expect and demand this in CSR strategy developed in global emerging economies and regions in the future." (Munro, 2013a, p. 98)

While *stakeholders* appear to be positive toward corporates supporting social enterprise development as part of CSR strategy, there are varying perspectives on the success of the social enterprise movement itself. Some researchers say the social enterprise movement has made limited progress in solving the systemic social problems it states it will address. Ganz et al. (2018) take this one step further by stating the movement actually *distracts from and undermines the critical role of an organized citizenry, political action, and democratic government from achieving systemic social change,* by offering itself as a private, market-based alternative. While long supported in America and the UK, other universities around the globe have more recently set-up centers for social enterprises. The Yunus Social Business Center, for example, has recently been set-up at Griffith University in Queensland, Australia, and at the La Trobe Business School in Melbourne, Australia. Both draw from the philosophy of Muhammad Yunus, aiming to drive system change through innovation, social entrepreneurship, and enterprise.

Corporates, however, are also supporting millennials and Generation Z (henceforth referred to as millennials), to solve systemic wicked problems (henceforth referred to as challenges), through supporting innovation, systems change and social enterprise development. Social entrepreneurship, therefore, is not just for the social sector, or start-up entrepreneur – corporations can also be social entrepreneurs as a way to assist others. Leading companies are seeking to create more robust forms of strategic corporate citizenship and are engaging in "corporate social entrepreneurship" (CSE) (Austin, Leonard, Reficco, & Wei-Skillern, 2006). Austin et al. (2006), in their book chapter titled *Social entrepreneurship: it's for corporations too* make precisely this point. CSE should be a priority topic in university curriculums alongside social entrepreneurship and social intrapreneurship, starting with understanding the components of CSR as the overriding strategy that can incorporate these types of entrepreneurship within organizations.

As millennials will make up over half the workforce by 2025, innovation and change is important to consider. As noted previously, it is acknowledged that millennials will seek "change" in society, they will "be the change" and they will have the power to effect change. In fact, "they will change how change is made" (Case Foundation, 2017). Research has also found that millennials reward or punish corporations based on corporate levels of CSR involvement alone (McGlone, Spain, & McGlone, 2011). The research presented in the CSR and Innovation section of this chapter suggests CSR can be used as a starting point for innovation, where innovative projects are perceived as risky in the start-up phase. Conducting innovative social enterprise start-up projects under CSR strategy as an SI or social project places the entrepreneurial project under the safe umbrella of the organization's CSR strategy. This allows for experimentation with innovation in a safe environment before being released to the general public. In this way CSR can provide innovation with a safety net. The corporate can provide a setting for the enterprise to experiment with a pilot project, which if successful, can be adopted as part of the organization's ongoing CSR strategy and further developed and made scalable when unleashed to society.

This chapter commences with a discussion on innovation and its evolution to social innovation and co-creation and its relationship with CSR. Following this is a discussion on social entrepreneurship, social enterprise, CSE and corporate social intrapreneurship (CSI) alongside CSR. Millennials and social change is also discussed as part of their interest in the social enterprise movement. Research regarding social solutions to wicked challenges and systemic problems is also covered.

Innovation as the Sustainable Engine

As mentioned in the introduction to this chapter, innovation is well acknowledged as the sustainable engine for a firm's growth and survival. Innovation is also fundamental and integral to the latest definition of CSR announced by the European Commission:

> "…the responsibility of enterprises for their impacts on society" (where) "enterprises must be given the flexibility to innovate and to develop an approach to CSR that is appropriate to their circumstances (and) maximize opportunities through transparency and social innovation as part of their CSR strategy" (European Commission, 2011).

However, innovation is a broad concept referring to scientific inventions, patents, technological breakthroughs, or even a simple new way to do things (Lee, Olson, & Trimi, 2012).

Although innovation is a frequently used term in business studies, economics, and management, the meaning of it is often broad and abstract. In fact some authors refer to it as "… a near meaningless buzzword having a positive connotation and implying some vague level of originality which everyone can agree is something desirable" (Nguyen and Hipsher, 2018). This is relevant as scholars state "language and word choices influence how individuals frame, analyze, and process information" (e.g., Imai, Kanero, & Masuda, 2016; Ronda-Pupo & Guerras-Martin, 2012; Tamariz & Kirby, 2016).

Therefore, to understand a term with such an abstract and capacious meaning, one must look at its context and "understand how the term is being used in that specific application." (Nguyen and Hipsher, 2018). In this vein, Osburg (2013) bases his definition of innovation on the work of Austrian economist Joseph Schumpeter, who believed Innovation can be understood as a "new" combination of production factors (Schumpeter, 1982). He then followed the work of Baldwin and Curley (2007) who view innovation as the creation and adoption of something new that creates value for the organization that adopts it. The authors also quote Drucker (1985) who states innovation can be a specific instrument of entrepreneurship, more specifically an act that endows resources with a new capacity to create wealth (Osburg, 2013, in; Osburg & Schmidpeter, 2013). In comparison, McLean (2005) defined innovation as a development and implementation process of finding new types of problem-solving ideas. Similarly, Van de Ven (1986) defined innovation as the "development and implementation of new ideas" and then stating the new ideas. To further highlight the confusion regarding when the term innovation is, or is not used, Nguyen and Hipsher (2018) state "new ideas which are not perceived as useful are not normally called innovation." This leads to the realization that innovation is not just a new idea. The idea has to be deemed useful first.

The academic research literature has generally found innovation to be of importance to economic performance, both at the national and firm level, and also at the individual level. The recent exploration of innovative firm performance by Tuan, Nhan, Giang, and Ngoc (2016), for example, suggests the higher the number of innovative activities, the greater the innovative output and overall performance (Nguyen and Hipsher, 2018). Increasingly it is thought that innovation is necessary to be able to compete in both global and local markets. Not only is it necessary for multinational enterprises (MNEs), it is also necessary for small and medium-sized enterprises (SMEs) and micro-entrepreneurs or individuals, which can also be supported by MNEs. Previously this was more often in developed countries, but the main focus now for innovation as documented by the United Nations sustainable development goals (SDGs) is for increasing innovation focused on developing countries (Munro, 2018).

To do this, innovation needs to be perceived within a business sense of "taking an idea from a state of conception to a state of commercialization" (Quinn, 1985). Lee et al. (2012) refer to a new stream of research and business practice that advocates "shared value," "should be the target of any Innovation" (Lee et al., 2012, p. 818). This may refer to the shared value of items in general or creating shared value (CSV) as in Porter and Kramer (2011). In some cases, innovation has become key to business strategy. Porter and Kramer's (2011) shared value does in fact advocate innovation as a key pillar for execution within their framework. This is discussed further in Chapter 4.

Innovation discourse in business strategy tends to evolve around the concept that new ideas must be created, implemented, and accepted before the ideas can be considered "Innovative." Doing this at the social level connects innovation with Social Innovation and therefore also CSR. The following sections outline this more clearly.

Social Innovation: A Broad Term

The concept of Social Innovation is becoming very much present in today's corporate discussions in both developed and developing countries (Osburg, 2013). Osburg discusses the significant differences in the way Social Innovation is understood. While some see it as the next big thing after CSR, others see it as a new term for CSR. Still others refer to improvements in the CSR process itself as Social Innovation (Rexhepi, Kurtishi, & Bexheti, 2013). A clear definition of Social Innovation is provided by the EU Commission, as part of their new definition of CSR, announced in 2011, stating that Social Innovations are:

> "... new ideas (products, services and models) that simultaneously meet social needs (more effectively than alternatives) and create new social relationships or collaborations" (EU-Commission, 2012).

In keeping with this, the European Business School (EBS) defines Social Innovation as ... *new solutions that address societal challenges in a way that is contextual, targeted, and promotes common welfare* (European Business School, 2012).

Today, innovation centers like the Australian Centre for Social Innovation, for example, no longer need to define Social Innovation in their public dissemination materials. Their website, for example, includes its mission, and uses its visual materials to somehow imply what it is. This example suggests Social Innovation is already incorporated into society and therefore well understood, needing little explanation. Whether Social Innovation is mainstream yet or not is debatable, it is, however, being disseminated as a well-developed concept. As explained in the introduction to this chapter, the leading business schools like Harvard and Stanford were the first to create centers for Social Innovation and other universities are now following suit. From a corporate perspective, some critics query that while innovation is part of the DNA of firms, it is not yet an integral part of CSR. Googins (2013), for example, argues that the traditional role of CSR supported and supports business in areas like licence to operate and basic citizenship duties with all of its subcomponents. While this has worked well in the past, it might not be sufficient in a more complex and future world (Googins, 2013).

The Edelman (2019) survey discussed in the introduction to this book, refers to a growing and general lack of trust in the community for corporates, media, and government. This is also viewed as a part of the problem for wicked social challenges today. In addition, corporates are increasingly asked to assist with social problems. Osburg (2013) draws attention to this in the statement, with a *decrease in power and resources of the public sector in many countries, business is increasingly asked to contribute to solving burning social issues, which goes far beyond traditional CSR, even for the leading companies in this area* (p. 18). Many argue, however, that CSR is a good starting point for innovation and solving social problems, and provides a structure to do this, which can then become the core social mission of the business. There is also evidence that a number of key corporates are already transitioning to this journey as can be seen among those corporates selected for the Fortune 2018 *Change the World* list, with 57 companies listed using innovation to help the planet and tackle social problems, such as Merck, Bank of America, ABB, and Weight Watchers International. This is an area receiving increased attention. However, as pointed out in the following section, more research in this area of innovation is yet to be conducted.

Innovation and CSR: A Lack of Research

As mentioned in the introduction to this chapter, a CSR strategy or product without considering innovation is no longer viable to long-term business (Grayson et al., 2008; Kim et al., 2014). There is still much to be done, however, to make the innovation movement mainstream. Adding to this is a lack of academic research combining innovation with CSR. Some researchers have in fact noted that academic discussions of innovation hardly ever impact on discussions of CSR and are rarely discussed in combination in the literature (MacGregor & Fontrodona, 2008). This is thought to be surprising given the degree of interdependence between the two areas (MacGregor, Fontrodona, & Hernandez, 2010). This section therefore updates this research information and focuses on innovation and CSR.

Among this research are a number of papers that support discussions of impact, CSR, and innovation. An interesting research paper, for example, regarding CSR and innovation is that of Mishra (2017). He analyzed 13,917 companies from 1991 to 2006 and found that innovative firms demonstrated what they termed, "high-CSR performance". These "high-CSR" innovative firms also enjoy significantly higher valuation post innovation. The findings suggest that firms with potential growth opportunities, defined by the number of registered patents and innovation citations, benefit by investing more in CSR activities. Hence, in this instance, innovation and CSR go hand and hand. Mishra (2017) agrees with this finding, stating: "it is beneficial for innovative firms to incorporate CSR performance into their strategies: that is, promote social responsibility to enhance the valuation effect of their innovative efforts" (Mishra, 2017, p. 303).

HP and Intel provide examples of significant Social Innovation. HP, for example, has a Global Social Innovation Group, using innovation to make a positive difference in the world. The Intel case study is mentioned throughout this book as an early example of both CSR and CSV. More research is necessary, however, to determine how often Social Innovation departments in large corporates, such as HP and Intel, can become part of the CSR department, and achieve attention from C-suite company leaders, or better still – have both CSR and Innovation dispersed throughout the corporation. Osburg (2013), for example, suggests "CSR Managers need to become Change Agents in leading the company toward transformation" (p. 20). They need to help the company realize the significance of innovation so that CSR is not just an "add on" exercise. While this is discussed in business social media mediums, there is less academic research measuring or reporting these changes. "CSR Managers needing to become Change Agents" sounds similar to the role of the Social Intrapreneur in corporations and strengthens the argument for *Innovative CSR* existing within CSR strategy. The role of the Corporate Social Intrapreneur in enhancing innovation is discussed later this chapter.

Continuing the theme of research examining CSR and innovation, MacGregor and Fontrodona (2008) put together a 15-month study involving 60 SMEs throughout Europe. The study built a Social Innovation model based on a conceptual understanding of CSR and innovation though presenting three hypotheses which map CSR on to innovation and vice versa. The results confirmed the importance of integrating CSR with Social Innovation. The authors found their Social Innovation model worked well with SMEs that wanted "to transform innovation chaos into formalized, sustainable value creation across the enterprise" (MacGregor & Fontrodona, 2008). The authors therefore decided that "CSR can act as an effective delivery mechanism for small company value generation" and that, for innovation "SMEs should pro-activate their CSR" (MacGregor & Fontrodona, 2008). These suggestions from MacGregor and Fontrodona (2008) are extremely important toward understanding CSR and innovation in SMEs. Future research should mirror this model to see if the findings for SMEs are similar to examining these issues among MNEs, as the concept of a Social Innovation model would be equally helpful to larger corporations.

On this note, Kim et al. (2014) examined 619 multinational firms from the DJ STOXX 600 and MSCI World indices, to examine CSR-driven innovation and the relationship between CSR and innovation activities of firms through innovative investments. In doing so, they proposed two hypotheses as follows:

(1) There is a significant relationship between CSR and innovative investments
(2) There are a number of significant and different effects of explore and exploit investments on the CSR activities of firms.

The researchers used the European financial rating agency Vigeo to measure CSR performance. Vigeo which evaluates CSR and risk factors for environmental, social, and governance (ESG) criteria for European firms listed on the DJ STOXX 600 and MSCI World indexes (Cavaco & Crifo, 2014). Their measure is based on CSR performance for six domains: *human rights, environment, human resources, business behavior, corporate governance, and community involvement.*

Kim et al. (2014) found significant effects for CSR activities on investment strategies of firms. The six CSR behaviors listed above show diverged effects according to the type of investment activities. For short-term and exploitative investments, for example, CSR activities related to *human resources, the environment, business behavior, and community involvement.* In contrast, *human rights and corporate governance* have a relationship with long-term-oriented investment. These findings suggest that understanding the connection between CSR behaviors and innovative investment activities helps understand the best way to design CSR strategies based on innovation and investment. For example, "exploitative investment" had a positive effect on the CSR variables *human resource, environment, business behavior, and community involvement.* "Explorative investment" also shows a positive effect on *human rights*, but a negative relationship with *corporate governance.* The result also show that CSR variables are more related to "exploitative investment" than "explorative investment", but that "R&D (research and development) investment" is positively related with *human rights and community involvement.* This suggests more innovation and investment would be well spent in the areas of CSR related to innovation evolving round the CSR areas *human rights and community involvement.* This is a positive finding for investment in innovative SIs and social projects which, by definition, tend to be community based. Based on these findings, however, more innovation needs to be diverted to the other CSR categories or activities listed, to maximize investment opportunities. As "short-term and exploitative investments" are related to the CSR activities – *human resources, environment, business behavior, and community involvement* – it may or may not be beneficial to increase these investments from short- to long-term investments. This issue needs to be tested further in future research.

Meanwhile, the findings of Kim et al. (2014) overall, identify a substantial relationship between CSR and innovation activities of firms. In relation to their findings they propose that:

"…innovative investment is needed to prepare tomorrow's profits not only by considering investments in technology and in R&D, but also by dealing with sustainability to human, social, environmental, technical, and economic investments" (p. 175).

While their findings provide an understanding of the effect of sustainable CSR management strategies on the innovation of firms, as stated above, these findings need to be replicated in future research. Future research should also examine types of innovation and *Innovative CSR* social projects developed under the CSR categories: human rights and community involvement, which the researchers have nominated, and examine these categories in particular in developing countries where the *needs* for many of these topic areas are often much greater.

'Innovative CSR': The Future for CSR

Preuss (2011) examined a framework for anchoring CSR in the academic literature for innovation by combining the two areas of innovation and CSR. Earlier researchers on innovation such as Roberts (2007) provides a slimmed down version of the definition of Innovation: *Innovation = Invention + Exploitation.* Preuss (2011) then combines the definition of innovation with a CSR definition to create a term for *Innovative CSR*:

"Innovative CSR = design of novel ways of addressing social and environmental concerns + integration of these into business operations and interactions with stakeholders" (Preuss, 2011, p. 42).

This suggests that normal and routine CSR conducted in novel and innovative ways would allow an opportunity to combine the two fields of CSR and innovation. To operationalize this, Preuss (2011) extends the 4Ps of innovation by Francis and Bessant's (2005) framework, to combine CSR and innovation as follows:

- CSR P1 Innovation in CSR project content
- CSR P2 Innovation in CSR processes
- CSR P3 Innovation in CSR positioning
- CSR P4 Innovation in the CSR paradigm

Source: Preuss (2011, p. 42).

Many companies are already incorporating these types of innovation into their CSR strategy; however, Preuss (2011) provides a framework to study this in the academic research literature. At the same time this methodology provides examples of innovative corporate case studies. These are listed below:

CSR P1

A bottom-of-the-pyramid (BOP) example, where business can provide a solution to global poverty through paying attention to the huge unmet demand among the world's poorest consumers (Prahalad & Hammond, 2002; Preuss, 2011, p. 23). This can include decreasing prices by making more innovative products; involving the poor in creating products; and therefore increasing their wages and livelihood.

CSR P2

A betting and gaming group, Gala Coral, collaborated with charity Sue Ryder Care (SRC), through a joint procurement scheme (Preuss, 2011, p. 23). Their games raise funds for SRC to provide expert care for people living with serious conditions such as cancer and Huntington's Disease. Extending initiatives across all corporate divisions allows these processes to be fully immersed throughout the organization.

CSR P3

An example is Illycaffè, an early coffee firm, to address social and environmental issues in its relationship with coffee growers. On their website they state, their relationship with coffee growers "improves their lives." Further they state they have created value for *all stakeholders* through the entire value chain, becoming "the first in the world to obtain 'Responsible Supply Chain Process' certification from DNV (Det Norske Veritas), which certifies the sustainability of the entire supply chain" (Illycaffè, 2017).

CSR P4

An example is AT&T and their Foundation, transitioning from corporate philanthropy to a business-case-driven approach. They established a family care fund, governed by a union-management committee, to support employee-led efforts to establish day care in their communities. Not only did the availability of day care facilities and quality of care improve, the initiative also became a model for resolving union management disputes (Smith, 1994, cited in, Preuss, 2011, p. 24).

Source: Extracts adapted from Preuss (2011).

The CSR P2 example above includes "collaboration" and partnering, as a key component of innovation and also the sustainable development goals (SDGs) (i.e., goal 17, partnerships for goals). The SDGs and their individual goals are discussed further in Chapter 3. The CSR P4 example above is an interesting example of innovation, and in this case positioning, and is a good example of the way forward to future mainstreaming of CSR through *Innovative CSR*. The above P4 examples should therefore be considered as interesting examples to study in future research.

Making sense of CSR from the starting point of innovation as Preuss (2011) suggests, may help managers and scholars consider why some approaches to CSR are fragmented and often disconnected from business and strategy (Porter & Kramer, 2006; Preuss, 2011). As mentioned previously, focusing on *Innovative CSR* would suggest CSR could be used as a safe starting point, to develop CSR SIs or social projects under the umbrella of CSR strategy which a corporation can deliver, but with an innovative twist. Implementing this under CSR will also promote knowledge creation and learning, to promote innovation further into the corporation and provide examples and suggestions to further current CSR SIs and social projects in the innovation domain.

Previous research has suggested that the SIs or social projects should be an integral part of CSR strategy and the corporation's core business (Munro, 2013b). This refers to the concept that CSR must become so interwoven into everyday activities it eventually becomes part of the company's identity (Berger, Cunningham, & Drumwright, 2007). That is how micro SIs and macro social projects can become recognized under the CSR umbrella if they become integral to the company. Being more innovative with these SIs and social projects will enhance and mainstream *Innovative CSR* more rapidly. Whether CSR can be made more mainstream through *Innovative CSR* needs to be assessed in future research. There are several ways of doing this. Future research should examine CSR strategy utilizing the 4Ps that Preuss (2011) mentions for *Innovative CSR* (including innovation in CSR project content, processes, positioning, and paradigm), and test for the prevalence of their use in a corporation's CSR strategy. Future research could also examine SIs or social projects which are innovative rather than static and determine if it is safer or less risky to develop these initiatives, as innovative projects under the umbrella of CSR strategy. The knowledge of a high success rate of allowing an enterprise to set-up an innovative pilot under the safety net of the organization's innovative CSR program, before allowing it to go mainstream, would inspire more social entrepreneurs to work with corporates and vice versa.

Innovation in Developing Countries

Organizations in developing countries come from economies that do not often have the facility for large-scale R&D departments or the investment capabilities to develop departments specifically to conduct innovation research. Companies are therefore likely to rely on other ways to combine existing technological knowledge with changing market conditions to create advantage which is different from their competitors (Nguyen & Hipsher, 2018). This is therefore a complex exercise. It may also mean they are more likely to rely on innovators of an entrepreneurial nature or rely heavily on Social Innovation, as this relates to the social and community needs already existing in developing countries (Munro 2013a, 2017). However, it would also appear that innovation in developing countries is likely to happen in self-made enterprises or in fact more often in very small enterprises, such as micro-enterprises. While much of the academic literature on innovation and the example case studies focus on technology firms in developing countries as a means of innovation, it would seem that innovation is also an important factor in determining economic success in developing countries. It may also be a different type of innovation, while technology, IT, and the innovative digital examples are the most often portrayed examples in the literature and social media. A very different picture emerges when we examine innovations under the restriction of limited resources in developing countries. This is therefore an important emerging opportunity to pursue in future research.

The developing country setting therefore is an interesting context to consider for innovation research. Fajnzylber, Maloney and Rojas (2006), for example, report that developing countries have a higher percentage of business activities which take place in an "informal economy" by self-employed micro-entrepreneurs. This very much changes the support structures that are required and needed, and also the type of innovation. MNEs based in host countries in developing countries can support this type of innovation by developing micro-entrepreneurs and upskilling them to take on the task through projects related to their SDGs and SIs embedded in their CSR strategy.

A key point made here in relation to this is by Duflo and Banerjee (2011). They state that unlike many entrepreneurs in developed economies (starting a new business by a desire for a different type of financial reward), most micro-entrepreneurs in developing and less developed economies are forced into becoming entrepreneurs because of lack of quality paid employment (Duflo & Banerjee, 2011, p. 225; Hipsher, 2010, 2012; Nguyen & Hipsher, 2018). This is therefore a primary innovation starting point which could be supported by MNEs hosted in the home country of these micro-entrepreneurs.

In developing country situations, research suggests that micro-enterprises have limited access to "innovative and effective business practices" due to the owners' own limited skill base, lack of knowledge, and limited finance (Nartisa, 2012). This is thought to result in businesses which lack differentiation (and therefore innovations per se) and have difficulty achieving sustainable levels of profits (Banerjee, Duflo, Glennerster & Kinnan, 2013). As mentioned above, this could, however, be supported by corporates in these countries under the umbrella of their *Innovative CSR* strategy.

The findings by academics researching in this area suggest that innovation which exists primarily in micro-enterprises in developing economies is likely to take on a significantly different meaning than a high-tech company in a developed economy, but is of equal importance in the study of innovation, and the transition of CSR to *Innovative CSR*. This area of research is an excellent opportunity for future research as the innovation scene begins to take off through millennial changemakers in both developed and developing countries. Future research should examine innovation in these settings and the significance of it to CSR within these settings.

Innovation for Competitive Advantage

Innovation plays a significant role in creating a firm's competitive advantage. Reed and DeFillippi (1990) argue there is a direct correlation between innovative development of a business and gaining competitive advantage. This can be examined through value creation. While many business graduates understand value creation, it is important to redefine it here to determine its value within an innovation setting. The following quote provides a traditional definition of value creation:

> "Creating value for customers helps sell products and services, while creating value for shareholders, in the form of increases in stock price, insures the future availability of investment capital to fund operations. From a financial perspective, value is said to be created when a business earns revenue (or a return on capital) that exceeds expenses (or the cost of capital)" (Reference for Business, 2018).

However, many analysts believe a broader definition for value creation is required which is separate from financial measures. For example, Sarmah, Islam, and Rahman (2015) state MNEs are engaged in value creation with the community through supporting CSR programs. These programs ensure maximum *stakeholder* participation in value creation processes, especially in the selection, design, and delivery of such programs (p. 314). Innovation is a part of this; however, due to the many *stakeholder* types and differing expectations, companies often face difficulties due to the lack of knowledge of their host communities. This is especially the case in developing countries where host countries are foreign territories for MNEs (Munro, 2017; Munro et al., 2018). Some say, "companies are trying to go beyond their CSR activities by proactively working with community to achieve corporate sustainability goals" (Sarmah et al., 2015, p. 315). This has increased in recent years with the expected uptake of SDGs and the rapidly approaching target completion for SDG implementation by 2030. Much of this involves collaboration with *stakeholders*, including governments, NGOs, development banks, and multifunctioning international actors across borders.

Co-creation and collaboration are solutions in aligning CSR programs with the need and expectations of *stakeholders* to achieve maximum benefit. To do this companies are devising action plans in consultation with internal and external *stakeholders* while exploring, creating, and delivering value to society (Clarkson, 1995). This can also be co-created in interaction with other parties (Ramaswamy, 2008; Sarmah et al., p. 31) and completed in an innovative setting. This is discussed further in the following section.

The Evolution of Innovation: Toward Collaboration and Co-creation

Before continuing to the different types of innovation, this section acknowledges the research literature examining the "evolution of Innovation" within business organizations. Lee et al. (2012), for example, refers to innovation evolving in three set stages. They refer to *closed-innovation,* where innovation happens purely within the organization. With the development of the global market, relying on self was the less accepted norm and new forms of interorganizational collaborative partnerships, alliances, and joint ventures arose. Lee et al. (2012) refer to this as *collaborative-innovation*.

With the rise of the global economy and the invention and development of the Information Communications Technology (ICT) industry supporting worldwide knowledge sharing, Chesbrough (2006) termed *open-innovation* as an inside-out and outside-in collaborative innovative effort for value creation. Lee et al. (2012) describe this as the building of a world-class value chain through a new innovation ecosystem where various complements can be combined into coherent value creating solutions seamlessly on collaborative arrangements (p. 824). Hence this combined the organization's own competencies of creativity with those of external expertise and the words "Innovation Ecosystem" appeared. This occurred around the same time as the introduction of the SDG framework when an emphasis on collaboration with support from external expertise and organizations also occurred. CSR is therefore increasingly operating within wider and more innovative ecosystems.

As part of this, with the rise of social networks and collective intelligence, we increasingly use social technologies to get what we need for or from individuals. The last stage referred to by Lee et al. (2012) is an *open-innovation system* called *co-innovation*. The *co-innovation* platform is built on the "convergence of ideas, collaborative arrangement, and co-creation of experience with stakeholders" (Lee et al., 2012, p. 824). Here, co-innovation refers to the collaboration of ideas and people, through finding solutions to new products, services, or ventures right through the value chain (Lee et al., 2012).

Research studies tend to agree that "building a co-innovation enterprise is not simple. It requires a new innovation culture, strategic vision, courage, direction, and sense of urgency" (Lee et al., 2012). However, many researchers are stating a corporation's needs are not only to help develop the new ecosystem for society's needs but also for an organization's competitive advantage. Therefore "co-innovation" is important. It is also an excellent opportunity for future research as much of this work requires a theoretical foundation to firmly establish the concept of co-innovation in the literature and then complete empirical research to determine the key success factors and outcomes of it.

Lee et al. (2012) have created a model which ties together co-innovation and CSV across new products and services, a new customer base, efficiency in the value chain, and creating new business models. However, Lee et al.'s (2012) theoretical model places co-innovation at the center as a co-innovation platform. Value is then created through five value creating avenues. These are based on convergence, collaboration, and co-creation with partners (Lee et al., 2012). In this process authors often focus on co-creation as a key avenue toward innovation, which of course also involves collaboration.

As has been published in academic papers, numerous conferences, and business commentary sites, "doing good is not enough" – it needs to be scaled up and made sustainable and this also requires collaboration. Osburg (2013) adds the collaborative part to the equation by adding the term *Open Innovation* to Social Innovation. He describes this as "a close collaboration of knowledge sharing inside and outside the firm" and that this is crucial for success. Further he states "apart from Governments, private firms, and various NGOs, it is mainly the

Social Entrepreneur who can become a strategic partner for the private sector by creating shared value" as part of collaboration (Osburg, 2013, p. 21). A large part of collaboration is the act of co-creation.

In relation to this, Prahalad and Ramaswamy in the late 1990s began discussing the importance of co-opting customer competence when developing new products and services, and also experiences (Prahalad & Ramaswamy, 2000). They went on to discuss how companies had to learn to "co-create" value with customers. Together, they wrote *The Future of Competition*, defining the implications of the shift in modern society toward the centrality of individuals and their human experiences (Prahalad, Ramaswamy, Fruehauf & Wolmeringer, 2004). This led to the discussion of digital and consumer relationships in terms of co-creation, whereby interactions are more important than activities. This then led to a later paper defining co-creation as follows:

> "Co-creation is the process by which products, services, and experiences are developed jointly by companies and their stakeholders, opening up a whole new world of value. Firms must stop thinking of individuals as mere passive recipients of value, to whom they have traditionally delivered goods, services, and experiences." (Ramaswamy, 2009, p. 11)

Following the definition of Ramaswamy (2009) it was suggested that organizations did in fact stop thinking of individuals as mere passive recipients of value, and instead, "seek to engage people as active co-creators of value everywhere in the system" (p. 11). Further, Ramaswamy (2009) explains that "the conventional firm-centric view of value creation has expanded beyond the activities of the firm toward one whose locus is now a function of *interactions* anywhere in the system – underpinning the new source of value (the 'where' of value creation)." The "where" being anywhere and therefore the opportunities vast. He provides two examples of this: *Nike+* and *Caja Navarra* (a bank in Spain). These are discussed further below.

"Where" is Anywhere – Nike Partnerships with Apple and Customers:

The *Nike+* "experience" kit consisting of a wireless device that transmits speed and distance information from a sensor-equipped Nike running shoe to an iPod Touch or special wrist- band. Then, through the website "nikeplus.com" runners can track their progress, set personal goals and challenge friends to races. As of June 2009, he quoted over a million runners uploading 130 million miles. Increasing Nike's market share with increased revenues through the *Nike +* ecosystem, in partnership with Apple and others.
Source: Adapted from Ramaswamy (2009).

This is a very early example of a partnership involving innovation through co-creation and collaboration for a customer's better health. Since 2009, many other innovative examples, also within an organization's CSR strategy (or shared value approach), have occurred on the market to assist those who are impoverished or without regular Internet connection, for example, but when innovatively assisted they also become a customer. Providing Internet and mobile phones for customers to be able to have a bank account in Kenya is an example often used in this setting. However, the *Nike* + example illustrates the shift beyond products and services to "human experience environments", not a visual 3-dimensional experience at this stage, but an IT innovation, nonetheless.

Further to understanding the incorporation of innovation within CSR strategy, it is important to explain "human experience environments" such as the *Nike* + example further. Ramaswamy (2009), explains that *human experience environments*:

> "...embody interactions of individuals with each other and with the company and its network partners' products and artefacts, places and spaces where interactions take place (whether online or offline), and interactions with the company and network partners' business processes" (Ramaswamy, 2009, p. 12).

This refers to partnerships and "collaborations" which are part of innovative CSR strategy and CSV examples, as discussed in Chapter 4. As explained for the Kenyan mobile phone example above, while the initiative increases the market share for *Nike* it also increases the health of the purchaser of the *Nike* shoes. However, it is most certainly a "co-creation" example, as customers further have an opportunity to co-create their own experience with Nike partners.

The *Caja Navarra* bank example in Spain provides an example of innovating co-creative engagement platforms as part of CSR community or SIs. This is also an example of interactions of innovation and engagement across a platform and a *human experience environment.*

Engaging Customers as Innovation Platforms – *Caja Navarra* bank:

> *Caja Navarra* bank is traditionally a regional not-for-profit bank designed *to support its local communities through social contributions.* Ramaswamy (2009) explains that it is "based on a dual financial and social mission, with part of its profits allocated for society's development and well-being." Their campaign "You Choose: You Decide," allows customers to specify their preferences among *seven initiatives of social actions* supported by the bank. Customers' credit cards are then personalized to show their choices, reinforcing their identification with the initiative and generating a strong emotional connection. By

engaging customers on this innovative platform, they were able to tell their customers what they did with their savings and let each customer choose where these funds should be invested.
Source: Adpated from Ramaswamy (2009).

This is a similar case study example to the Bendigo bank who won an *Australian Shared Value Award* in 2017 for their innovative shared contributions to community SIs through customer choice. Stated as a shared value example, this further illustrates the overlap of terms with collaboration, co-creation, innovation, CSR, and CSV. As expressed by Osburg, collaboration and co-creation is important to the social enterprise and is a large part of the methodology used in business models for social enterprise start-ups. Many of these innovative initiatives are supported by corporates as part of their CSR programs. This leads us to a discussion on social entrepreneurship and the inclusion of social enterprises and Social Innovation in CSR strategy.

Defining and Understanding: Social Enterprise, Innovation, and Social Entrepreneurship

One of the best explanations with regards to Social Innovation and social entrepreneurship is the research and writings of Drucker (1985). He confirms innovation lies at the heart of entrepreneurship and adds that "this is irrespective of context (i.e., public, private or third-sector organisations)". Innovation, therefore, is seen as fundamental to *social entrepreneurship*, and as an entrepreneurial activity undertaken for a 'social purpose,' changing the way social needs are addressed. In contrast, *social enterprise* represents a business established for a 'social purpose,' to create positive social change (Luke & Chu, 2013). Although seemingly different, the terms are often used interchangeably as they are also similar: "both blur the boundaries between for (profit) and not-for-profit activities and combine commercial activities with social objectives" (Chell, 2007; Mair & Marti, 2006, cited in, Luke & Chu, 2013, p. 764).

Researchers, however, often examine these terms separately to create better understanding of each. The term "enterprise," for example, is associated with commercial business activity (Chell, 2007; Dart, 2004). The term "entrepreneurship" is associated with opportunity identification, innovation, and risk (Shane, 2003; Venkataraman & Sarasvathy, 2001), and bringing something new to the market (Davidsson, 2006; Luke & Chu, 2013). Historically, "entrepreneurship" was recognized as the basic engine that gives rise to new ventures – the driving force behind the dramatic growth and development of the business sector (Austin et al., 2006, p. 169). Developing from this is an accepted full definition for 'social enterprise': *"A 'social enterprise' is an organisation that exists for a social purpose and engages in trading to fulfil its mission, using market-based techniques to achieve social ends"* (Barraket, Collyer, O'Connor, & Anderson, 2010, cited in, Luke & Chu, 2013, p. 765). In contrast, 'social entrepreneurship' is defined as: *"Entrepreneurship with a social goal. Wherein 'social entrepreneurs' are regarded as change agents"* (Dees, 1998; Thompson, 2002, cited in Luke & Chu, 2013, p. 766).

An accepted definition that combines both concepts is as follows:

> "Social entrepreneurship is the way of using resources to create benefits for the society while the social entrepreneur is the person who seeks to benefit society through innovation and risk taking" (Tracey, Phillips, & Haugh, 2005).

More recently, further definitions of social entrepreneurship have been provided by the European Commission (2014) who include *social impact* as a development within their 2011 definition of CSR:

> "A social enterprise is an operator in the social economy whose main objective is to have a social impact rather than make a profit for their owners or shareholders. It operates by providing goods and services for the market in an entrepreneurial and innovative fashion and uses its profits primarily to achieve social objectives. It is managed in an open and responsible manner and, in particular, involves employees, consumers and stakeholders affected by its commercial activities" (European Commission, 2014).

Luke and Chu (2013) throw an interesting light on the difference between social enterprise and social entrepreneurship and have backed this by research. They examined 10 non-governmental organizations. Their findings on social enterprise revealed a focus on the 'purpose' of social business, while findings on social entrepreneurship revealed an emphasis on the 'processes' underlying innovative and entrepreneurial activity for 'social purpose.' The implications of this type of research allows an understanding of the action to achieve social change, and the risk when outcomes are not achieved. This is a considerable opportunity for future research. In particular, research should explore strategy within social enterprises, to consider ways to financial sustainability to address long-term sustainable social change and to measure social impact as part of this. Luke and Chu (2013) also touch on issues surrounding the potential collaboration of social enterprises with corporates delivering CSR. This is discussed further in the following section.

Social Entrepreneurship and CSR

The research of Crisan and Borza (2012) examines how social entrepreneurship and CSR are related and interconnected. They quote:

"Corporate Social Responsibility (CSR) brings many benefits being considered an important lever in supporting social entrepreneurship (Austin et al., 2006). Also, CSR has a significant role in the social value creation process for both, businesses and social purpose organizations" (Crisan & Borza, 2012, p. 106).

Crisan and Borza (2012) in their discussion of social entrepreneurship refer to CSR policies as "business decisions" that surpass economic and technical initiatives of the organization. They also refer to CSR initiatives as major activities undertaken by a firm in order to sustain social causes and to fulfill its commitment to CSR. They provide the following examples: health (assisting AIDS and cancer causes), safety (crime prevention), education (education for those in need), job creation (training practice), environment (recycling), economic and social development (low interest loans for purchase of apartments), and other basic human needs and desires (combating hunger, poverty, discrimination) (Wills, 2009, cited in Crisan & Borza, 2012, p. 106). While acknowledging that CSR is important to supporting social entrepreneurship, Crisan and Borza define them separately, with CSR policy being particularly important to the process: *CSR policies help firms to fulfill economic and social responsibilities ensuring wellbeing and social welfare (Hockerts, 2007). CSR policies can be considered as being companies' commitment to improve society through business practices (Kotler & Lee, 2005)* (cited in Crisan & Borza, 2012, p. 106).

As part of their research, Crisan and Borza (2012) refer to the social entrepreneurship definition by Tracey et al. (2005). Tracey et al. (2005) focus on corporate social involvement (CSI), defining CSI as investing in collaborations and partnerships "with non-profit and public sector in order to create healthy and favourable conditions, targeting both, community and business" (Crisan & Borza, 2012, p. 106). From their research analysis, Crisan and Borza (2012) conclude that social entrepreneurship is the field that allows observation of how social problems can be solved in a sustainable way. They view social entrepreneurship as the interaction between NGO and other organizations (including corporates), through CSR, CSI, and sustainable and independent activities. They suggest that with these types of collaborations with the private sector (who have the experience and ability to develop the commercial side of social organizations), social outcomes can be successfully created.

Crisan and Borza (2012) reached their conclusions after examining 394 enterprises. Their final conclusion acknowledges that social entrepreneurship can be sustained by companies through CSR (partnership, collaboration, and founding an organization with a social mission). They also suggest CSR and social entrepreneurship have distinct conceptual approaches, but CSR can assist with greater recovery of social opportunities (Crisan & Borza, 2012). It would therefore make sense for corporates to be conducting social entrepreneurship projects as part of their CSR social strategy, and this may garner them strong support from *stakeholders,* and the millennials and collaborators involved in these projects. This is an important area to examine further and provides extensive opportunities for future research integrating CSR, Social Innovation, and social entrepreneurship.

Confirming this perspective is CSR research Professor and guru, Archie Carroll, who discusses social entrepreneurship in relation to CSR. He expresses *social entrepreneurship* as:

> "...the process of pursuing solutions to social problems while using time-tested business principles to help achieve total organizational success" (Carroll, 2015, p. 94). Further Carroll states, social entrepreneurship may occur in either for-profit or non-profit organizations: *"Non-profit social entrepreneurs are primarily interested in achieving positive social change as their primary mission while needing to generate acceptable financial returns to sustain the enterprise. For-profit social entrepreneurs' factor in and integrate social objectives in their business missions from the very beginning."* Carroll (2015, p. 94)

Carroll (2015) then provides CSR-based examples of for-profit corporations who have followed a social mission excellence with financial excellence. These very early examples include: The Body Shop, Ben & Jerry's Ice Cream, Whole Food Markets, and Tom's of Maine. There is, however, a plethora of additional examples developed in recent years, and this is an opportunity for future research to integrate these examples of CSR-based Social Innovation and social entrepreneurship projects, through systematic literature reviews, to determine the strength of these examples.

Carroll's (2015) definition above also focuses on the nonprofit social entrepreneur contrasted with the for-profit social entrepreneur. This provides an opportunity to examine how corporations can support social entrepreneurs under their CSR strategy. In doing so, it is important to acknowledge that social entrepreneurship has an external and internal role. The role of the internal social entrepreneur, for example, is to identify social problems inside the company and to solve them in order to reach SDG targets (Amelio, 2017; Drayton, 2002). This internal role is more often labeled *social intrapreneur*; however, there are a number of *preneurs* to consider, and these are discussed below.

The Evolution of the 'Preneur': From Social Entrepreneur to Corporate Social Entrepreneur and Corporate Social Intrapreneur

This section discusses what is considered to be the offspring of social entrepreneurship; that is, CSE and CSI. To understand the evolution and integration of these terms, for corporate entrepreneurship (CE) contrasted with social entrepreneurship, it is first necessary to understand that traditional approaches to management were not as innovative as the new ventures which are appearing today. Corporate managers therefore attempted to bring more innovative and entrepreneurial initiatives into their organization through CE which was aimed at finding market opportunities and then later repeating this in the social sector as social entrepreneurship grew to encompass CSE, as portrayed in the extract below:

> "…'corporate entrepreneurship' is aimed at spotting and redefining market opportunities through innovative strategies, processes and organizations that would generate new competitive advantage. Parallel to this trend, the social sector saw the emergence of the practice of 'social entrepreneurship', which aimed at achieving greater social impact through innovation and adaption of the discipline and tools from the business world in support of a social mission." (Austin et al., 2006, p. 169).

A further definition of CE is provided by Covin and Miles (1999) as *the presence of innovation with the objective of rejuvenating or redefining organizations, markets, or industries in order to create or sustain competitive superiority.* In parallel, the concept of social entrepreneurship emerged (Austin and Reficco, 2009). Dees (1998), for example, defined social entrepreneurship as *innovative activity with a social purpose in either the private or nonprofit sector, or across both.* CSE was then born to integrate and build on these concepts (Austin and Reficco, 2009).

> Adding corporate to entrepreneurship suggests that CSR is possibly a complementary theme or part of corporate entrepreneurship. Further, Googins and Rochlin (2006) comment on this evolution: *"What is clear is the widespread agreement on the need for a more active and strategic citizenship"* within CSR. As part of this following, the concept of corporate social entrepreneurship (CSE) began to gain more acceptance (Austin & Reficco, 2009).

The term corporate social entrepreneurship (CSE) was first used by Hemingway (2004) over 15 years ago in a paper published with her dissertation; however, it is yet to be fully accepted as a separate field from social entrepreneurship, CE, and CSR (Hadad & Cantaragiu, 2017). The term is believed to have evolved from CSR, with early beginnings as philanthropy, which some authors referred to as social entrepreneurship (Ostrander, 2007). CSR proponents may find this association with CSR through philanthropy hard to accept, as the full definition of CSR is not just philanthropy. Philanthropy is just one component of CSR which has since evolved to include more active and innovative SIs, and should be expressed as such.

The term corporate social entrepreneurship has numerous definitions. Hadad and Cantaragiu (2017) systematically gathered together all existing definitions and listed the following themes for a corporate social entrepreneur:

(a) an employee in a corporation
(b) promotes a socially responsible agenda to be achieved alongside business profits
(c) solves social problems

Source: Hadad and Cantaragiu (2017, p. 257).

Hadad and Cantaragiu (2017) also state the themes and description of the corporate social entrepreneur listed above can be applied to describe the companies that act as corporate social entrepreneurs. There is also an emphasis on social responsibility and solving problems, but with the addition of the word 'entrepreneur.' This suggests a more active role from the top-down. It also removes the word "responsibility" from its label, which Carroll (2015, 2018) describes as a way to make terms like sustainability and corporate citizenship more "palpable" for corporations and the general public to accept.

Like all entrepreneurship, CSE involves opportunity and innovation. However, unlike either CE or social entrepreneurship, CSE is more about mobilizing internal and external resources in order to generate both economic and social value (Austin et al., 2006). CSR proponents consider CSE under the umbrella of CSR through the development of social projects at a level that measures impact and the benefits for beneficiaries of social projects. Austin, Leonard, Reficco, & Wei-Skillern, 2005 (and Austin et al., 2006), therefore, define CSE as:

> "…the process of extending the firm 's domain of competence and corresponding opportunity set through innovative leveraging of resources, both within and outside its direct control, aimed at the simultaneous creation of economic and social value."

What is interesting about this definition is the acknowledgment of innovation as an entrepreneurial feature in the simultaneous *creation* of economic and social value. While the simultaneous *creation* concept is an aspect of CSR, it is emphasized often more fully in the CSV literature but shows the similarity between these two terms. Overall, the authors, Austin and Reficco (2009) state that the fundamental purpose of CSE is to accelerate a company's transformation to be better generators of doing societal good, but no real statement of how to do this is given.

With regard to the list of features above for the role of the corporate social entrepreneur, which can also define the company's role in CSE, this is considered similar to the definition of corporate citizenship which is also acknowledged by both the person and the company, as explained in Chapter 1 and Chapter 2. It may also be possible that an individual in the role in CSE can achieve both roles in an organization: CSR and CSE, while pursuing social projects under the umbrella term of CSR. The examination of these roles and their crossover is an excellent opportunity for future research. Also, the examination of the frequency of the prevalence of the CSE term and role in companies is necessary, as past researchers have found a lack of research published on the term, with some researchers suggesting limited uptake of the term by corporations.

In addition, research studies state the only publicly available guidelines enabling organizational CSE was drafted by Crets (2012) and focuses on environmentally sustainable business, recycling, and reducing waste (Hadad & Cantaragiu, 2017) rather than the social side of sustainability and entrepreneurship. Historically, this meant there was less mention of the social aspects and social challenges in the definitions for CSE, as listed above. This leaves a substantial gap in the literature and an excellent research opportunity to explore. The role of the CSE individual in companies mentioned above leads us to a discussion of a second role within companies – the corporate social intrapreneur.

The Relationship of Corporate Social Intrapreneurship to CSR

As previously mentioned, the offspring of social entrepreneurship is CSE and CSI. Looking at the origins of social intrapreneurship, the term intrapreneurship is thought to have been created in 1978 by Gifford and Libba Pnchot. However, it is clear it was not fully taken on board at that time. More recently, Mair and Marti (2006) refer to social intrapreneurship as social entrepreneurship in a new or already established organization. Carroll (2015) takes a similar slant, with the statement, "Social intrapreneurship includes firms that did not have a social agenda as part of their initial charter, but later developed a highly visible social agenda" (Carroll, 2015, p. 94).

Other authors associate the term with the role a person takes on board within a company, working from within, regardless of whether a social agenda exists already or not. There is a sense of this in the second part of Carroll's definition, where he also associates the work of the social intrapreneur with CSR and cites some early examples of this in the literature:

> "Social intrapreneurs work from within companies to advocate social programming that addresses social or environmental challenges. Companies that illustrate this category might include Timberland, Starbucks, Microsoft, Patagonia and others. Through innovation and risk taking these firms have become high-profile exemplars of CSR and sustainability and their numbers are increasing" (Carroll, 2015, p. 94).

Elkington and Love claim to have been the first to coin the term in 2008, when they published *The Social Intrapreneur Report* (Hadad & Cantaragiu, 2017). Their previous research on social entrepreneurs and their connections with already established social entrepreneurs, such as Accenture, Banco Real, Coca-Cola, Ford, Morgan-Stanley, and Nike, assisted this work. As part of their findings, they state intrapreneurs: "were still struggling to find a common identity, even if they share(d) a common purpose" (Grayson, McLaren, & Spitzeck, 2011, p. 1). It is widely acknowledged that giving a name to a social phenomenon gives people the resources necessary to unite and construct a self-identity. This identity can then be easily understood and accepted by others also seeking an identity or a group to identify with (Munro, 2017).

In relation to this and from the perspective of the identity of a social intrapreneur, the research of Grayson et al. (2011) in this area emphasized there are people who present themselves as "social intrapreneurs" in their professional CVs and seek to find "others" of the same kind to unite forces and share personal experiences with. Social media is very good for this. To make their point, the authors provide some early examples from social media sites, for example: socialintrapreneur.weebly.com (the personal page of James Espiritu); plus the Skoll World Forum 2013 participants: Regula Schegg, Strategic Business Developer for Hilti Foundation; James Inglesby, Category Manager for Unilever Nigerian and Co-Founder of Clean Team Ghana, to name a few (Grayson et al., 2011).

The authors concluded that "social intrapreneurs" are constructed through various research papers or articles about themselves on social media (Grayson et al., 2011). This industry area has moved on significantly since 2011, hence this provides an excellent opportunity for future research to further define social intrapreneurship and social entrepreneurship through an examination of different resources from practitioners and academics alike, including the many different sources through current social media.

Bringing 'Change' through Innovation and 'Preneurship'

For Innovation and Entrepreneurship to be powerful enough to bring about 'change' in the social world, it needs to differentiate between other types of research and different kinds of people or 'Preneurs'. Social *intrapreneurs*, for example, are contrasted with social *entrepreneurs*, and also their employed counterparts working in CSR departments or acting as corporate volunteers or "green" team members. Their distinctive nature, as defined by Hadad and Cantaragiu (2017, comes from defining two dimensions: one, social intrapreneurs act within already established business boundaries, and two, they are focused on bringing profits to their companies (p. 261).

More specifically in *The Social Intrapreneur – A Field Guide for Corporate Changemakers* the social intrapreneur is defined as:

> "a) someone who works inside major corporations or organisations
> to develop and promote practical solutions to social or

environmental challenges; b) someone who applies the principles of social entrepreneurship inside a major organisation; c) one characterised by an 'insider-outsider' mind-set and approach" (SustainAbility, 2008, p. 4).

Confirming this, Hadad and Cantaragiu (2017) summarise the prerequisites of the *social intrapreneurship* as: employee, corporation, and solutions oriented toward social and environmental challenges and progress. Some definitions also include, "disruption" terminology which is extremely important in the *'be the change'* movement and the innovation setting. This is referred to in the definition below:

> "...the social intrapreneur is an employee who uses corporate politics to get disruptive ideas to market and to more customers sooner, with greater environmental or social impact. Synthetizing the already designed definitions, we identify a social intrapreneur as being an employee who leverages corporate politics to come up with a practical/innovative solution to a social problem to create social value and profits. As for social intrapreneurship, this is the action of a social intrapreneur who seeks to outreach the community in order to blend societal and business values as to address social challenges" (Hadad and Cantaragiu, 2017, p. 262).

"Disruption" as listed in the quotation above can refer to disrupting the current system, the capitalist system, of how we operate and do business. It is also an acknowledged part of the integrated values system approach coined by Visser (2014) which includes disruption as one of the five forces of his fragmentation framework, where *Disruption* refers to any instability that threatens human life, safety, and security (Visser, 2018, p. 7). However, here we refer to it as people disrupting the system, with activism on social media and/or to disrupt the way institutions or events are run and how policies are implemented. The "disruption" Visser refers to also makes sense when he includes five types of "innovative solutions" in his concept, one of them being the production of *Secure* innovations to lower risk and aid recovery from threats and disruptions and ensure continuity in society. Visser's approach is explained further in Chapter 6.

To understand the connection between social *intrapreneurs*, social *entrepreneurs* and innovation within a CSR context, it is important to note this involves a level of risk-taking, as mentioned in the quote from Carroll below:

"Social intrapreneurship includes firms that did not have a social agenda as part of their initial charter, but later developed a highly visible social agenda. Social intrapreneurs work from within companies to advocate social programming that addresses social or environmental challenges." (Carroll, 2015, p. 94).

Again, numerous researchers like Carroll have recognized innovation and intrapreneurship are significant parts of CSR social agendas. This topic area is therefore a significant opportunity for future academic research to look at social entrepreneurship and intrapreneurship within a CSR context, including the different job roles in each speciality and the overlap between roles that exists. In particular, there is a need to update research on corporates in this area as many of the case study examples such as Timberland and Starbucks, referred to earlier by Carroll (2015), are outdated and overused in the literature. In addition, the idea of "risk-taking" is probably less daunting in the current 'change movement' evolving in society today, and needs to be further researched with newer examples in the current context.

Millennials and the Social Enterprise Movement

As mentioned above, there has been a mainstream movement toward the development of social enterprises to co-create and deal with wicked challenges and create 'change' in society to solve social problems by seeing these problems as challenges and as an opportunity, and then providing an opportunity through a business idea or social enterprise. Millennials (as defined below) are particularly interested in making change and taking control of their own destiny. In addition, the growing social movements described in Chapter 1 lean toward conscious capitalism, 'purpose,' 'change,' innovation, collaboration, and social entrepreneurialism in the business sector and general community and are generational and necessary.

From a research perspective, it is important to define the millennial age range and their perspective and current mindset relative to this. Millennials are defined by their birth years between 1981 and 1996 (aged 23–38 years old in 2019) and are in the current workforce. Generation Zs were born between 1997 and 2012 (aged 7–22 years old in 2019) with the oldest in the range, in the workforce or just entering it (Mental Floss, 2018). Their interests are clearly in business for 'purpose,' 'be the change,' and the social entrepreneurialism spheres, and university curriculums are adapting to accommodate this. Next up is Generation Alpha born from 2010, same year as the iPad, with instant access to information and innovation – they will enter a very different world and workforce.

Millennials and Generation Z (henceforth referred to as millennials), a large part of the current workforce, will play a key role in innovation going forward and this includes what happens in CSR. Research by Howe and Strauss (2000) reveals millennials as optimists, cooperative, and civic minded. It is expected they will demand that employers adjust to their needs and build careers and families at the same time. Fair Play on pay and benefits will also be at the forefront (Howe & Strauss, 2000; Reavis, Tucci, & Pierre, 2017). It is also expected that millennials will demand changes focused on their needs, and as activists they will seek to influence community, political, economic, and environmental issues (Howe & Strauss, 2000; Reavis et al., 2017). As previously mentioned in earlier chapters, millennials are looking for things to support because they want to feel like they're making a 'change' in the world. They will also 'change' the corporate culture they move into and/or run their own companies shaped by 'change'. They will as a priority want corporations to have a social conscience (Sharp, 2014) as an overriding feature, and more specifically, the same social conscience as them.

Looking back at the desires of millennials and their support for common good, authors of various studies support the prediction of Howe and Strauss (2000). That is: "as millennials continue to age and rise in organizations; social, political, and business institutions will be challenged" (Reavis et al. 2017, p. 82). Further research such as *The Millennial Impact Report (2017)* reveals millennials do not have much trust in government to do what's right. Instead, they put more faith in themselves to create "the change" they want to see (The Millennial Impact Report, 2017). The report confirms millennials are an invigorated generation for social causes and are interested in issues at the macro level, consistently identifying education, wages, health care, employment, and the economy as the areas of most concern to them. They act, however, at the micro level, getting engaged primarily with issues that are or have been close to their personal lives. They do not see themselves as activists like their parents, but as "everyday changemakers" (Case Foundation, 2017). Large expectations perhaps, but this is also at the heart of CSR and at the heart of innovation. With millennials expected to create their own jobs in the future, and their vision as 'changemakers', the business model for start-ups and social enterprises therefore makes sense. However, millennial and Generation Z aged students need an understanding of CSR and how corporate businesses operate alongside a start-up business, as many corporates are embracing the opportunity to support social enterprises along their supply chain or as part of their CSR social projects and SIs. Corporates working with social enterprises is discussed in the following section.

In the interim, the university curriculum for learning how to set-up a social enterprise involves learning how to solve wicked challenges. As mentioned in the beginning of this chapter, many universities have set-up centers with social hubs and labs to create start-up social enterprises and attract the interest of millennials. The Yunus Social Business Center, for example, recently set-up at Griffith University and at La Trobe Business School in Melbourne, Australia was mentioned earlier. These centers, in general, aim to drive systems change through social entrepreneurship and enterprise, where research and teaching is focused on the field of social enterprise, entrepreneurship, and innovation. This is a large opportunity for universities, but it is also an opportunity for corporates to grow their network, resources and strategy.

Corporates, Millennials, and Social Innovation

As corporations, particularly MNEs, work primarily in and across global markets they undoubtedly come across deep and complex problems. As mentioned earlier, these multidimensional type problems for corporations can involve global challenges such as the earth's limited natural resources (Lindahl & Widén, 2015; Waddel, McLachlan & Dentoni, 2013; Rockström, Steffen, Noone, Persson, Chapin III, Lambin, 2009; Waddock, 2012), and also social problems such as famine, extreme poverty, and consequently a lack of physical resources and education. These types of complex and difficult problems, referred to here as wicked challenges, are examined within a CSR context. Businesses taking on board wicked challenges existing in society and developing solutions to solve them at scale, and with meaningful impact that can be measured, is part of CSR strategy. This includes an organization's SIs and social projects as part of their CSR activities.

Some researchers have a harsher critique and refer to businesses being made responsible for the wicked challenges they have created rather than the problem already being part of a broken system, and a new opportunity to resolve. The organization's corporate footprint is discussed further below. However, research typically shows wicked challenges normally occur in a social context, where there are diverse and differing views and perceptions of who is responsible and what the cause is. There are no right answers to solving wicked challenges (Camillus, 2008), and so it would appear they have been named accordingly: *Wicked problems (challenges), refer to issues which are highly complex, have innumerable and undefined causes, and are difficult to understand and frame* (Dentoni, Hospes, & Ross, 2012, p. 2). As explained earlier, these problems are also referred to as challenges and opportunities.

It should also be added with regards to the complexity of wicked challenges that there may be no "directly traceable causes" (Gioia, 1992, p. 381). For instance, poverty has been linked to both a lack of income and a deficit in human capabilities (Sen, 1999). While this may create a third problem of lack of education to solve the problem, it also makes it difficult to delimit wicked challenges, identify villains, and offer definitive solutions (Reinecke & Ansari, 2016; Waddock, 2008). Despite the multilayered context surrounding many of these wicked challenges, as stated above, the corporate is often held accountable. One reason is the corporate footprint on society. Businesses are viewed by some researchers as a major influence in the processes that have led to today's social, economic, and environmental problems (Albareda, 2008; Belz & Peattie, 2012;

Porter & Kramer, 2011, cited in, Lindahl & Widén, 2015). Hence, the current perspective that corporations need to redesign their business models, to not only create value for themselves but also for society, is increasingly the status quo.

Research has shown that collaboration must take place within *multi-stake-holder* networks to fully understand and be a part of a resolution to wicked challenges (Lindahl & Widén, 2015). As previously mentioned, these levels of collaboration can be achieved by corporates and/or MNEs under the CSR banner as social projects and SIs as referred to in the research paper in Chapter 2. Social projects can also be scaled up to make enormous impact where both parties benefit, making the project sustainable, ongoing, and collaborative at the same time. Some researchers refer to CSV as one of the methodologies to do this. The next section looks at the potential for social projects and SIs to adopt social enterprise projects as part of the organization's CSR strategy.

Corporates Working with Social Enterprises

Current social media on the topic of innovation and entrepreneurship will confirm there is significant opportunity for social enterprises and corporates to work together and support each other in solving wicked challenges. It is possible to develop or scale social enterprise projects to meet large populations and corporate demand. However, both the social enterprise and the corporate face similar challenges. Both are working with large complex challenges, and both are working within a system not yet aligned or functioning to support the delivery of profit for purpose (or 'business for purpose' as discussed in Chapter 1).

While waiting for the system to change, corporates are building social enterprises into their supply chain. They are doing this by supporting social enterprises through development assistance or procurement and educating their suppliers to do the same. PwC calls this "Buying Social" to fit. In doing so, this also fits a company's commitment to diversity and inclusion, encouraging social mobility and supporting disadvantaged groups in society. Social enterprises also collaborate to familiarize themselves with the standards and controls used by big businesses, to ensure the quality and security they need can be delivered in ways that are not overly burdened for smaller start-ups (PwC, 2018). Another risk related to the delivery capacity of smaller social enterprises is they may not supply or distribute across an entire country where a corporate operates. To assist with this, PwC, for example, embrace a "multi-local" approach, so that different (but similar types of) social enterprises can be collaborated with, in different parts of the country. They also set-up a social enterprise hub that houses a social enterprise training course and a related trade association and includes a social enterprise restaurant. Numerous corporations have pursued this method of integrating social enterprises into their supply chain or supporting social enterprises under their CSR strategies, supporting them with their start-up strategy and income, and/or including them in their ongoing community programs. SAP, Barclays Bank and UBS provide recent case study examples of this, in the following section.

SAP Social Enterprise Case Study:

SAP announced in September 2018, they have entered a three-year partnership, with the Social Enterprise World Forum (SEWF), acting as their global technology partner. The organizations will work together to fulfill the SEWF's 'purpose' to support the growth and development of social enterprises throughout the world and is considered to be the first-of-its-kind partnership. Central to the partnership, SAP will work closely with SEWF and Social Enterprise UK, to develop a Massive Open Online Course (MOOC) demonstrating the commercial and social impact corporates can obtain by investing in social enterprises according to SAP News. In addition, SAP and the SEWF will explore ways to drive greater social impact by introducing more social enterprises into corporate supply chains (SAP News, 2018). SAP employees will also support the partnership at an individual level through volunteering their time and skills. Each year, for example, SAP teams around the world will volunteer their time and skills to social enterprises in the regions where the SEWF is held.

Source: Adapted from an extract SAP News, UK Press Room/ Corporate (2018).

Joint Social Enterprise Case Study:

Amey, PwC, BP and Santander, have spent collectively more than £45m with social enterprises since the *Buy Social Corporate Challenge* was launched in 2016. Social Enterprise UK, which organises the scheme, is calling UK businesses to spend £1bn with social enterprises. This will help support jobs for people facing challenges entering the job market, such as those with mental and physical disabilities or from vulnerable populations. A procurement software platform is being developed that will "streamline the onboarding of social enterprises.'

Source: Extract from CIPS (2018), Supply Management News.

Barclays Bank Social Enterprise Case Study:

Barclays is contributing to reducing homelessness by purchasing coffee from a social venture *Change Please*, supported in the Big Venture Challenge programme. As a professional barista, *Change Please* provides a service to events, festivals and corporate functions and operate a number of coffee carts around London. All baristas were formerly homeless, referred through a partnership with The Big Issue, and now earn a London Living Wage. They also received training, banking opportunities help to secure a house, and are then provided with additional job opportunities through *Change Please* partners.
Source: Square Space (2017).

UBS Global Visionaries Social Enterprise SDG Case Study:

An excellent case study for a corporate looking at their obligations and developing social projects to fit is UBS, who set-up Global Visionaries to welcome entrepreneurs to work towards one or more of the 17 UN SDGs. The entrepreneurs are given the opportunity to find innovative solutions to societal issues, across sectors: health; education; equality and the environment. UBS in return supports them by providing organizational support through their own corporate employee skill set, including finance, plus providing them with promotional tools through UBS marketing channels and social media campaigns. They also help the entrepreneurs scale up their projects for positive change by connecting them with their network of UBS partners and clients.
Source: UBS (2020).

Conclusion

As mentioned in the introduction of this chapter, CSR without considering innovation is no longer a viable proposition (Grayson et al., 2008; Kim et al., 2014). It is well acknowledged that innovation is crucial to a firm's growth and survival. As mentioned previously, innovation is also fundamental to the latest definition of CSR announced by the European Commission (2011), which is listed earlier this chapter. As innovation lies at the heart of entrepreneurship (Ganz et al., 2018), this chapter has discussed issues relating to Social Innovation and CSR, and social entrepreneurship to create social enterprises, alongside CSE, CSI, and intrapreneurs within a company structure.

It is important to acknowledge that social entrepreneurship is not just for the social sector, or start-up entrepreneurs – corporations can also be social entrepreneurs. Leading companies are seeking to create more robust forms of strategic corporate citizenship and are engaging in what we refer to as "corporate social entrepreneurship" (Austin et al. 2006). The book chapter by Austin et al. (2006) titled *Social entrepreneurship: it's for corporations too*, states precisely this point. CSE should be a priority in university curriculums alongside social entrepreneurship and social intrapreneurship, starting with understanding the components of CSR as the overriding strategy that can incorporate these types of entrepreneurship within organizations.

As stated earlier, Austin and Reficco (2009) explain the emergence of CSE from three other conceptual frameworks: entrepreneurship, CE, and social entrepreneurship. In doing so, they refer to the early vision of Schumpeter (1942), that entrepreneurship should shift from individuals to corporations, as corporates have greater resources for R&D. Austin and Reficco (2009) state this has already happened. However, over time corporate bureaucracy was seen as stifling innovation which slowed this movement. With the new movement of Social Innovation and 'purpose' that corporates are also embracing, there is a possibility that the concept of CSE is in development and gathering momentum. "Companies worldwide are facing a combination of push and pull factors that propel them toward more robust forms of CSR" (Austin et al., 2006) with the authors further suggesting corporates therefore have a good reason to invest in CSE. This is certainly an area for future research in light of the rapid social entrepreneurial movement and the corporate move toward innovation.

Many researchers agree that entrepreneurs have contributed significantly to society, as well as the economy and population, through job creation, utilization of business opportunities, and product innovation (Majid & Koe, 2012; İyigün, 2015); however, the impact is less often measured. The rise of sustainable development due to concerns for the environment has prompted popular demand for corrective and preventive action by entrepreneurs in areas such as pollution, land degradation, and climate change (Chick, 2018). This has also given rise to the social and sustainable entrepreneur. As discussed in this chapter, future research should look at the benefits of corporates supporting and actioning projects by sustainable entrepreneurs, as part of their integrated CSR and sustainability strategy. To determine the success rate and benefits to both parties, measuring their social impact is a necessity, and this is a growing area for future research.

As mentioned in the introduction to this chapter, the research presented in the CSR and Innovation section of this chapter suggests CSR can be used as a starting point for innovation, where innovative projects are perceived as risky in the start-up phase. Conducting innovative social enterprise start-up projects under CSR strategy as a Social Project or SI, places the entrepreneurial project under the safe umbrella of the organization's CSR strategy. This allows for experimentation with innovation in a safe environment before being released. In this way CSR can encourage and enhance innovation toward social problems with a safety net. The corporate can therefore provide a setting for the enterprise to experiment with pilot projects, which, if successful, can be adopted as part of the organization's ongoing CSR strategy and further developed and made scalable when unleashed to society.

Preuss (2011) confirms this with his research, suggesting:

> "...if the *Innovative CSR* project succeeds, the company will have improved its legitimacy with society, and perhaps the project could also become a crystallisation point for other forms of innovation" (p. 25).

Hence, CSR has provided the initial safety net for innovation to succeed and can lead to additional innovative projects, which are scalable and financially beneficial. This is similar to the CSV projects suggested by Porter and Kramer (2011) in Chapter 4 of this book. CSR can therefore be a starting point for innovation and innovation within CSV projects.

As proposed in this chapter, corporates are in an excellent position to assist millennials by taking them under their wing and allowing their innovative social enterprise to develop as part of CSR strategy. Exploring future research opportunities in this area is key to creating an upward trend in CSR-related social causes in a millennial-based society. However, there is a need for future research to unpackage the clichés surrounding the current research on millennials by providing research data that is conceptually driven, scrutinized, and peer reviewed. This will help secure future progress in the social and environmental domain of society and continue to unpack new solutions to social issues through innovation combined with millennial interest, might and will. If millennials are the way to future innovation – and will be the greatest influencers in corporations going forward – they need to be involved in CSR, innovation, and entrepreneurship as part of corporate strategy and not just in a social enterprise training setting.

Innovation has also become a popular topic when advocating for technological advancement and enhancing innovative processes in firms in developing countries and economies. From a research perspective, innovation is less understood in emerging economies and less-developed countries. However, innovation, entrepreneurship, creativity and creating competitive advantage, and knowledge are some of the main drivers for social and economic development (Nguyen & Hipsher, 2018). This chapter has suggested this can be achieved under the banner of *Innovative CSR*. Future research should focus on examining the different types of *Innovative CSR* in emerging markets which can benefit these countries, their micro enterprises, and also tick the box on the SDG targets by 2030 for developing countries.

Another area of discussion in this chapter are the many wicked challenges needing innovative solutions at a scale that corporates in collaboration can deal with. As this book primarily focuses on the "social side of CSR", a discussion of Social Innovation is befitting as they share a commonality. That is, "a wish to do social good for society." Getting to the root cause of the systemic problem is another branch of Social Innovation, which requires a greater depth of understanding, which is possible by adding Social Innovation to CSR social projects.

As explained earlier, corporates are often blamed for wicked challenges, which may be viewed partially as a result of their ecological footprint. These problems, however, are also multilayered with many undefined causes (Dentoni et al. 2012), as explained earlier. Scholars have attempted to explain how businesses have increasingly taken on regulatory roles to address social and environmental challenges; however, less attention has been given to the process of how businesses are made responsible for wicked challenges (Reinecke & Ansari, 2016). This provides an excellent research opportunity to examine how much Social Innovation is possible under the canopy of CSR in corporations, while also studying more *Innovative CSR* programs and case studies.

This topic of innovation in CSR is therefore a significant opportunity for future academic research to examine social entrepreneurship and intrapreneurship, and the corporate versions of this within a CSR context, including the different job roles in each speciality and the overlap between roles that exists. In particular, there is a need to update research in this area as many of the case study examples used in the academic literature such as Timberland and Starbucks utilizing entrepreneurship and intrapreneurship as part of their CSR strategy are overused and outdated. Corporates supporting external entrepreneurs by bringing innovative programs into their businesses and mentoring social entrepreneurs to scale up and unleash projects to the public when ready is key.

Also important is the role of the social intrapreneur. They as an employee can use their corporate politics from within to get 'disruptive' ideas to market. This includes solving wicked problems through developing CSR social and environmental projects and initiatives, and also shared value (CSV) and/or integrated value (CIV) social and environmental projects and initiatives, under this umbrella. The social intrapreneur can help deliver and implement these projects within the organization. Their rate of success in doing this, and method(s) of successful implementation is an interesting area for future research, alongside systematic measurement of the social impact of these projects on wicked problems, within the communities where they operate.

Supporting an external entrepreneur in business synergies as part of CSR strategy also provides significant future research opportunities, especially with regard to measuring the social impact and benefit of these activities. As mentioned earlier, business consultants and millennial entrepreneurs frequently use terms related to innovation – such as 'disruption,' 'be the change' movement, and 'business for purpose.' Academics must mirror these themes in their research of corporate strategy, to keep pace with the business community and continue to produce cutting-edge research in this rapidly growing area.

References

Albareda, L. (2008). Corporate responsibility, governance and accountability: From self-regulation to co-regulation. *Corporate Governance: The international journal of business in society*, *8*(4), 430–439.

Amelio, S. (2017). CSR and social entrepreneurship: The role of the European union. *Management Dynamics in the Knowledge Economy*, *5*(3), 335–354. doi:10.25019/mdke/5.3.02

Austin, J. E., Leonard, H., Reficco, E., & Wei-Skillern, J. (2005). Social entrepreneurship: it's for corporations too. In A. Nicholls (Ed.), *Entrepreneurship: New paradigms of sustainable social change*. Oxford, GB: Oxford University Press.

Austin, J. E., Leonard, H., Reficco, E., & Wei-Skillern, J. (2006). Corporate social entrepreneurship: The new frontier. In M. Epstein & K. Hanson (Eds.), *The accountable corporation. Volume 3: Corporate social responsibility*. Westport, CT: Praeger.

Austin, J., & Reficco, E. (2009). Corporate social entrepreneurship. *International Journal of Not-for-Profit Law*, *11*(4), 305.

Baldwin, E., & Curley, M. (2007). *Managing it innovation for business value: Practical strategies for it and business managers*. Santa Clara, CA: Intel Press.

Banerjee, A. V., Duflo, E., Glennerster, R., & Kinnan, C. (2013). The miracle of microfinance? Evidence from a randomized evaluation. Massachusetts Institute of Technology Department of Economics Working Paper Series.

Barraket, J., Collyer, N., O'Connor, M., & Anderson, H. (2010). Finding Australia's social enterprise sector. Social Traders. Melbourne. Retrieved from http://www.socialtraders.com.au/FASES%20ful%20final%20report%20July%202010.pdf

Belz, F.-M., & Peattie, K. (2012). *Sustainability marketing: A global perspective* (2nd ed.). Hoboken, NJ: Wiley.

Berger, I. E., Cunningham, P. H., & Drumwright, M. E. (2007). Mainstreaming corporate social responsibility: Developing markets for virtue. *California Management Review*, *49*(4), 132–157.

Camillus, J. C. (2008). Strategy as a wicked problem. *Harvard Business Review*, *86*(5), 1–10.

Carroll, A. B. (2015). Corporate social responsibility. *Organizational Dynamics*, *44*(2), 87–96. doi:10.1016/j.orgdyn.2015.02.002

Case Foundation. (2017). Millennials: The rise of the everyday changemaker. March 14, 2017 Retrieved from https://casefoundation.org/blog/millennials-the-rise-of-the-everyday-changemaker/

Cavaco, S., & Crifo, P. (2014). CSR and financial performance: Complementarity between environmental, social and business behaviours. *Applied Economics*, *46*(27), 3323–3338. doi:10.1080/00036846.2014.927572

Chell, E. (2007). Social enterprise and entrepreneurship: Towards a convergent theory of the entrepreneurial process. *International Small Business Journal*, *25*(1), 5–26.

Chick, A. (2018). Green entrepreneurship: A sustainable development challenge. In R. Mello (Ed.), *Entrepreneurship for everyone*. London: SAGE Publications.

Chesbrough, H. W. (2006). *Open innovation: The new imperative for creating and profiting from technology*. Boston, MA: Harvard Business Press.

CIPS. (2018). Johnson & Johnson aims to spend £15m with social enterprises. Retrieved from https://www.cips.org/en-AU/supply-management/news/2018/april/johnson-johnson-aims-to-spend-15m-with-social-enterprises/

Clarkson, M. E. (1995). A stakeholder framework for analyzing and evaluating corporate social performance. *Academy of Management Review, 20*(1), 92–117.

Covin, J. G., & Miles, M. P. (1999). Corporate entrepreneurship and the pursuit of competitive advantage. *Entrepreneurship: Theory and Practice, 23*(3), 47–63.

Crisan, C. M., & Borza, A. (2012). Social entrepreneurship and corporate social responsibilities. *International Business Research, 5*(2),106–113. doi:10.5539/ibr.v5n2p106

Crets, S. (2012). *Enterprise 2020: Don't stifle your corporate social entrepreneur.* CSRWire, May 22. Retrieved from www.csrwire.com/blog/posts/415-enterprise-2020-dont-stifle-your- corporate-social-entrepreneur

Dart, R. (2004). The legitimacy of social enterprise. *Nonprofit Management and Leadership, 14*(4), 411–424.

Davidsson, P. (2006). *Researching entrepreneurship.* Boston, MA: Spinger.

Dees, J. G. (1998). The meaning of social entrepreneurship. In Comments and suggestions contributed from the social entrepreneurship funders working group. Harvard Business School, Boston, MA.

Dentoni, D., Hospes, O., & Ross, R. B. (2012). Managing wicked problems in agribusiness: The role of multi-stakeholder engagements in value creation: Editor's introduction. *International Food and Agribusiness Management Review, 15*(B), 1–12.

Drayton, W. (2002). The citizen sector: Becoming as entrepreneurial and competitive as business. *California Management Review, 44*(3), 120–132.

Drucker, P. F. (1985). *Innovation and entrepreneurship.* New York, NY: Harper Trade.

Duflo, E., & Banerjee, A. V. (2011). *Poor economics: A radical rethinking of the way to fight global peverty.* New York, NY: Public Affairs.

Edelman. (2019). *2019 Edelman Trust Barometer.* Retrieved from https://www.e-delman.com/trust-barometer

EU-Commission. (2012). Social innovation. Retrieved from http://ec.europa.eu/enterprise/policies/Innovation/policy/social-Innovation/index_en.htm

European Business School. (2012). Strengthening social innovation in Europe – A journey to affective assessment and metrics. Retrieved from http://www.ebs.edu/socialinnovation.html?&L1

European Commission. (2011). A renewed EU strategy 2011-14 for corporate social responsibility. Communication from the commission to the European parliament, the council, the European economic and social committee and the committee of the regions. Retrieved from https://eur-lex.europa.eu/legal-content/EN/TXT/?uri='''CELEX%3A52011DC0681

European Commission. (2014). Directive 2014/95/EU of the European Parliament and the Council of 22 October 2014 amending Directive 2013/34/EU as regards disclosure of non-financial and diversity information by certain large undertakings and groups. The European Parliament and the Council of the European Union, Strasbourg. Retrieved from http://data.europa.eu/eli/dir/2014/95/oj

Fajnzylber, P., Maloney, W., & Rojas, G. M. (2006). Microenterprise dynamics in developing countries: How similar are they to those in the industrialized world?

Evidence from Mexico. *The World Bank Economic Review*, *20*(3), 389–419. doi: 10.1093/wber/lhl005

Francis, D., & Bessant, J. (2005). Targeting innovation and implications for capability development. *Technovation*, *25*(3), 171–183.

Ganz, M., Kay, T., & Spicer, J. (2018). Social Enterprise Is Not Social Change: Solving systemic social problems takes people, politics, and power—not more social entrepreneurship. *Stanford Social Innovation Review*, (Spring 2018).

Gioia, D. A. (1992). Pinto fires and personal ethics: A script analysis of missed opportunities. *Journal of Business Ethics*, *11*(5–6), 379–389. doi:https://doi.org/10.1007/BF00870550

Googins, B. (2013). Transforming corporate social responsibility: Leading with innovation. In T. Osburg & R. Schmidpeter (Eds.), *Social innovation – solutions for a sustainable future*. Heidelberg: Springer.

Googins, B. K., & Rochlin, S. A. (Eds.). (2006). *Corporate citizenship: Top to bottom*. Westport, CT: Praeger.

Grayson, D., McLaren, M., & Spitzeck, H. (2011). Social intrapreneurs-an extra force for sustainability. The Doughty Centre Cranfield School of Management, Befordshire. Retrieved from https://dspace.lib.cranfield.ac.uk/bitstream/handle/1826/7429/Social_intrapreneurs.pdf?sequence=1

Grayson, D., Rodriguez, M., Lemon, M., Jin, Z., Slaughter, S., & Tay, S. (2008). A new mindset for corporate sustainability. White paper. Cranfield School of Management, Befordshire. Sponsored by British Telecommunications and Cisco Systems.

Hadad, S., & Cantaragiu, R. (2017). Corporate social entrepreneurship versus social intrapreneurship: Same idea, different trajectories ? *Management & Marketing*, *12*(2), 252–276. doi:10.1515/mmcks-2017-0016

Hemingway, C. A. (2004). Personal values as a catalyst for corporate social entrepreneurship. Paper presented at the 17th annual European business ethics network conference, University of Twente, Encshede, The Netherlands.

Hipsher, S. (2010). Theoretical view on microenterprise entrepreneurial motivators. In J. Munoz (Ed.), *Contemporary micro-enterprise: Concepts and cases*. Northampton, MA: Edward Elgar Publishing Ltd.

Hipsher, S. (2012). Motivations of entrepreneurs in the informal economy: Examples from Cambodia. In M. Thai & E. Turkina (Eds.), *Entrepreneurship in the informal economy: Models, approaches and prospects for economic development*. London: Routledge.

Hockerts, N. K. (2007). *Managerial Perceptions of the Business Case of Corporate Social Responsibility, CSR&Business in Society CBS Working Paper Series no. 03-2007*, CBS Center for Corporate Social Responsibility, Dissertation no. 2750.

Howe, N., & Strauss, W. (2000). *Millennials rising*. New York, NY: Vintage Books.

Illycaffè. (2017). Who we are. Trieste. Retrieved from https://www.illy.com/en-us/company/company/illy

Imai, M., Kanero, J., & Masuda, T. (2016). The relation between language, culture, and thought. *Current Opinion in Psychology*, *8*, 70–77. doi:10.1016/j.copsyc.2015.10.011

Iyigün, N. Ö. (2015). What could entrepreneurship do for sustainable development? A corporate social responsibility-based approach. *Procedia - Social and Behavioral Sciences*, *195*, 1226–1231. doi:10.1016/j.sbspro.2015.06.253

Khan, F. R., & Lund-Thomsen, P. (2011). CSR as imperialism: Towards a phenomenological approach to CSR in the developing world. *Journal of Change Management, 11*(1), 73–90. doi:10.1080/14697017.2011.548943

Kim, Y., Brodhag, C., & Mebratu, D. (2014). Corporate social responsibility driven innovation. *Innovation: The European Journal of Social Science Research, 27*(2), 175–196. doi:http://dx.doi.org/10.1080/13511610.2014.915191

Kotler, P., & Lee, N. (2005). *Corporate social responsibility: Doing the most good for your company and your cause.* Hoboken, NJ: John Wiley & Sons.

Lee, S. M., Olson, D. L., & Trimi, S. (2012). Co-innovation: Convergenomics, collaboration, and co-creation for organizational values. *Management Decision, 50*(5), 817–831. doi:10.1108/00251741211227528

Lindahl, E., & Widén, J. (2015). Collaboration to address a wicked problem: The case of certified palm oil.(environmental economics and management - master's programme). Swedish University of Agricultural Sciences, Uppsala.

Luke, B., & Chu, V. (2013). Social enterprise versus social entrepreneurship: An examination of the 'why' and 'how' in pursuing social change. *International Small Business Journal, 31*(7), 764–784. doi:10.1177/0266242612462598

MacGregor, S. P., & Fontrodona, J. (2008). Exploring the fit between CSR and innovation. IESE Business School – University of Navarra.

MacGregor, S. P., Fontrodona, J., & Hernandez, J. (2010). Towards a sustainable innovation model for small enterprises. In C. LouchE, S. Idowu, & W. Filho (Eds.), *Innovative CSR: From risk management to value creation.* London: Routledge.

Mair, J., & Marti, I. (2006). Social entrepreneurship research: A source of explanation, prediction, and delight. *Journal of World Business, 41*(1), 36–44.

Majid, I. A., & Koe, W. (2012). Sustainable entrepreneurship: A revised model based on triple bottom line. *International Journal of Academic Research in Business and Social Sciences, 2*(6), 293–310.

McGlone, T., Spain, J. W., & McGlone, V. (2011). Corporate social responsibility and the millennials. *Journal of Education for Business, 86*(4), 195–200. doi:10.1080/08832323.2010.502912

McLean, L. D. (2005). Organizational culture's influence on creativity and innovation: A review of the literature and implications for human resource development. *Advances in Developing Human Resources, 7*(2), 226–246. doi:10.1177/1523422305274528

Mental Floss. (2018). *New guidelines redefine birth years for Millennials, Gen-X, and 'Post-Millennials'.* Minute Media. March 1, 2018. Retrieved from http://mental-floss.com/article/533632/new-guidelines-redefine-birth-years-millennials-gen-x-and-post-millennials

Mishra, D. R. (2017). Post-innovation CSR performance and firm value. *Journal of Business Ethics, 140*(2), 285–306.

Munro, V. (2013a). Stakeholder preferences for particular corporate social responsibility (CSR) activities and social initiatives (SIs): CSR initiatives to assist corporate strategy in emerging and frontier markets. *The Journal of Corporate Citizenship, 2013* (51), 72–105.

Munro, V. (2013b). Stakeholder understanding of corporate social responsibility (CSR) in emerging markets with a focus on Middle East, Africa (MEA) and Asia. *Journal of Global Policy and Governance, 2*(1), 59–77. doi:10.1007/s40320-013-0026-3

Munro, V. (2017). *Identification of CSR micro social initiatives within a developed and developing country context.* PhD thesis, Griffith University, Australia. Retrieved from https://www120.secure.griffith.edu.au/rch/items/5e1def2f-25a0-4c9b-aa72-8c4b8761cb80/1/

Munro, V. (2018). Changing the boundaries of expectations: MNE uptake of universal principles and global goals. In S. A. Hipsher (Ed.), *Examining the private sector's role in wealth creation and poverty reduction.* Hershey, PA: IGI Global.

Munro, V., Arli, D., & Rundle-Thiele, S. (2018). CSR engagement and values in a pre-emerging and emerging country context. *International Journal of Emerging Markets, 13*(5), 1251–1272. doi:10.1108/IJoEM-04-2018-0163

Nagler, J. (2012). Entrepreneurs: The world needs you, *Thunderbird Internal Business Review, 54*(1), 3–5. doi:10.1002/tie.21433

Nartisa, I. (2012). Openness and knowledge as leading tendencies in development of micro enterprises. *Economics and Management, 17*(4), 1579–1584. doi:10.5755/j01.em.17.4.3032

Nguyen, H. T., & Hipsher, S. A. (2018). Chapter 10: Innovation and creativity used by private sector firms in a resources-constrained environment. In S. A. Hipsher (Ed.), *Examining the private sector's role in wealth creation and poverty reduction.* Hersey, PA: IGI Global.

Osburg, T. (2013). Social innovation to drive corporate sustainability. In O. Thomas & S. René (Eds.), *Social innovation. CSR, sustainability, ethics & governance* (pp. 13–22). Berlin, Heidelberg: Springer.

Osburg, T., & Schmidpeter, R. (Eds.). (2013). *Social innovation, CSR, sustainability, ethics & governance.* Berlin; Heidelberg: Springer.

Ostrander, S. A. (2007). The growth of donor control: Revisiting the social relations of philanthropy. *Nonprofit and Voluntary Sector Quarterly, 36*(2), 356–372.

Porter, M. E., & Kramer, M. R. (2006). Strategy and society: The Link Between Competitive Advantage and Corporate Social Responsibility. *Harvard Business Review, 84*(12), 78–92.

Porter, M. E., & Kramer, M. R. (2011). The big idea: Creating shared value. *Harvard Business Review, 89*(1–2), 1–17. http://www.nuovavista.com/SharedValuePorterHarvardBusinessReview.PDF

Prahalad, C.K., & Hammond, A. (2002). Serving the world's poor, proitably. *Harvard Business Review, 80*(9), 48–57.

Prahalad, C. K., & Ramaswamy, V. (2000). Co-opting customer competence. *Harvard Business Review, 78*, 79–87.

Prahalad, C. K., Ramaswamy, V., Fruehauf, H. C., & Wolmeringer, G. (2004). *The future of competition: Co-creating unique value with customer.* New York, NY: Harvard Business Press.

Preuss, L. (2011). Innovative CSR: A framework for anchoring corporate social responsibility in the innovation literature. *The Journal of Corporate Citizenship, 42*(Summer 2011), 17–33.

PwC. (2018). Buying social. *PwC Network.* Retrieved from https://www.pwc.co.uk/who-we-are/social-enterprise/buying-social.html

Quinn, J. B. (1985). Managing innovation. Controlled chaos. *Harvard Business Review, 63*(3), 73–84.

Ramaswamy, V. (2008). Co-creating value through customers' experiences: The Nike case. *Strategy & Leadership, 36*(5), 9–14.

Ramaswamy, V. (2009). Co-creation of value — towards an expanded paradigm of value creation. *Marketing Review St*, *26*(6), 11–17.

Reavis, M. R., Tucci, J. E., & Pierre, G. S. (2017). Corporate social responsibility and millennials' stakeholder approach. *Journal of Leadership, Accountability and Ethics*, *14*(4), 74–83.

Reed, R., & DeFillippi, R. J. (1990). Causal ambiguity, barriers to imitation, and sustainable competitive advantage. *Academy of Management Review*, *15*(1), 88–102. doi:10.5465/AMR.1990.4308277

Reference for Business. (2018). Zero sum game. *2020 Advameg, Inc.* Retrieved from https://www.referenceforbusiness.com/management/Tr-Z/Zero-Sum-Game.html#ixzz5WUvLZXkw

Reinecke, J., & Ansari, S. (2016). Taming wicked problems: The role of framing in the construction of corporate social responsibility. *Journal of Management Studies*, *53*(3), 299–329. doi:10.1111/joms.12137

Rexhepi, G., Kurtishi, S., & Bexheti, G. (2013). Corporate social responsibility (CSR) and innovation–the drivers of business growth?. *Procedia-Social and Behavioral Sciences*, *75*, 532–541.

Roberts, E. B. (2007). Managing invention and innovation. *Research-Technology Management*, *50*(1), 35–54.

Rockström, J., Steffen, W., Noone, K., Persson Å., Chapin III, F. S., Lambin, E. … Schellnhuber, H. J. (2009). Planetary boundaries: Exploring the safe operating space for humanity. *Ecology and Society*, *14*(2), 32. Retrieved from http://www.ecologyandsociety.org/vol14/iss2/art32/.

Sabeti, H. (2011). The For-Benefit Enterprise. *Harvard Business Review*, *89*(11), 98–104.

SAP News. (2018). SAP partners with the Social Enterprise World Forum to help the social enterprise sector run better and improve peoples' lives. Retrieved from https://news.sap.com/uk/2018/09/sap-partners-with-the-social-enterprise-world-forum-to-help-the-social-enterprise-sector-run-better-and-improve-peoples-lives/

Sarmah, B., Islam, J. U., & Rahman, Z. (2015). Sustainability, social responsibility and value Co-creation: A case study based approach. *Procedia - Social and Behavioral Sciences*, *189*, 314–319. doi:10.1016/j.sbspro.2015.03.227

Schumpeter, J. (1942). *Capitalism, socialism and democracy*. New York, NY: Harper.

Schumpeter, J. A. (1982). *The theory of economic development: An inquiry into profits, capital, credit, interest, and the business cycle*. New Brunswick, NJ: Transaction Publishers.

Sen, A. (1999). *Development as freedom*. Oxford: Oxford University Press.

Shane, S. (2003). *A general theory of entrepreneurship: The individual–opportunity nexus*. Northampton, MA: Edward Elgar.

Sharp, K. (2014). Millennials' bold new business plan: Corporations with a conscience. *Salon*, January. Retrieved from http://www.salon.com/2014/02/09millennialsboldnewbusinessplancorporationswithaconscience/

Smith, C. (1994). The new corporate philanthropy. *Harvard Business Review*, *72*(3), 105–114.

Square Space. (2017). How corporates can engage with social entrepreneurs: Collaborating to create impact. The Foundation for Social Entrepreneurs. London. Retrieved from https://static1.squarespace.com/static/56d2eebbb654f9329ddbd20e/t/58cef9cd17bffcb09bcdd777/1489959379700/Corporates+engaging+with+social+ventures+UnLtd.pdf

SustainAbility. (2008). The social intrapreneur: A field guide for corporate change-makers. *SustainAbility*, Retrieved from www.echoinggreen.org/ sites/default/files/ The_ Social_Intrapreneurs.pdf. Accessed on March 12, 2014.

Tamariz, M., & Kirby, S. (2016). The cultural evolution of language. *Current Opinion in Psychology, 8*, 37–43. doi:10.1016/j.copsyc.2015.09.003

The Millennial Impact Report. (2017). Why do Millennials choose to engage in cause movements? Retrieved from http://www.themillennialimpact.com

Thompson, J. L. (2002). The world of the social entrepreneur. *International Journal of Public Sector Management, 15*(5), 412–431.

Tracey, P., Phillips, N., & Haugh, H. (2005). Beyond philanthropy: Community enterprise as a basis for corporate citizenship. *Journal of Business Ethics, 58*(4), 327–344.

Tuan, N., Nhan, N., Giang, P., & Ngoc, N. (2016). The effects of innovation on firm performance of supporting industries in Hanoi, Vietnam. *Journal of Industrial Engineering and Management, 9*(2), 413–431. doi:10.3926/jiem.1564

UBS. (2020). https://www.ubs.com/global/en/wealth-management/globalvisionaries/ about.html.

Van de Ven, A. H. (1986). Central problems in the management of innovation. *Management Science, 32*(5), 590–607. doi:10.1287/mnsc.32.5.590

Venkataraman, S., & Sarasvathy, S. (2001). Strategy and entrepreneurship: Outlines of an untold story. In M. A. Hitt, R. E. Freeman, & J. S. Harrison (Eds.), *The Blackwell handbook of strategic management* (pp. 650–668). Oxford: Blackwell.

Visser, W. (2014). *CSR 2.0: Transforming corporate sustainability and responsibility.* New York, NY: Springer.

Visser, W. (2018). Creating integrated value: From systems thinking to sustainable transformation in business and society AMS Sustainable Transformation Paper Series, 3 (Inauguration Lecture of the Chair in Sustainable Transformation) Antwerp Management School 2019, University of Antwerp, Antwerp.

Waddell, S., McLachlan, M., & Dentoni, D. (2013). Learning & transformative networks to address wicked problems: A GOLDEN invitation. *International Food and Agribusiness Management Review, 16*(A), 23–31.

Waddock, S. (2008). *The difference makers: How social and institutional entrepreneurs created the corporate responsibility movement.* Sheffield: Greenleaf Publishing.

Waddock, S. (2012). More than coping: Thriving in a world of wicked problems. The *International Food and Agribusiness Management Review, 15*(B), 127–132.

Wills, B. (2009). *Green intentions: Creating* a green value stream to compete & win, New York, NY: CRC Press Taylor & Francis Group.

Chapter 6

The Future of CSR and the New Ecosystem for CSR 4.0

Abstract

With the World Economic Forum's 2019 theme based on the new era – Globalization *4.0: Shaping a New Architecture in the Age of the Fourth Industrial Revolution* – this chapter takes into consideration innovation as defined in the previous chapter and builds on the escalation of innovation required for the Fourth Industrial Revolution and to reach the sustainable development goals (SDGs) deadline by 2030. Proposed is an entire ecosystem change of how the world lives, eats, makes money, sleeps and breathes. This chapter considers these changes with an explanation of CSR 1.0 and CSR 2.0 to CSR 3.0, providing case studies of these, plus discussing the transition from Globalization 3.0 to 4.0, and the various known and unknown system changes that may be required including integrated value creation (IVC). We live in exciting times where IVC and other systems, such as the well-being economy, exponential economy, shared economy, innovation and resilience economy, may be part of a new ecosystem. This chapter concludes with a discussion of these themes, and the development of CSR 4.0 mapped on to Globalization 4.0 within a deeply transformed systems approach to create transformed value (CTV). Emerging research opportunities as a result of these changes are discussed throughout this chapter.

Introduction

As mentioned in the Introduction to this book, this chapter examines the future of CSR and the new ecosystem required to inject 'purpose' into that system. In Thomas Friedman's 2005 article, *It's a Flat World, After All,* he defines succinctly the stages of globalization as a journey through time, commencing with Globalization 1.0 in 1492, Globalization 2.0 in 1800, and Globalization 3.0 in 2000, which is now superseded since his 2005 article, by Globalization 4.0.

Innovation and CSR in the previous chapter helped set the scene for a discussion on the future of CSR in this chapter. The evolution of CSR and its many

CSR for Purpose, Shared Value and Deep Transformation, 203–229
Copyright © 2020 Emerald Publishing Limited
All rights of reproduction in any form reserved
doi:10.1108/978-1-80043-035-820200009

surrogate, complementary, and alternative terms through the journey of time are discussed in the first chapter of this book. It is somewhat fitting therefore that this book ends with an eye toward the future expectations for CSR. This chapter begins with a discussion of the waves of CSR transformation, and finishes with a discussion on the systems change required for the Fourth Industrial Revolution. Additional research opportunities are identified as part of this process. By way of understanding this, the current chapter briefly returns to a discussion on the evolution of CSR, by outlining three already documented waves in the literature and one new proposed wave documented especially for this book.

The first wave in the 1960s had corporate *philanthropy* at its core. This was not always aligned with business strategy (Vogel, 2005), with corporates selecting causes not associated with their core business (Smith, 1994). It is well documented that over time these CSR initiatives became referred to as "bolted on" (Grayson & Hodges, 2004; Weaver, Trevino, & Cochran, 1999), rather than integrated. In response to this, the second wave of CSR in the 1980s developed a *strategic* approach (Burke & Logsdon, 1996; Porter and Kramer, 2006; van de Ven & Jeurissen, 2005). Companies were expected to organize CSR from a business case perspective. This meant benefitting both the firm and its key *stakeholders* through CSR policies, activities, and practices (Carroll & Shabana, 2010). The business model was expected to include both economic and noneconomic contributions (Weber, 2008). Companies could then benefit from CSR opportunities which were not part of original business models (Carroll & Shabana, 2010). The literature refers to this as CSR becoming "mainstreamed" (Grayson & Hodges, 2004; Preuss, 2011). By the early 2000s, *mainstreaming* CSR, was reported as the third wave of CSR. This meant it was integrated into corporate policy and became part of corporate identity (Berger, Cunningham, & Drumwright, 2007). This further developed into what some authors term CSR 2.0 (e.g., Visser, 2011). This chapter argues that there is a fourth wave of CSR, one that transforms "Strategic CSR" through CSR 2.0 (Visser, 2011) and CSR 3.0 (e.g., Prafitri, 2017), to propose CSR 4.0. This part of the fourth wave coincides with the Fourth Industrial Revolution and Globalization 4.0, requiring a bigger system change – an ecosystem change – and one that requires a network or web of interactions to integrate *change* through every transaction. This is explained further in this chapter, and first outlined in the following series of phases.

Phases of CSR

Phase 1: CSR Transitioning to Strategic CSR

As discussed above, and in chapter one, the 1980s saw CSR move to a more *strategic* approach in response to criticism, that CSR was merely philanthropic, and "bolted on" (Grayson & Hodges, 2004; Weaver et al. 1999). It is thought that Baron (2001) was the first to use the term *strategic CSR* to capture value for the organization. He stated, "it is the motivation for the action that identifies socially, as opposed to privately, responsible action" (p. 17). McWilliams and Siegel (2011) further explained it as motivation "to serve society, at the cost of profits, the action is socially responsible (CSR), but if the motivation is to serve the bottom line, then the action is privately responsible" (p. 1481). With this perspective in mind it is understandable why creating shared value (CSV) or integrated value creation (IVC) as a motive is more attractive to managers and the general public if there is a direct return of profit to the company. As can be seen in the Appendix of this chapter, many of the more developed CSR examples currently include a return of profit to the company.

McWilliams and Siegel (2011) also provide an example of *Strategic CSR* which could be argued returns profit to the company. The example they give is paraphrased here. *If an organization helps provide day care which lowers the number of juvenile crimes in a community, this is value to society.* However, the organization may provide the day care only because it increases the availability of workers and lowers the cost of absenteeism. They therefore state, the true motivation of managers can therefore not be determined. As the organization is only concerned with the creation and capture of value, they define strategic CSR as "any 'responsible' activity that allows a firm to achieve sustainable competitive advantage, regardless of motive" (p. 1481). There is little research, however, on defining and measuring the conditions under which CSR can contribute to sustainable competitive advantage. The ISO 2600, however, was published to demonstrate how *Strategic CSR* could be measured and is discussed later this chapter.

Examining the issue of competitive advantage further, Crane, Palazzo, Spence, and Matten (2014) comment that before Porter and Kramer coined the term shared value, they were promoting *Strategic CSR*. An example of this is their 2006 article tilted: *Strategy and Society: The Link Between Competitive Advantage and Corporate Social Responsibility*. Here, they discuss that corporations should analyze their opportunities for social responsibility using the same frameworks that guide their core business choices. They provide examples such as Whole Foods Market, Toyota, and Volvo, and explain how these companies do not perceive CSR as a *cost* (a constraint or a charitable deed), but instead, as a source of *innovation* and *competitive advantage* (Porter and Kramer, 2006).

In their article on *Strategic CSR,* Porter and Kramer (2006) describe the "many opportunities to pioneer innovations to benefit both society and a company's own competitiveness can arise in the product offering and the value chain" (Porter and Kramer, 2006, p. 88). They use the example of Toyota, Urbi, and Microsoft as mentioned in Table 6.1 overleaf.

The Microsoft Strategic CSR example is similar to Intel's CSR and CSV example, as discussed previously in several chapters in this book. Intel also creates collaborations with governments and makes scalable and systemic changes to school systems in entire countries. Porter and Kramer refer to integrating inside-out and outside-in practices, pioneering value chain innovations and addressing social constraints to competitiveness as the tools to create economic and social value (Porter and Kramer, 2006). This inside-out and outside-in practice is also reflected on in an earlier academic paper mentioned in Chapter 4 on *Bangchak Petroleum Public Company Limited*, alongside several CSV case study examples in the Appendix of

Table 6.1. Examples of *Strategic CSR*.

---

(1) Toyota – in response to automobile emissions electric cars were released. This gave them environmental benefits and competitive advantage while individual car owners saved money on gas and put out less pollution

(2) Urbi – a Mexican construction company builds houses for disadvantaged buyers using flexible mortgage payments through payroll deductions, while also accessing a new market where previously could not get loans

(3) Microsoft – partners with the American Association of Community Colleges (AACC), to obtain workers in an IT shortage, while also contributing $50 million over five years in money and IT products to colleges, plus employee volunteers, curriculum development, and additional institutes. Hence, staff used their core professional skills, rather than a "paint a school" using unrelated core skills, while also maintaining and recruiting staff, benefiting the community with training and increased computer sales back to Microsoft.

Source: Adapted from Porter and Kramer, 2006.

Chapter 4. The inside-out and outside-in practice of *Strategic CSR* later evolved into the three pillars of Porter and Kramer's CSV, launched in 2011.

Hence, at an earlier stage Porter and Kramer (2006), referred to *Strategic CSR* as "unlocking the 'shared value' by investing in social aspects of context that strengthen company competitiveness" (p. 89). As several authors have commented (e.g., Crane et al., 2014 and Voltan, Hervieux & Mills, 2017), Porter and Kramer used the term *Strategic CSR* back in 2006 before the CSV term was unveiled in 2011. This confirms why some authors and members of the business community may still refer to these more strategic initiatives and CSV initiatives – as a form of CSR. This also confirms the ongoing evolution of CSR depending which label you select to define it.

Phase 2: An Interpretation of CSR 1.0 Relative to CSR 2.0

Beyond the evolution of traditional CSR and its surrogate, complementary, alternative, and competing terms discussed in Chapter 1, Integrated Value Professor Wayne Visser termed philanthropic CSR as old CSR and labeled it CSR 1.0 (Visser, 2011), and at the time defined a new CSR, referred to as CSR 2.0 (Visser, 2015). Today most organizations have moved on from the first phase of CSR, philanthropy or cash-cheque giving, as it was often quoted. There are therefore very few current working case study examples of this available. However, Visser challenges this traditional type of CSR and proposes the need to move to a more transformative CSR labeled CSR 2.0. A number of case study examples labeled as such by Visser (2011) are included in the Appendix of this chapter.

Visser first coined the term CSR 2.0 in 2008 in what he labeled *The New Era of Corporate Sustainability and Responsibility.* This was followed with his book, *The Age of Responsibility* in 2011. Labeling old CSR as CSR 1.0 allowed him to compare it to the old Internet, Web 1.0, which he says moved from a passive audience consumption approach to a more collaborative mode of Google–Facebook Web 2.0 interactions. CSR 1.0 was therefore seen as passive public relations, rather than an interactive, *stakeholder*-driven model. Further, Visser's analogy referred to Web 1.0 as dominated by standardized hardware and software, whereas Web 2.0 encouraged Co-creation and diversity, similar to the mental shift required for what he termed CSR 2.0.

It is not the scope of the current book to cover all the differences suggested between CSR 1.0 and CSR 2.0; however, one perspective in relation to multi-national corporations (MNCs) and enterprises (MNEs) is of interest here. That is, Visser's further interpretation of CSR 1.0, to include smaller initiatives rather than scalable initiatives, which tend to be more western based (rather than global). Hence, many of these differences fit with the natural evolution of CSR as identified in Chapter 1. This also fits with the development of innovation and MNE CSR strategy in Chapter 2 and 5, where there is now a need to develop CSR strategy and initiatives which are Eastern based and scalable, especially when moving into emerging markets and developing countries. Many organizations and large corporates, for example, now include helping social enterprises develop, as part of their CSR strategy and as a core aspect of their organization's 'purpose.' This is similar to many organizations who are now less likely to compartmentalize CSR in departments (as prescribed in CSR 1.0) and more likely to have incentives spread through the organization (CSR 2.0). Several examples of this are provided in Chapter 5.

Visser also included *Strategic CSR* under the CSR 1.0 banner. *Strategic CSR* referred to by Visser and other authors has been covered earlier this chapter. Following this Visser termed *Systemic CSR* as the transformation phase from CSR 1.0 to CSR 2.0. As mentioned in the first chapter of this book, he defines *Systemic CSR* under his term for *The Age of Responsibility,* commencing in 1994. This Age is characterized by *Systemic CSR* which "focuses its activities on identifying and tackling the root causes of our present unsustainability and irre-sponsibility" (Visser, 2010, p. 3). This is achieved through CSR within innovative business models which revolutionize "their processes, products and services and lobbying for progressive national and international policies" (Visser, 2010, p. 3). CSR 2.0 as defined by Visser is further documented by explaining the five prin-ciples of CSR 2.0 (Table 6.2).

Many of these principles are noted in past discussions of CSR and also corporate citizenship, business ethics, and corporate sustainability (Visser & Kymal, 2015). However, providing a specific measure for each of these principles would provide a way to test levels of CSR 1.0 or 2.0 in an organization's implementation of CSR and is an excellent opportunity for future research. Measures for each of these principles as evidence of impact in these areas would

Table 6.2. The Five Principles of CSR 2.0.

* *Creativity* – refers to innovation and creativity
* *Scalability* – refers to producing the idea at scale
* *Responsiveness* – not just to disasters, also lobbying, greater transparency, taking more active roles
* *Glocality* – refers to global localization
* *Circularity* – the recent release of the documentary *Closing the Loop* (2018) by Visser is an example

Source: Adapted from Visser, 2010.

be valuable to determining uptake of CSR 2.0 in organizations, and in doing so, would help confirm the exact definition of each principle.

Visser's book *The Age of Responsibility* lists over 300 organizations which he suggests are practising CSR 2.0. The Appendix of this chapter provides a case study snapshot of these organizations, plus other examples from the general literature. As mentioned earlier, studying the impact of each principle listed above, and doing this as a longitudinal study, would be an excellent opportunity for future research. This would allow researchers to determine organizational change over time, mapped on to expectations and societal change.

Phase 3: The Development of CSR 3.0

As discussed in the previous chapter (Chapter 5), mixing the current wave of innovation with CSR brings us to a discussion of CSR 3.0 proposed by only a few authors at this stage, with others seeing it as a natural progression of all versions of CSR. In this respect, CSR 3.0 has overlapping themes with CSR 2.0.

In their article for the *Stanford Business Review*, James et al. (2008) refer to social innovation as going beyond new products, technologies, or modes of production and provides perspectives on social innovation as a form of idealism, legislation, social movement(s), and/or a combination of this. Social innovation is discussed in Chapter 5, as is some of Osburg's thoughts on social innovation. However, in this section, social innovation is related to creating value, or more fully the process of transforming ideas or inventions into solutions that create value for *stakeholders* and *shareholders* (Osburg, 2013, p. 14) and tackles social issues as a way of creating value for business and society (Crets & Celer, 2013, p. 86; cited in; Prafitri, 2017). In this respect, CSR as we know it can be seen as an important driver for strategic innovation and long-term value creation, as suggested by Crets and Celer (2013) and Prafitri (2017).

Dr Rizki Prafitri connects CSR 3.0 with social innovation but suggests that CSR 3.0 is similar to the weakness identified in CSR 2.0, while still insisting that CSR 3.0 is a development of CSR 2.0. In her discussion of CSR 3.0, she states that while "CSR 3.0. helps companies generate value by addressing social problems," she wonders how the latest generation of CSR (3.0) will provide alternatives for companies, stating for it "to be ethical, good and avoid harm for society and environment is still debatable" (Prafitri, 2017, p. 24). The win-win solution to the world's problems has become a predominate theme in business discourse and is discussed further in the final conclusion of this book.

An *EBSCOhost* literature search at the time of writing this book revealed little available in the academic research literature for CSR 3.0. This leaves a significant gap in the literature and provides an excellent future research opportunity to determine in what form CSR 3.0 exists or whether it is a different or an already existing version of CSR or another term such as CSV or IVC. Similarly, a recent search on *Google Scholar* revealed only one academic article on the topic of CSR 3.0 in the first 100 searches. The listing is a book chapter written by Osburg (2013) on social innovation (Osburg and Schmidpeter, 2013), but makes only one mention of CSR 3.0 referring to social innovation, as the new CSR or CSR 3.0.

> "Management buy-in will be critical in order to fully embrace the relevance of Social Innovation for the Business as a whole. If Social Innovation is considered to be the next CSR 3.0, the concept will remain within the CSR Departments and not get the needed attention from company leaders. The huge risk is that Social Innovation becomes a new buzzword that people think will go away in few years. Academia can play a leading role in that respect to drive the concept forward and make it last." (Osburg, 2013, p. 20)

Academic articles in general may refer to moving on from CSR but not CSR 3.0 specifically. Rosabeth Moss Kanter, for example, provides a slight twist on this by attempting to explain a form of CSR evolution – moving beyond existing CSR initiatives of charity and volunteering, by referring to "corporate social innovation" as a way of moving forward (Kanter, 1999). However, she does not refer specifically to CSR 3.0. Continuing with the CSR 3.0 theme of innovation by Osburg (2013), the association, *CSR Europe* (2015), also refers to innovation in their report on CSR. They describe an *Enterprise 2020* company as a company that is fully integrated within a CSR framework, referring to social innovation as a part of this. This they say allows for new ideas and new collaborations (CSR Europe, 2015).

As previously mentioned in other chapters of this book, *CSR Europe* is the leading European business network for CSR. Their most recent report continues with the theme of *collaboration* alongside *innovation*, for impact and maturity and for sustainability in corporations (CSR Europe, 2018). As part of their latest report on CSR, and their current expectations for CSR, they state that collaboration and innovation is vital to pursue the systemic changes needed in society and within business to achieve the Sustainable Development Goals (SDGs; CSR Europe, 2018). This confirms innovation and collaboration as a development of CSR.

A search on general *Google* to determine general *business community* perception of CSR 3.0 brings forward a few articles. An article by Dumont in the *Singapore Business Review* in March (2012), *Don't mess with CSR 3.0,* suggests the importance that the business community leverage from a third and more evolved form of CSR. The article was written by Jean Michel Dumont, Chairman of Ruder Finn Asia. The article is light on definition and detail and is written with an underlying theme of CSR's ability to communicate messages of change via social media and other mediums. However, it does suggest three slightly different definitions of CSR which may have existed in mainstream *business community* understanding of CSR at the time. Dumont (2012) defines the three different stages of CSR as follows:

(1) CSR 1.0 – pushing the message out, building awareness passively.
(2) CSR 2.0 – beginning engagement with dialogue and interaction, building communities with transparency and accountability.
(3) CSR 3.0 – is involving communities across geographical, age and socio-economic boundaries, reducing lag time, sustaining *stakeholders'* interest and taking ownership.

Source: Dumont, 2012.

Dumont (2012) describes CSR 3.0 as the latest evolution of CSR. His article does not explain this in any concrete or empirical form. What this does suggest, however, is that if the *business community* takes on a perspective that a more integrated and collaborative CSR exists, in the form of CSR 3.0, this should then be studied in the *academic community* and considered in future academic research.

Another article of note on a general *business community* google search is from the US Chamber of Commerce Foundation website in 2013. The article is written by Richard Crespin, a former Senior Fellow of the US Chamber of Commerce Foundation, Director of the Corporate Citizenship center, and CEO of CollaborateUp and Crespin Enterprises. The article commences with definitions of CSR 1.0, 2.0 and 3.0, which places shared value (Kramer and Porter, 2011) in the CSR 2.0 category, and places a more networked and integrated systems concept example in the CSR 3.0 category. This sentiment is captured in the following quote:

> "If CSR 1.0 was 'do good because it is good,' and CSR 2.0 was 'shared value – do good in alignment with your business strategy,' then CSR 3.0 is 'networked value – do good in alignment with your business strategy and tap into the power of your value chain and social network. Fully utilizing this network, companies, NGOs and governments can create greater social and financial net worth for both the company and the country'" (Crespin, 2013).

While the term CSR 2.0 and CSR 3.0 are possibly overlapping, like many of the CSR terms discussed in Chapter 1, there is a suggestion of a more advanced

CSR in a more integrated system. Crespin (2013), for example, states that the allure of CSR 2.0 was the potential for additional revenue generation in "do-gooding," whereas CSR 3.0 adds a more integrated "network" aspect to CSR. To support this view, Crespin (2013) cites the example of *DSM* North America's President Hugh Welsh, reporting some of his speech and examples given at the US Global Leadership Coalition's (USGLC) annual conference in 2013:

"We don't do philanthropy" ... *"this is our business."* DSM strengthens food supply chains in Africa as part of Partners in Food Solutions (PfS), a public-private-civil partnership between Cargill, General Mills, Royal DSM, Buhler, and USAID. Formed in 2008, the PfS objective is to create an organization that will make long-term investments in Africa, but at the danger of delayed payoff. However, PfS will become a vital tool in their ability to grow within the region. Crespin spoke to a senior aerospace executive who explained, *"we're the best in the world at designing the next generation of aeronautics,"*, *"but it takes 30 years for us to develop these products and we have no idea where the markets will be 30 years from now" she continued. "That's why we need strong relationships on the ground in those countries now, helping us build up the social capital we need so that when we do come to market, we've got the relationships we need."*
(*Source:* Adapted from Crespin, 2013)

The collaborative, scalable, and global features in this example refer to aspects of CSR 2.0. and also, CSV. Hence, as stated earlier, there is some overlap between terms. However, the suggestion is made that CSR 3.0 is more network oriented at a more complex level. In addition, the statements made by Crespin in 2013 are fast becoming the norm for doing business especially since the introduction of the United Nations SDGs in 2015 – and in particular SDG 17 (Partnerships for the Goals). The collaboration and network required to implement SDG 17 would be synonymous with Crespin's suggested version of CSR 3.0. Further, as explained in Chapter 3, there are interconnections between all the goals requiring various levels of partnership, networking, and collaboration (CSR Europe, 2018). Hence, the example given by DSM and PfS above, shows collaborations with potentially a more interconnected "web" of collaborations. In relation to this Crespin concludes that the "network effect" of CSR 3.0 is: "using the broad reach of your company's network to open minds and open markets" and claims this is what "the US Chamber of Commerce Foundation's Business Civic Leadership Center (BCLC) means by the 'Network Effect'" (Crespin, 2013).

Crespin (2013) provides additional CSR 3.0 examples that are relevant to this discussion. They are listed in the Appendix of this chapter. Crespin (2013) concludes his article by comparing CSR 3.0 to innovation. Again, he refers to CSR 3.0, specifically in relation to network building across communities with inclusion of innovation:

> "All around the world, leading companies are creating what the US Global Leadership Coalition has called "Smart Power Innovations." By bringing all their corporate assets to the table, including their supply chain, brand, and social capital, and combining them with governments and NGOs, these organizations are forging new pathways to prosperity; turning their networks into net worth." Crespin (2013)

This discussion reveals the movement in CSR within the business community, toward a more integrated, networked, and partnership orientated CSR as suggested for CSR 3.0 (Crespin, 2013; Dumont, 2012; Prafitri, 2017) and CSR 2.0 (Visser, 2015). At best the discussion regarding CSR 3.0 acknowledges what forward-thinking companies are doing and how they are updating their CSR strategies to fit the current global changes in the way business is done. This section, however, has noted that the definition of CSR 3.0 provided by Crespin (2013) is similar to the definition provided by the *Singapore Business Review* article, by Dumont (2012). Both are suggesting that CSR 3.0 is not CSV (Kramer and Porter, 2011). The definition in fact sounds closer to aspects of IVC (Visser, 2014), discussed in the next section. These developments in CSR strategy have become more collaborative and integrated since the launch of the SDGs in 2015. This is discussed further in Chapter 3. Future research needs to measure specific differences which may exist between CR 2.0 or 3.0.

Integrated Value Creation

The term integrated value creation was coined by Visser in 2014. He states the concept has roots in CSR, corporate citizenship, business ethics, and corporate sustainability (Visser & Kymal, 2015). Many of these terms have already been discussed in Chapter 1, as part of the evolution of CSR and its many complementary and alternative themes.

While Professor Visser states his definition of IVC is not yet set in stone, he currently defines it as:

> "...the simultaneous building of multiple 'non-financial' capitals (notably infrastructural, technological, social, ecological and human capital) through synergistic innovation across the nexus economy (including the resilience, exponential, access, circular and wellbeing economies) that result in net-positive effects, thus making our world more secure, smart, shared, sustainable and satisfying" (Visser, 2017a).

The IVC concept is a part of value creation. Like CSR, value creation has also evolved. He states, however, that CSR 2.0 is still applicable to his current model of Integrated Value. Visser also makes the point that CSV is not the same as creating integrated value but is an important part of the puzzle, whereby integrated value would not be possible without previous concepts and other forms of value creation. IVC is therefore said to build on and share aspirations with many preexisting concepts of value creation. These include: Shareholder value (Friedman, 1970); Stakeholder value (Freeman, 1984); Four capitals (Ekins, 1992); Triple bottom line (Elkington, 1994); Blended value (Emerson, 2000); Bottom of the pyramid (Prahalad & Hart, 2002); Sustainable value (Hart & Milstein, 2003); Five capitals (Porritt, 2007); Shared value (Porter & Kramer, 2011); and Integrated value (Visser, 2017a). (Source: Visser, 2018).

As noted directly above in the list of value creation concepts, Visser adds integrated value to the end of this list as the most recent value creation term after shared value and refers to it as: economic development. While contributing to the enrichment of *shareholders* and executives in an economic context, the company also invests in infrastructure, creates jobs, and provides skills development (Source: Visser, 2010, 2012). Again, scholars may argue this is similar to previous forms of value creation such as CSV, rather than building on CSV and other value creation terms.

In his various blogs and articles, Visser refers to new methodologies emerging from IVC, including: KPMG's True Value, PwC's Total Impact Measurement & Management, B-Lab's B Impact Assessment, and Puma's Environmental Profit & Loss (KPMG, 2014; Visser, 2018). Visser and Kymal (2015) believe these types of concepts are the type that business managers can understand and get excited about, through the language of integration and value creation. Other commentators and researchers may perceive this as just a new label or a new language for an older term. Visser and Kymal (2015) tackle this criticism by commenting that CIV is not just a new language or design of a new label, it's about implementation. They state IVC is a "methodology for turning the proliferation of societal aspirations and *stakeholder* expectations into a credible corporate response, without undermining the viability of the business" (Visser & Kymal, 2015, p. 12). Further the authors state IVC aims to be "a tool for innovation and transformation, which will be essential if business is to become part of the solution to our global challenges, rather than part of the problem" (Visser & Kymal, 2015, p. 12).

In summary, the authors explain that IVC is about "rethinking how we conceive of and measure value in our societies, economies and businesses" (Visser, 2018, p. 3). Visser also claims that the difference with resilience, exponential, access, circular, and well-being economies, discussed later in this chapter, is that IVC "places more emphasis on the innovation opportunities that exist" (Visser, 2018, p. 3).

Systems Thinking through Integrated Value, Innovation, and Implementation

As Professor of Integrated Value and Chair in Sustainable Transformation, Antwerp Management School from 2018, Visser is currently working on the

214 CSR for Purpose, Shared Value and Deep Transformation

development of the IVC concept and practice. Integrated value provides an excellent opportunity for future research as there has been little written on it yet in the academic literature. There is also an emerging opportunity to study the companies said to be currently interweaving integrated value into their business case and examine how this they may develop over time and in the long term.

To date organizations considered to be implementing IVC type case studies include: BASF, Unilever, Tesla, and Interface. BASF are also contributing to the measurement of integrated value. These case study examples and the measurement example for BASF are included in the Appendix of this chapter.

Visser confirms the current belief that we need to apply systems thinking, "to see and to act on the interconnectedness of our economic, technological, human, social and ecological systems" (Visser 2018, p. 3). Visser uses the definition of Capra and Luisi (2015) who define systems thinking as: "thinking in terms of relationships, patterns and context." It is the interconnection between the relationships in our ecosystem which needs to be examined to determine the root cause of the social and environmental challenge. In the current capitalist system, Visser refers to the need to "redesign our global economic and business systems to be inclusive, empowering and restorative" (Visser, 2018, p. 5). As discussed in Chapter 3, and in the conclusion of the book, many of these developments are already happening through implementation of the SDGs and growth of the language and terminology surrounding this movement.

Visser has developed his framework to included five forces of fragmentation listed as follows in brief: *Disruption* (any instability that threatens life); *Disconnection* (any form of isolation that prevents communication); *Disparity* (inequities that increase social friction); *Destruction* (production and consumption that leads to decline and disruption); *Discontent* (unhealthy lifestyles and toxic environments that impair well-being) (Visser 2018, p. 7). He then refers to different forms of innovation to find solutions to the five forces of fragmentation. These in brief are: *secure* solutions to reduce *disruption*; *smart* solutions to tackle *disconnection*; *shared* solutions to reduce *disparity*; *sustainable* solutions to reverse *destruction;* and *satisfying* solutions to address *discontent* (Visser, 2018).

Some of these innovative solutions have been built on by past authors. For example, *shared* refers to innovation in the access economy (Eckhardt and Bardhi, 2015), and is sometimes referred to as the sharing economy (Botsman & Rogers, 2010). *Sustainable* refers to innovation in the "circular economy" (Webster, 2015).

Similar to Kramer and Porter's (2011) CSV, Visser (2018) refers to the need for speed, scale, and effectiveness in our response to current global situations using innovation that is *secure, smart, shared, sustainable,* and *satisfying*, within his IVC framework. The methodology developed by Visser and Kymal (2015) to achieve this is presented in several publications (e.g., Visser, 2017a). A comparison of the methodology for IVC with other systems such as CSV would be an excellent opportunity for future research. To do this, the case studies for IVC in the

Appendix should be systematically reviewed in the academic and business literature as they provide an example of the IVC process.

The conclusion for this chapter provides an explanation of the transition to the next CSR phase, CSR 4.0, within a new value creation setting which requires creating a deeply transformed value (CTV) system.

Conclusion

In summary, many academics, authors and researchers recognize that companies have moved beyond mere Philanthropy and "static CSR" without renaming the type of CSR (e.g., CSR 1.0 or CSR 2.0). Testament to this are the many case study examples listed in the Appendix of Chapter 1, which are labeled purely as "CSR" and no other version of this, such as CSR 1.0 or CSR 2.0. Examples of the associations and services listing these nominated companies as "CSR" case studies, includes: the *CSR Hub, Forbes* (2017), the *Hiring Success Journal* (2017, 2018), and *Fortune* (2018) magazine. These case studies reveal that numerous companies have moved beyond philanthropic CSR to a more "strategic CSR." Researchers also discuss companies beyond what is termed transformative CSR or CSR 2.0 (Visser, 2013) to CSR 3.0 as discussed in this chapter, followed by an examination of IVC and other value creation systems, to enable these changes to happen. This chapter therefore considers CSR 2.0 and 3.0 (Crespin, 2013; Dumont, 2012; Prafitri, 2017) as a development of CSR or a transitional phase for CSR.

This chapter considers the argument that the difference between CSR 1.0 and CSR 2.0, and the potential transition to CSR 3.0 is a natural occurrence over time. This is illustrated by the many case study examples throughout this book. As discussed earlier this chapter, CSR 2.0 is considered to be more collaborative, and CSR 1.0 is considered to be more philanthropic than CSR 2.0. In addition, CSR 1.0 includes smaller initiatives rather than scalable initiatives and tends to be more western based rather than global and therefore less likely to move into developing markets as CSR must do within MNCs and MNEs. Many of these differences fit with the natural evolution of CSR that is also discussed in Chapter 1 with a research example in Chapter 2.

In addition, the innovative solutions suggested here, and the new economies discussed in this chapter, are already in play in society. PwC (2015), for example, ran a study in the US and found 44% of the US population were familiar with the "sharing economy" (Botsman & Rogers, 2010) as referred to with the innovative *Shared* solution above. Their online survey defined the sharing economy as one that "allows individuals and groups to make money from underused assets. In this way, physical assets are shared as services" (PwC, 2015b, p. 5). A shared solution example is a car owner renting out their car to others while not using it. There are already many everyday examples of the sharing economy, such as: Airbnb, Uber, Amazon Family Library, Spotify, and Sound-Cloud, to name a few.

In 2018, Visser's film *Closing the Loop* on the "circular economy" was released, educating viewers on what is required to achieve this type of economy. The film provides many existing and future examples of sustainable innovation to transact in this type of society. As we enter the Fourth Industrial Revolution, other economies or systems are being presented, including: satisfying innovation in a "well-being economy" (Fioramonti, 2017) and smart innovation in an "exponential economy" (Carlson & Wilmot, 2006) and innovation that makes us secure in a "resilience economy" (Buheji, 2018). In brief, Professor Fioramonti's (2017) "well-being economy" discusses breaking free from the growth economy and putting wellbeing of all at its center. Fioramonti (2017) says a well-being economy would boost small businesses and empower citizens as the collective leaders of tomorrow. The exponential economy (Myhrvold, 2007), for example, is the realm of business and innovation characterized by exponential technological growth and is responsible for an increasing share of productivity and overall economic growth. The "exponential economy," for example, requires exponential improvement processes through "smart" innovations (Carlson & Wilmot, 2006) and the examination of high-value innovations via multidisciplinary collaborations.

The era of Globalization 4.0 and the Fourth Industrial Revolution has innovation at its very core. Some of the threats associated with this refer to resilience as a priority. In a paper by Briguglio, Cordina, Farrugia, and Vella (2009), economic resilience as a term is used to refer to the ability to recover from or adjust to the negative impacts of external economic shocks. Visser (2017b) utilizes the Stockholm Resilience Center (2017) definition. They define resilience as the capacity of a system, be it an individual, or an economy, to deal with change. They refer to shocks and disturbances, such as a financial crisis or climate change, to spur renewal and innovative thinking. Hence, "secure innovation," as referred to as one of Visser's innovative solution types, can assist us to survive and thrive in period of greater economic, social, and environmental turbulence. Buheji (2018) describes the power of a resilience economy and the need to "change the world" movement as part of this. With a "resilience economy," Buheji (2018) says the world would witness more harmony while enhancing its capacity to respond to a sudden crisis; however, the sharing and scaling up of those innovations need to happen much faster, especially in the current global setting.

As IVC proposed by Visser (2014) is still unfolding there is limited academic research and less working case studies available to discuss this concept. This is also because it is very difficult to practice in the current economic, global, and political systems. Researchers like Visser, for example, state the current "dysfunctional" economic and financial system, and also the policies, tools, standards, and innovations that will make integrated value mainstream are only just being developed (Visser, 2017c). But like CSV and the introduction of the SDGs, both promote opportunity in social challenges. Visser also sees an opportunity if business, economics, and the entire system of capitalism can be reinvented. The Wold Economic Forums held each year in Davos are attempting to make inroads into changes in these areas. IVC is therefore one way of thinking about the transformation of the current system (Visser, 2017c) among the other systems proposed above.

Regardless of which system, corporate leaders have awoken to the fact that social problems present both daunting constraints to their operations and vast opportunities for growth. Many are struggling, however, to find ways to implement strategies to solve these problems whether it be through CSR 2.0, CSR 3.0, CSV, or IVC. Implementation of the SDGs has potentially enabled a framework to make progress in this area. However, a "system change" needs to be created or installed, and innovation advances developed to allow a more inclusive and innovative CSR to evolve. To do this the entire ecosystem needs to change to usher in a new era.

The systems change referred to by Visser, as an IVC approach, has created a setting for CSR 2.0 and CSR 3.0 to flourish. Globalization 4.0 expands this opportunity to encourage further development of CSR, mapped on to a "system change" requiring even greater transformation, and the creation of a deeply transformed value (CTV) systems approach. From this it is expected we will see a more deeply transformed system, and a more developed CSR. This book proposes the development of CSR 4.0 mapped on to Globalization 4.0. As mentioned briefly in the Preface of this book, if we consider CSR to be like Globalization 4.0, as a journey of time through different eras, the evolution of CSR and its complementary, surrogate, and alternative themes are also still evolving and part of this evolution. Rather than saying CSR 1.0 (or 2.0) is becoming *extinct*, there is instead an evolution of past CSR to CSR 3.0 and now CSR 4.0, mapped on to significant social movements in society regarding new eras of change and globalization (Globalization 4.0) as part of the next Industrial Revolution (the fourth). This will require inclusion and development of previous value creation approaches, under a more deeply transformed value systems approach, to create transformed value (CTV). CTV proposes an 8-part framework as a setting for CSR 4.0 development. An analysis of these new concepts will provide numerous research opportunities going forward.

As listed below, this book proposes a framework for CSR 4.0, in changing the way organizations and companies operate, and do business, within an evolving CSR framework and shared and integrated setting. Like other conceptual evolutions, this framework will evolve over time. The key principle and themes for CSR 4.0 are listed in Table 6.3 below.

Table 6.3. The CSR 4.0 Framework, Principles and Themes.

---

(1) 'Purpose': as an essential priority

- Profit with 'business-for-purpose' is the number one priority – for physical, mental health, and well-being – in the communities where businesses operate and reside

Table 6.3. *(Continued)*

(2) Innovation, Inclusion, and Collaboration: with all partners

- An evolved CSR which is more 'innovative' – focusing on innovation and agility to solve wicked problems and challenges – and a more 'inclusive,' cross-generational and collaborative CSR, enabling Social Initiatives (SIs) and social projects to 'scale up' and 'transform value' in a new system

(3) Identification, Engagement, and Co-creation: with all 'stakeholders'

- To leave no one behind – all participants in the organization and surrounding community are involved in 'identifying' SIs and social projects – and are 'engaged' in co-creation and innovative exercises to identify and implement SIs and social projects

(4) Shared and Integrated Value: at a deeper level

- SIs and social projects that are shared (CSV) and integrated (IVC) and more evolved in a deeply 'transformed' system to 'create transformed value' (CTV)

(5) Deeply Transformed and Networked: in a new ecosystem

- A network of organizations with multilayered collaborations in a newly transformed system. This intricate and detailed network involves CSR 4.0 as part of a new system, a new ecosystem, and a new way of doing business for Globalization 4.0, which encourages integration of all systems, networks, and deeper transformation

(6) Measurable SDGs: ongoing assessment and renewal

- Full implementation of the 17 SDGs – or a selection of meaningful Global Goals related to (local) core business – which are authentically embedded and operational throughout the organization with real and ongoing measurement in place and constant renewal to fit the challenges of a new and agile ecosystem

(7) Systems Orientation: at the C-suite and employee level

- An entire top-down bottom-up systems approach – involvement and commitment from the C-suite and collaboration with all employees and 'preneurs' – to change the entire operating system of the company (i.e., throughout the organization, its community and its supply chain(s) – for deeper transformation)

(8) Circular Social Missions: with environmental loops

- The core mission is 'purpose': to create change in society through solutions to wicked challenges which are circular and have *both* social and environmental initiatives, at its core. This mission is central to the way the organization does business: including every service it operates; and every function it undertakes.

This new framework for CSR 4.0 is an operational model for 'purpose' and 'change.' It needs to be developed and tested within organizations and corporations, followed by a longitudinal study implemented to measure change and impact over time. It is proposed that this is the future transformation for CSR within a deeply transformed value system (CTV). From an organizational perspective, corporate social entrepreneurs and intrapreneurs within the corporation are the link to implementing social projects at scale within a CSR 4.0 framework. The top-down bottom-up approach of CSR 4.0, plus its broader stakeholder engagement, means intrapreneurs will reach C-suite team members with a stronger voice, seamlessly allowing then to operationalize social projects throughout the organization. Future research should discover ways to enhance the profile of the corporate 'preneur' and examine their ability to execute these projects at scale.

The overall theme for CSR 4.0 is to embrace 'purpose' within a deeply transformed value system (CTV). In doing so, it must also embrace innovation, inclusion, collaboration, co-creation, and engagement, in a shared, integrated, and deeply transformed networked system, which is sustainable, Global Goal related, agile, measurable, authentic and systems orientated, with a circular social and environmental mission at its core.

CSR 4.0 is therefore an evolution of CSR guided by social and environmental movements related to the Fourth Industrial Revolution and current global circumstances. As Globalization 4.0 ushers in, CSR 4.0 will develop further in response. The CSR 4.0 framework therefore provides an emerging area for future research to develop and consider. The Appendix of this chapter provides examples of current corporate case studies on the way to this transition, and the overall conclusion for this book provides additional perspectives to be considered.

References

Baron, D. P. (2001). Private politics, corporate social responsibility, and integrated strategy. *Journal of economics & management strategy, 10*(1), 7–45. doi:10.1162/105864001300122548

Berger, I. E., Cunningham, P. H., & Drumwright, M. E. (2007). Mainstreaming corporate social responsibility: Developing markets for virtue. *California Management Review, 49*(4), 132–157.

Botsman, R., & Rogers, R. (2010). *What's mine is yours: The rise of collaborative consumption.* New York, NY: Harper Collins.

Briguglio, L., Cordina, G., Farrugia, N., & Vella, S. (2009). Economic vulnerability and resilience: Concepts and measurements. *Oxford Development Studies, 37*(3), 229–247. doi:https://doi.org/10.1080/13600810903089893

Buheji, M. (2018). *Understanding the power of resilience economy: An inter-disciplinary perspective to change the world attitude to socio-economic crisis.* Bloomington, IN: Author House.

Burke, L., & Logsdon, J. M. (1996). How corporate social responsibility pays off. *Long Range Planning, 29*(4), 495–502.

Capra, F., & Luisi, P. L. (2015). *The systems view of life: A unifying vision.* Cambridge: Cambridge University Press.

Carlson, C. R., & Wilmot, W. W. (2006). *Innovation: The five disciplines for creating what customers want.* New York, NY: Crown Random House.

Carroll, A. B., & Shabana, K. M. (2010). The business case for corporate social responsibility: A review of concepts, research and practice. *International Journal of Management Review, 12*(1), 85–105. doi:10.1111/j.1468-2370.2009.00275.x

Crane, A., Palazzo, G., Spence, L. J., & Matten, D. (2014). Contesting the value of "creating shared value". *California Management Review, 56*(2), 130–153. doi: 10.1525/cmr.2014.56.2.130

Crespin, R. (2013). CSR 3.0: Capitalism with a twist of networked value. Retrieved from https://www.uschamberfoundation.org/bio/richard-crespin

Crets, S., & Celer, J. (2013). The interdependence of CSR and social innovation. In T. Osburg & R. Schmidpeter (Eds.), *Social innovation: Solutions for a sustainable future* (pp. 77–88). New York, NY; Heidelberg: Springer.

CSR Europe. (2015). Enterprise 2020 manifesto: The future for Europe we need Brussels. Retrieved from https://www.csreurope.org/enterprise-2020-manifesto

CSR Europe. (2018). Collaboration for Impact: Maturity and integration of sustainability in European sector associations. Retrieved from https://www.csreurope.org/collaboration-impact-maturity-and-integration-sustainability-european-sector-associations

Dumont, J. M. (2012). Don't mess with CSR 3.0. *Singapore Business Review. March 5, 2012.* https://sbr.com.sg/media-marketing/commentary/don%E2%80%99t-mess-csr-30

Eckhardt, G. M., & Bardhi, F. (2015). The sharing economy isn't about sharing at all. *Harvard Business Review, 28*(01). Retrieved from https://hbr.org/2015/01/the-sharing-economy-isnt-about-sharing-at-all

Ekins, P. (1992). A four-capital model of wealth creation. In P. Ekins & M. A. Max-Neef (Eds.), *Real-life economics: Understanding wealth creation* (pp. 147–155). London; New York, NY: Routledge.

Elkington, J. (1994). Towards the sustainable corporation: Win-win-win business strategies for sustainable development. *California Management Review, 36*(2), 90–100.

Emerson, J. (2000). *The nature of returns: A social capital markets inquiry into elements of investment and the blended value proposition* (Vol. 1). Division of Research, Harvard Business School.

Fioramonti, L. (2017). *Wellbeing economy: Success in a world without growth.* Johannesburg: Pan Macmillan SA.

Freeman, R. E. (1984). *Strategic management: A stakeholder approach.* Boston, MA: Pitman.

Friedman, M. (1970). The social responsibility of business is to increase its profits. *New York Times Magazine, 13 September 1970,* 122–126.

Grayson, D., & Hodges, A. (2004). *Corporate social opportunity! Seven steps to make corporate social responsibility work for your business.* Shefield: Greenleaf Publishing.

Griffin, J. J., & Mahon, J. F. (1997). The corporate social performance and corporate financial performance debate: Twenty five years of incomparable research. *Business & Society, 36*(1), 5–31.

Hart, S. L., & Milstein, M. B. J. A. o. M. P. (2003). Creating sustainable value. *Academy of Management Perspectives, 17*(2), 56–67.

James, A. P., Jr, Deiglmeier, K., & Miller, D. T. (2008). Rediscovering social innovation. *Stanford Social Innovation Review,* (Fall 2008), 34–43.

Kanter, R. M. (1999). From spare change to real change: The social sector as beta site for business innovation. *Harvard Business Review, 77*(3), 122–132.

KPMG. (2014). A new vision of value: Connecting corporate and societal value creation. Retrieved from https://home.kpmg.com/xx/en/home/insights/2014/09/a-new-vision-connecting-corporate.html

Myhrvold, N. (2007). The exponential economy. *Xconomy*. October 29, 2007.

McWilliams, A., & Siegel, D. S. (2011). Creating and capturing value: Strategic corporate social responsibility, resource-based theory, and sustainable competitive advantage. *Journal of Management, 37*(5), 1480–1495. doi:10.1177/014920631038 5696

Osburg, T. (2013). Social innovation to drive corporate sustainability. In O. T. & S. R. (Eds.), *Social innovation. CSR, sustainability, ethics & governance* (pp. 13–22). Berlin, Heidelberg: Springer.

Osburg, T., & Schmidpeter, R. (Eds.). (2013). *Social innovation, CSR, sustainability, ethics & governance*. Berlin, Heidelberg: Springer.

Porritt, J. (2007). *Capitalism as if the world matters*. London: Earthscan.

Porter, M. E., & Kramer, M. R. (2006). Strategy and society: The link between competitive advantage and corporate social responsibility. *Harvard Business Review, 84*(12), 78–92.

Porter, M. E., & Kramer, M. R. (2011). Creating shared value. *Harvard Business Review, 89*(1/2), 62–77.

Prafitri, R. (2017). Creating shared value (CSV) in East Java, Indonesia: A critical analysis of CSV impacts on dairy farming communities. PhD thesis, Murdock University. Retrieved from http://researchrepository.murdoch.edu.au/id/eprint/42583

Prahalad, C. K., & Hart, S. L. (2002). The fortune at the bottom of the pyramid. *Strategy+Business, 26*(First quarter).

Preuss, L. (2011). Innovative CSR: A framework for anchoring corporate social responsibility in the innovation literature. *The Journal of Corporate Citizenship, 42*(Summer 2011), 17–33.

PwC. (2015). The sharing economy: Consumer intelligence series. Delaware. Retrieved from https://pwc.com/CISsharing.

Rahdari, A. (2016). Fostering responsible business: Evidence from leading corporate social responsibility and sustainability networks. In M. A. Camilleri (Ed.), *CSR 2.0 and new era of corporate citizenship*. Hershey, PA: IGI Global.

Smith, C. (1994). The new corporate philanthropy. *Harvard Business Review, 72*(3), 105–114.

van de Ven, B., & Jeurissen, R. (2005). Competing responsibly. *Business Ethics Quarterly, 15*(2), 299–317.

Visser, W. (2010). The age of responsibility: CSR 2.0 and the new DNA of business. *Journal of Business Systems, Governance and Ethics, 5*(3), 7–22.

Visser, W. (2011). *The age of responsibility: CSR 2.0 and the new DNA of business*. London: Wiley.

Visser, W. (2012). CSR 2.0: Reinventing corporate social responsibility for the 21st century. *Management eXchange,* (May 13).

Visser, W. (2013). Creating shared value: Revolution or clever con? *Blog Briefing*. June 17, 2013. Retrieved from http://www.waynevisser.com/wp-content/uploads/2013/08/blog_csv_csr_wvisser.pdf

Visser, W. (2014). *CSR 2.0: Transforming corporate sustainability and responsibility*. New York, NY: Springer.

Visser, W. (2015). *Sustainable frontiers: Unlocking change through business, leadership and innovation*. Sheffield: Greenleaf Publishing.

Visser, W. (2017a). Integrated value: What it is, what it's not and why it's important. *Huffington Post.* September 30, 2017.

Visser, W. (2017b). Innovation pathways towards creating integrated value: A conceptual framework. International Humanistic Management Association, Research Paper Series 17–41. doi:10.2139/ssrn.3045898

Visser, W. (2017c). Integrated value the aspirational goal of purpose-inspired organisations. AMS Sustainable Transformation Briefing Series, 2 Antwerp Management School, University of Antwerp, Antwerp.

Visser, W. (2018). Creating integrated value: From systems thinking to sustainable transformation in business and society. AMS Sustainable Transformation Paper Series, 3(Inauguration Lecture of the Chair in Sustainable Transformation) Antwerp Management School, University of Antwerp, Antwerp.

Visser, W., & Kymal, C. (2015). Integrated value creation (IVC): Beyond corporate social responsibility (CSR) and creating shared value (CSV). *Journal of International Business Ethics, 8*(1), 1–14.

Vogel, D. (2005). Is there a market for virtue? The business case for corporate social responsibility. *California Management Review, 47*(4), 19–45.

Voltan, A., Hervieux, C., & Mills, A. (2017). Examining the win-win proposition of shared value across contexts: Implications for future application. *Business Ethics: A European Review, 26*(4), 347–368. doi:10.1111/beer.12159

Weaver, G. R., Trevino, L. K., & Cochran, P. L. (1999). Integrated and decoupled corporate social performance: Management commitments, external pressures, and corporate ethics practices. *Academy of Management Journal, 42*(5), 539–552. doi: 10.2307/256975

Weber, M. (2008). The business case for corporate social responsibility: A company-level measurement approach for CSR. *European Management Journal, 26*(4), 247–261.

Webster, K. (2015). *The circular economy: A wealth of flows. Isle of Wight*: Ellen MacArthur Foundation.

Case Study Appendix

Case Study Examples for: CSR 2.0, CSR 3.0 and IVC.

Case Study Appendix I

CSR 2.0 Case Study Examples

Wayne Visser's book *The Age of Responsibility:* provides over 300 organizations practising CSR 2.0 at the time of writing his book in 2011. Many of these are included as CSR examples in Chapter 1, as they are typically labeled as CSR examples in general. However, Visser (2011) defines them under his key principles as CSR 2.0 examples as follows:

- Creativity – A little World, Ashoka, Freeplay, FUNDES, Google
- Scalability – General Electric, Grameen Group, Suntech, Tata Group, Wal-Mart

- Responsiveness – Hydro Tasmania, Rio Tinto, The Body Shop, the Prince's Charities
- Glocality – Anglo American, BHP Billiton. Cemex, SC Johnson, Sony
- Circularity – Coca-Cola, Fuji Xerox, Nike, Patagonia, Tesco
- Change – Johnson Matthey, McDonalds, Nokia, Shell and Google (again).

Source: Visser, 2011.

Case Study Appendix II

CSR 3.0 Case Study Examples

CSR 3.0 is discussed in this chapter as a concept that is relatively untouched in the literature and in some cases is merged with CSR 2.0 examples. In addition to the CSR 3.0 examples included in this chapter, Crespin (2013) provides several additional examples. They are considered to be more digitally oriented, integrated, and networked than CSR 2.0 examples.

A Government Example

    While president, Barack Obama announced a "Power Africa" initiative, investing $7 billion to help bring 10,000 megawatts of power capacity to Sub-Saharan Africa, this investment grows a network, but also leverages a previously untapped network, while also getting companies like GE to provide $9 billion in private sector investment.

An IT Sector Example

    The Microsoft White Space Project is part of their 4Afrika Initiative, which takes unused portions of the television spectrum, called "white space," alongside solar-powered base stations to bring wireless broadband Internet connections to rural Africans. The program was piloted with the Kenyan Ministry of Information and Communications and Kenyan Internet service provider Indigo. With broadband Internet, Africans in return will be able to use Microsoft products.

Source: Adapted from Crespin (2013) .

    The Microsoft example Crispin provides as a CSR 3.0 example is a similar case study example to Intel's initiatives, which was part of their CSR strategy back in 2011 when I researched the company's CSR strategy. In other literature it is now one of the most quoted creating shared value (CSV) examples, showing again the overlap in terminology and case study examples between CSR and CSV.

Case Study Appendix III

IVC Case Study Examples

Visser (2017a, 2017b, 2018) explains that achieving Integrated Value is extremely difficult in practice, due to the current economic and financial system in place. He further states that many of the policies and tools required are still in the early stages of development. Therefore, only a few organizations are experimenting with and practicing elements of IVC. Visser (2017b, 2017c) provides the following corporate examples:

(1) Tesla's economic integration in disruptive business models across multiple innovation pathways
(2) Organizational integration behind the remarkable progress of Interface toward its "2020 Mission Zero"
(3) Strategic integration at Unilever

Source: Adapted from Visser (2017b, 2017c)

Case study examples of these companies are included below, followed by an IVC measurement case study from BASF.

Tesla

Tesla is in transition to sustainable energy, creating products such as electric cars, powerpack batteries, solar panels, solar roof tiles, and integrated renewable energy solutions for homes.

The company fits the five pathways for innovation specified by IVC strategy. It is *secure, smart, shared, sustainable, satisfying* (Visser, 2017a). Visser explains how Tesla had achieved this, in his conceptual framework paper on the innovation pathways toward IVC. Firstly, he explains it's "secure" because its electric cars are on autopilot and have found to reduce accidents 10 times greater than a human driver. He explains it's "smart" because the cars are digitally connected, with live performance monitoring, software updates, and computer managed driving. Thirdly, he explains it's "shared" because autonomous cars will scale car sharing by allowing car owners to add their car to the shared Tesla fleet (Visser, 2017a). The "sustainable" feature is that the cars eliminate fossil fuels while Tesla also promotes renewable energy by creating its storage batteries, solar panels, and solar tiles. Lastly, he explains, Telsa fits the "satisfying" pathway because the cars directly clean the air for drivers and passengers (with a HEPA filtration system), and cuts carbon emissions though electrification (Visser, 2017a).

Interface

The second IVC example is **Interface**, the modular carpet company. It is quoted as the world's first environmentally sustainable and restorative company (Interface website, 2018). Over 24 years ago it launched Mission Zero, to eliminate its negative environmental impacts by 2020. Its American manufacturing sites now operate using 96% renewable energy and operates on 84% renewable energy globally (Hasek, 2016). Interface has also started to supplement its landfill gas, and is the first of its kind to sign an Environmental Product Declaration (EPD), with 99% of Interface products globally with an EPD (Hasek, 2016). Its carpet products are made of 81% total recycled content, and 100% recycled content nylon face fiber (Green Lodging News, 2016).

The most recent framework the company lists on its website is the Climate Take Back® plan, creating a climate fit for life through four elements: Live Zero (aim for zero negative impact in the environment); Love Carbon (stop seeing it as an enemy but instead as a resource); Let Nature Cool (support the biospheres ability to regulate climate); Lead the industrial revolution (transform industry into a force for a future they want) (Interface, 2018).

Unilever

Unilever is the third IVC case study suggested by Visser (2017a). As previously mentioned, it is also often referred to by many academics as a CSV example and a CSR example. This quote also shows the overlap between CSR, CSV, and IVC, where Unilever's IVC strategy is referred to as CSR:

> "An effective corporate social responsibility (CSR) strategy adds to Unilever's efforts for a sustainable business in the consumer goods industry. Stakeholders' interests are satisfied through appropriate approaches that ensure holistic corporate citizenship and responsibility fulfilment. The company's corporate social responsibility (CSR) strategy, through the Unilever Foundation and related programs, satisfies stakeholders' interests in the consumer goods business" (Panmore Institute, 2017).

While other researchers use examples of its strategy to state it as a CSV example and/or one of the best IVC examples available, it seems it's also considered under the CSR banner but with differing levels of shared and integrated value woven throughout its current initiatives. Academic research would add greatly to this discussion by examining more case study examples and the extent of the SIs examined for each case. This is an excellent opportunity for future research in this area.

The Unilever Sustainable Living Plan. The Unilever Sustainability Living Plan (USLP) is selected by Visser (2018) as the most Integrated Value example available. It is scalable, integrated, global, and ongoing. To achieve this Unilever has three key goals:

(1) Improve health and well-being for more than 1 billion by 2020
(2) Reduce environmental impact by half by 2030
(3) Enhance livelihoods for millions by 2020

Source: A report by Unilever Indian subsidiary *Hindustan Unilever* (HUL), titled the *Unilever Sustainable Living Plan – HUL Summary of Progress, 2017,* Hindustan Unilever Limited, 2017.

The three goals above are supported by six key initiatives. These are listed in Chapter 5 in relation to the UN SDGs.

At the more integrated level the report (the Unilever Sustainable Living Plan – HUL Summary of Progress, 2017) includes the following pillars:

---

(1) Fairness in the workplace

- 100% global implementation of UN Guiding Principles on Business and Human Rights
- 100% of procurement in line with responsible sourcing and mandatory requirements on human and labor rights
- Framework for fair compensation
- Improve employee health, nutrition, and well-being
- Reduce workplace injuries and accidents

(2) Opportunities for women

- Build a gender-balanced organization
- Promote safety and education for women in communities
- Enhance access to training and skills
- Job test preparation platform for exams, reducing barriers to essential skills
- Expand opportunities in the value chain – enhancing opportunity to rural women microentrepreneurs – and inspire and equip youth with English training

(3) Inclusive business

- Improve livelihoods of smallholder farmers
- Contribute to development of local communities: livelihoods, water conservation, health and hygiene awareness.
- Improve incomes of small-scale retailers and provide entrepreneurship opportunities to 10,500 people across India

(4) *Waste*

- 100% eco-friendly recycling of nonhazardous waste generated at factories
- 100% of the nonhazardous waste recycled in environment-friendly ways
- Reusable, recyclable, or compostable plastic packaging
- Reuse packaging and reduce office waste – achieving "zero waste to landfill" status

(5) *Greenhouse gases*

- Become carbon positive in manufacturing and reduce greenhouse gas emissions
- Reduce energy consumption in their offices

---

(6) *Sustainable sourcing*

- Sustainable palm oil with targets for reaching 100%
- Palm derivatives – support no deforestation and no development on peat lands
- Supporting economic and social impact with transparency and no exploitation of people or communities
- Produce sustainable tea – to reach 90%–100% by 2020
- Sustainable fruit and vegetables

(7) *Water*

- Reduce water abstracted by manufacturing sites
- Hindustan Unilever Foundation – "Water for Public Good" program

(8) *Nutrition*

- Continuously work to improve taste and nutrition using globally recognized dietary standards.
- Reduce salt levels and trans fat
- Remove sugar and reduce calories
- Provide healthy eating information
- Improve nutrition and hygiene of workers and smallholder farmers in tea supply chains

Source: Adapted from Hindustan Unilever Limited, 2017.

BASF Measurement IVC Case Study Example

BASF have made a start toward finding ways to measure their impact in their report which measures what they term 'Value-to-Society.' Visser (2018) cites this as an IVC example. They are also one of the few companies attempting to measure IVC, and in doing so, provide a valuable case study example.

They report that with their Value-to-Society approach, they are

> "...entering a new area of performance measurement going beyond established qualitative and quantitative assessments. For the first time, we quantify and value the financial and non-financial external effects of our business activities in society in a common unit." (BASF, 2018a).

According to BASF (2018a), their 'Value-to-Society' report measures impact of their entire supply chain, their own operations, plus their direct customers using three category measurements:

(1) Economic: net income, amortization depreciation
(2) Social: taxes, wages and benefits, human capital, health, and safety

(3) Environmental: air emissions, greenhouse gas emissions, land use, waste (solid), water consumption, and water emissions.

Source: Adapted from BASF, 2018a.

Further the social category above includes a section on their website for *employees and society:*

- Employee development: occupational health, safety, and security issues
- Human rights: As a founding member of the UN Global Compact, they support the UN Guiding Principles on Business and Human Rights
- SDGs: They provide information on how they are supporting all 17 SDGs.
- Social Engagement: Corporate Citizenship, BASF Stiftung, Starting Ventures, Education and Corporate volunteering

Source: Adapted from BASF, 2018b.

Under *Corporate Citizenship* listed above, they also include donations to education and employee volunteering in education science labs in schools and universities plus corporate volunteering in "connected care projects" such as employees building school projects, painting walls, and so on. Under the heading for Social Engagement above, BASF list two further projects, *BASF Stiftung* and *Starting Ventures*:

The ***BASF Stiftung project***: works with UN organizations and maintains a global network of partnerships to develop each international development project. Current UN partners in the Asia Pacific region alone include: Deutsche UNESCO, UNHCR, UNICEF, UNO, UN-Habitat, UN World Food Program (WFP), and also World Vision and Save the Children. The emphasis is on innovative approaches and the conception of development projects, plus funding and involvement in implementation. Projects range from education for working children in Bangladesh, education in rural areas (China), school meals (Cambodia), keeping girls in school through WFP scholarships in Cambodia, Vitamin A food program and clean water in India through to flood, cyclone, and earthquake relief in Japan, Myanmar, and Nepal.

Source: Adapted from BASF (2018a).

The BASF social project called *Starting Ventures* is reported to develop business solutions and empower people with low incomes to achieve a better quality of life. They state these projects contribute to their long-term business success as it improves the lives of low-income populations, which then creates opportunities to develop new business and strengthen their supply chain (BASF, 2018c). Further BASF report *Starting Ventures* demonstrates how they live their corporate 'purpose': to "create chemistry for a sustainable future" (BASF, 2018c). However, it is unclear through examining their *Value-to-Society* approach how they measure the impact of this and include it in the overall three categories above, as many of these projects just started in 2018, so this may be a part of their *Value-to-Society* calculation in the future. Measurement opportunities such as this need to be considered in future research development.

Case Study References

BASF Global. (2018a). BASF's value-to-society: Results 2013-2017 at group level. Retrieved from https://www.basf.com/en/company/sustainability/management-and-instruments/quantifying-sustainability/we-create-value/impact-categories.html

BASF Global. (2018b). Employees and society. Retrieved from https://www.basf.com/en/company/sustainability/employees-and-society.html

BASF Global. (2018c). Starting Ventures. Retrieved from https://www.basf.com/en/company/sustainability/employees-and-society/societal-commitment/starting-ventures.html

Crespin, R. (2013). CSR 3.0: Capitalism with a twist of networked value. Retrieved from https://www.uschamberfoundation.org/bio/richard-crespin

Green Lodging News. (2016). Interface closing in on 2020 mission zero goal. News Blog. Retrieved from https://www.greenlodgingnews.com/interface-closing-in-on-2020-mission-zero-goal/

Hasek, G. (2016). Interface closing in on 2020 mission zero goal. *Green Lodging News*.

Hindustan Unilever Limited. (2017). Unilever sustainable living plan. Retrieved from https://www.hul.co.in/Images/uslp-india-progress-report 2017-21may2018_tcm1255-522773_en.pdf

Interface. (2018). How will we start to create a climate fit for life? Retrieved from https://www.interface.com/APAC/en-AU/campaign/negative-to-positive/Climate-Take-Back-Plan-en_AU

Jeffrey, S., Rosenberg, S., & McCabe, B. (2018). Corporate social responsibility behaviors and corporate reputation. *Social Responsibility Journal, 14*(5), 2–15. doi: 10.1108/srj-11-2017-0255

Panmore Institute. (2017). Unilever's corporate social responsibility & stakeholders. Retrieved from http://panmore.com/unilever-corporate-social-responsibility-stakeholders

Visser, W. (2011). *The age of responsibility: CSR 2.0 and the new DNA of business.* London: Wiley.

Visser, W. (2017a). Innovation pathways towards creating integrated value: A conceptual framework. International Humanistic Management Association, Research Paper Series 17–41. http://dx.doi.org/10.2139/ssrn.3045898

Visser, W. (2017b). Integrated value the aspirational goal of purpose-inspired organisations. AMS Sustainable Transformation Briefing Series, 2 Antwerp Management School, University of Antwerp, Antwerp.

Visser, W. (2018). Creating integrated value: From systems thinking to sustainable transformation in business and society. AMS Sustainable Transformation Paper Series, 3 (Inauguration Lecture of the Chair in Sustainable Transformation) Antwerp Management School, University of Antwerp, Antwerp.

Chapter 7

Overall Summary and Conclusion

Abstract

Each chapter in this book provides its own conclusion with a dedicated summary and conclusion at the end of each chapter. This final chapter therefore provides a brief aerial overview of the book with additional recommendations for future research and transformation.

Industrial and Social Revolutions: They Come and Go

To recap to the beginning of this book, Chapter 1 opens with a discussion of the journey of corporate social responsibility (CSR) through time, toward sustainable development goal (SDG) development and the onset of the Fourth Industrial Revolution. The chapter describes how CSR has been influenced by a series of social movements and sentiments from both the academic and business community and reviews the responses to this in the academic literature. Commencing as early as the fourth and fifth century BC, Chapter 1 takes us through various social periods mapped on to each era and industrial revolution of the time. From the First Industrial Revolution of water and steam power (1769–1830) through to the Second Industrial Revolution of electric power and mass production (1870–1914), we entered the Third Industrial Revolution of electronics and IT in 1969. This is now superseded by the Fourth Industrial Revolution, with the rapid development of innovation touched on in the digital and Third Industrial Revolution. As described by Professor Schwab (2016), founder and executive chair, of the *World Economic Forum*, the Fourth Industrial Revolution is the blurring (of) lines between physical, digital, and biological spheres and its rapid acceleration of innovation is 'disruption.' His 2016 article was first published in 2015 in an article in *Foreign Affairs* (Schwab, 2015) and repeated again to support the theme of the *World Economic Forum* in both January 2019 and January 2020.

As the Fourth Industrial Revolution was seen to leapfrog the Third Industrial Revolution, so is Globalization 4.0 thought to leapfrog Globalization 3.0. This book proposes that as CSR continues to evolve, CSR 4.0 will also leapfrog previous versions of CSR. While CSR 2.0 is still adopted by many corporates, with some upgrading to CSR 3.0 primarily through an innovation focus, this upgrade

CSR for Purpose, Shared Value and Deep Transformation, 231–240
doi:10.1108/978-1-80043-035-820200010

will be preempted by CSR 4.0 mapped on to Globalization 4.0. The era of Globalization 4.0 is expected to develop new systems and ways of doing business, solving the world's systemic problems together, bringing everyone on board and leaving no one behind. The UN proposal for SDG implementation by all corporates, kick-started the movement toward inclusion of the 17 Global Goals by 2030.

This obviously is a complex task, and to some appears an infinite one, requiring new systems and integrated networks and major disruption to the way we do business. Each Global Goal provides opportunities for *all stakeholders* to '*create change.*' It is also an opportunity for academic studies to uncover potential expectations, weaknesses, and strengths and to test theory and study live examples in action. This very much needed research will allow for credible and trustworthy recommendations to be made and provide direction for future studies which have a major impact.

While jobs are threatened by an increasingly robotic and automated world, cyber security threatens individuals and the institutions to which they belong. While '*change*' is both positive and negative, there is also disruption to industry value chains. A positive example of this is the 'shared economy' mentioned in Chapter 6, with early adopters: Airbnb, Uber, Amazon Family Library, SnapGoods, and Spotify, now common place. This is a good example of keeping industries viable for the future through 'disruptive transformations.' However, many sectors will need to undergo systemic change, everything from Energy, Fashion, and Transportation through to IT, Health, Agriculture, and Finance. Part of the development of the SDGs across sectors is to deliver a new blueprint for business. A new responsibility. This includes transforming CSR to reach the UN SDG deadline by 2030.

As with the evolution of CSR through the journey of time explained in Chapter 1, this evolution is at an industrial revolution level. Each layer is mapped on to one more social movement and industrial revolution with new challenges to solve and new methodologies and technologies to be labeled. In this knowledge, there is hope for humankind as an enduring force through the ages. What is encouraged is that solutions to these wicked challenges be a global discussion. A discussion of 'shared' destiny is the appreciation that we as human beings have skills in common that a robotic world does not yet have. That is, the ability to have feelings, show empathy, and share compassion. Professor Klaus Schwab in his articles mentioned previously states "this new collective and moral consciousness" is based on a 'shared sense of destiny,' which can "lift humanity" (Schwab, 2015, 2016). As mentioned in previous chapters of this book, this global discussion will *change* the way we do business, *change* companies from the bottom up, and *change* the very ecosystem we live in.

From an academic perspective and at every stage of academic theory, practice, and management, there have been those who have challenged and advanced our understanding of the scope and ambition of corporate responsibility, shared value and sustainability. For example (and as previously mentioned), Ed Freeman (1984) introduced us to 'stakeholder theory,' John Elkington (1994) to the 'triple bottom line,' and Rosabeth Moss Kanter (1999) introduced us to 'social innovation.' As mentioned in Chapter 4, Jed Emerson (2000) introduced us to 'blended value,' C.K. Prahalad and Stuart Hart to 'bottom of the pyramid' (BOP), and 'inclusive markets' (Hart & Prahalad, 2002). In addition, Michael Porter and Mark Kramer introduced us to 'creating shared value' (CSV) (Porter & Kramer, 2011) and Wayne Visser introduced us to 'integrated value creation' (IVC) (Visser, 2017). On a similar note, this book introduces us to creating transformed value (CTV) and proposes that CSV, IVC, CSR 2.0, CSR 3.0, CSR 4.0, and the many other terms discussed in Chapters 1 and 2 of this book are all part of the same picture, on similar missions, at different times. Each has a role to play integrating society toward a common theme or cause, at greater or lesser speeds. Future research, however, needs to determine how corporates cope with Globalizations 4.0 and if there will be a further evolution beyond CSR 4.0, in response to further developing social and environmental movements. Ongoing discovery of the *changes* required to adapt the entire ecosystem, of which we live within, will be a key priority going forward.

Changes to Corporate Social Responsibility

This book acknowledges that CSR has evolved from a 'static' form of CSR to a more innovative, inclusive, and active one. In the academic world (and parts of the business world), CSR has not gone out of favor or fashion. As mentioned in the introduction and earlier chapters, CSR has a long and important history and has transformed over time to match changing social movements in different settings, and on occasions it is referred to by different, similar, alternative, and sometimes competing terminology in different geographic regions.

The academic literature suggests that CSR and its many forms is currently still given priority by C-suite corporates and investors. A paper published in the latter half of 2018, for example, examined how CSR behaviors can lead to corporate membership on the Fortune magazine's *World's Most Admired Companies* list. This paper by Jeffrey, Rosenberg & McCabe (2018) examined ESG statistics published by MSCI-KLD to predict the behaviors that lead to a most admired status. After controlling for corporate financial performance, the analysis found that specific 'social responsibility' behaviors contributed to membership on the list, confirming that CSR behaviors are still important to a firm's reputation (Jeffrey et al. 2018). The authors conclude that companies should continue with CSR activities to improve their reputation with investors and stakeholders. Future research must examine corporate activities not just against the ESG measures of the past but also measure the social impact of their community activities and projects, including their CSR Social Initiatives (SIs), social projects, and support for social enterprise start-ups.

Various CSR case studies from the Fortune's *Most Admired Companies* are listed in the Appendix of Chapter 6. Their initiatives and CSR examples correspond to various stages of CSR, labeled as CSR, CSR 2.0, CSR 3.0, moving toward being part of an increasingly holistic systems approach, such as IVC, CSV, and ultimately creating 'change' at a deeper transformed value (CTV) level.

Creating Value

This book therefore commenced with a discussion of traditional CSR and CSR 2.0 followed by CSR 3.0 and CSR 4.0 and the creation of value in different settings, such as shared value (CSV) and integrated value (IVC). This book concludes that what is required is a networked collaboration across *all stake-holders*. A complex 'web' of interactions and interrelations at a deeper level – across *all* actors. As discussed in Chapter 3, the SDGs encourage collaboration across networks to solve systemic problems and many corporations have incorporated these initiatives under their CSR platform. More recent research has criticized the level of impact achieved to date (see later this chapter and Chapter 3). There are additional issues relating to systems development for an entire ecosystem evolution. Commencing the Fourth Industrial Revolution, means the literature needs to reflect 'purpose' and examine other economies and systems such as satisfying innovation in a 'well-being economy' (Firoamonti, 2017), smart innovation in an 'exponential economy' (Carlson and Wilmot, 2006), and innovation that makes us secure in a 'resilience economy' (Brugmann & Prahalad, 2007). A discussion of each of these is beyond the scope of the current book, which attempts to unravel the vast topic area of historical and contemporary CSR, incorporating innovation and 'purpose' in a changing world. The current book's focus has given priority to the traditional academic literature alongside recommendations for future research, while also noting topics included in current university curriculums and business settings, amidst global world forums, round-table summits, and social media commentary.

A win-win solution to the world's problems is also a prominent theme. This is not a new objective in CSR discourse. Scholars and practitioners have attempted to develop win-win solutions in business-society relationships for many years (Prafitri, 2017). However, it is the belief of some commentators that CSR is still designed to create value for *shareholders* alone, and in doing so limits the ability of companies to create social value for society and its wider *stakeholders*. Many CSR researchers would disagree with this, presenting CSR project examples created by Intel and Unilever under the name of CSR over a decade ago. Porter and Kramer introduced the theory of CSV in 2011 as a more direct win-win solution and relationship with society. It was hoped this might overcome some of the criticisms of traditional CSR and deal with any academic backlash created by the development of CSV. However, as stated previously, many of these case studies, in particular Intel and Unilever, were originally quoted as CSR examples before CSV was launched as a concept in 2011. All are valid case studies.

Perhaps it is the limits of corporate rationality itself that determine the limits of CSR (or CSV) in a win-win situation. If a corporation "can do good only to help itself do well, there is a profound limit on just how much good it can do" (Bakan, 2004, p. 50). For CSR to produce social outcomes that are not constrained by corporate rationality, this requires change in the normative framework of public decision making at the highest level and requires a systems change (Banerjee, 2014). This is hoped for in the new decade toward 2030 and beyond.

Toward 2030 and Beyond

As we enter the Fourth Industrial Revolution, we are reminded of our 'purpose' and shared commitment to *all stakeholders*. Professor Schwab's article *The*

Universal Purpose of a Company in the Fourth Industrial Revolution, clearly states that the purpose of a company is to:

> ...engage *all* its stakeholders in shared and sustained value creation. In creating such value, a company serves not only its shareholders, but all its stakeholders – employees, customers, suppliers, local communities and society at large. The best way to understand and harmonize the divergent interests of all stakeholders is through a *shared commitment* to policies and decisions that strengthen the long-term prosperity of a company (Schwab, 2019).

In the wake of the new decade, 2020–2030, research has revealed the SDGs and Global Goals may not be heading in the direction intended. *The UN Global Compact (UNGC)-Accenture Strategy CEO Study on Sustainability (2019)* reports similar research findings to those discussed in Chapter 3. At the time of writing this conclusion, the *UNGC-Accenture study* (2019) was quoted as being the world's most comprehensive and up to-date business contribution to the SDGs (SDG Business Hub, 2020), so it is important to mention their findings briefly here.

The data were collected from 1000 CEOs in 21 industries across 99 countries and obtained their perspectives on the opportunities and challenges since the adoption of the SDGs in 2015 (UNGC, 2020). As mentioned in the preface of this book, the results comparing the 2016 *UNGC-Accenture Strategy CEO study* with the 2019 study suggest a shift in perspective, from one of hope and opportunity in the earlier launch stages of the SDGs in 2015/2016 to one of current reality in 2019. As mentioned briefly in Chapter 3, the 2016 study reported that CEOs believed the SDGs would provide a clear framework for companies to lead the sustainable development agenda (UNGC-Accenture, 2019). In 2019, however, the study reports CEOs do not believe that current business execution is meeting the challenges of the Global Goals. In 2016, the study reported 78% of CEOs interviewed saw opportunities to contribute to the Global Goals through their core business, in comparison to the 2019 finding that only 21% feel businesses overall are playing a critical role in contributing to the Global Goals (UNGC-Accenture, 2019). Of interest, however, 71% believe that if there is increased commitment and action, business can still play a critical role in contributing to the Global Goals. As a result, the report concludes a need for "bold action" with three calls to action "to accelerate business contribution." Businesses must:

(1) *Start local:* in their own companies and industries and partnerships
(2) *Change how they collaborate:* with honesty about challenges and reporting real impact, while also being more *noncompetitive* and increasing local partnerships
(3) *Define responsible leadership:* to pinpoint what is needed for this generation of leaders

Source: UNGC-Accenture (2019).

Inclusive and Responsible Leadership toward 2045

Focusing on the last call to action listed above, an additional nine 'emerging leadership qualities' were identified for this generation and beyond (UNGC-Accenture, 2019). These are pertinent to the development of 'corporate responsibility' and working toward a sustainable future for *all*. Integral to this is the need for organizations and markets to 'pioneer systems change,' within their own ecosystems first. UNGC-Accenture (2019) suggests this will then drive market demand for sustainability and overall 'systems change.'

This final chapters and conclusion of this book therefore focus on the need for 'systems change' highlighting the need to build cultures of responsibility and sustainability. An opportunity for academic and corporate research is to examine these leadership styles to promote noncompetitive collaboration between corporates, engage investors, and "lift up (entire) industries" (UNGC-Accenture, 2019) within ecosystems. The concept of engaging *all stakeholders* is a multifaceted helix opportunity, starting with internal *stakeholders* (the employees), as outlined in Chapter 2. Here we see that employees of a multinational corporation are also community members of society and national citizens of the developing countries where these corporations reside, and therefore extend to all networks in these host countries and cities.

> A company that has a multinational scope of activities not only serves all those stakeholders who are directly engaged, but acts itself as a stakeholder – together with governments and civil society – of our global future. *Corporate global citizenship* requires a company to harness its core competencies, its entrepreneurship, skills and relevant resources in collaborative efforts with other companies and stakeholders to improve the state of the world (Schwab, 2019).

Multinational corporations have the capability to take everyone with them (all stakeholders), not just their 'shareholders.' Their ability to be 'multinational' is 'being' global, and therefore integral to their key definition of being multinational. This book therefore argues that CSR is developing under a new blueprint, a new global road map for 'systems change.' The current version to be effective in this new 'system change' is CSR 4.0 as described in Chapter 6. This is a multifaceted approach but requires that CSR mirrors current expectations and the protocol of a *corporate global citizen.*

At an individual citizen level, the responsibility lies with each and every one of us. This is particularly evident in SDG 12 (Responsible Consumption and Production), and therefore what we select, purchase, and consume throughout the retail, food, and fashion chain is one example.

The opportunity provided by the SDGs is to take sustainability and responsibility personally. To *be the change* and lead authentically. Future research must be invested in these endeavors to further identify different individual stakeholder perspectives beyond the CEO, toward the opinion of their employees, the community they are from (its public citizens), and the younger generation, such as

Generation Z—yet to finish high school and university. As we have seen with Greta Thunberg and activists of a similar age, they are arising and becoming inspired around the globe to stand up and have a say about their future world.

Fitting this perspective is the presentation at the *World Economic Forum* (2020) by Mariah Levin (head of the *Forum for Young Global Leaders*), who encourages corporate leaders toward *Better Business* with three key objectives:

(1) Examine your *responsibility*
(2) Identify and truly engage your *stakeholders*
(3) Include different *generations*

Source: Levin (2020)

The inclusion of generations, in particular younger generations, Generation Z (and Generation Alpha to come), is a key theme mentioned throughout this book, and particularly in Chapter 5. Levin (2020) in her presentation emphasizes the strengths and solutions that each generation can bring, stating what is required is the need for inclusion of "leaders across generations with humility and openness." Only then she states we will be able to "tackle our greatest issues" (Levin, 2020).

The Time for Purpose and Change is Now

By way of conclusion, I quote one of the key findings of the recent *UNGC-Accenture (2019) study* mentioned above which states 63% of CEOs see "the Fourth Industrial Revolution and its technologies—digital, physical and biological—as a critical accelerator to achieving socioeconomic impact" (UNGC-Accenture, 2019). By 2045, we will be closer to this technological reality. Generation Z will be mid-career at this time. By joining the conversation now, they can be part of determining their future. This is also an excellent opportunity for future academic and corporate research to determine not only cross-border and cross-sector, but also cross-generational trends and needs to meet future 'systems demand.' We need to ask – What is 'honestly' required by corporates? and what is truly collaborative for Globalization 4.0?

Transformational change will not happen by corporate activity alone. As previously mentioned, it requires public input and critique, plus customers to change their 'personal' behavior and take responsibility for their actions on consumption—in every sector from fashion and home construction to daily travel and food choices. We all need to drive systems change toward the 2030 UN SDG deadline and toward the 2050 net-zero ambitions, referred to at the 2020 UN *World Economic Forum* in Davos. CSR 4.0 will be part of this systems change and therefore evolve in a more sophisticated, integrated, and dynamic world. As Globalization 4.0 ushers in, CSR 4.0 will develop further in response.

As this book introduces the term CSR 4.0 and the need to create transformed value (CTV), future research should examine '*change*' in response to this. We need to consider—how much will an organization's strategy need to *change* in response to an entire ecosystem *change*? How will organizations cope with compulsory *change*, or the *change* a revamped or reinvented ecosystem will bring?

> *Change* will not come if we wait for some other person, or if we wait for some other time. We are the ones we've been waiting for. We are the *change* that we seek. Barack Obama (The New York Times, 2008).

Incremental *change*, however, is no longer enough. The breadth of information available to us today and the impact at which we receive it are predicted to escalate as the Fourth Industrial Revolution continues. The information and technology revolution means individuals need to upskill, and businesses need to be prepared for tougher competition to survive the innovative growth curve. However, a market correction, or more correctly an ecosystem correction, may prevail first. It is hoped that current discussions and actions will adapt to *change* at the speed and scale required.

Meanwhile, leading corporates continue to move toward 'positive purpose.' It has long been recognized that multinational corporations in particular have the capacity to do this and the resources to help (McIntosh, 2015; Munro, 2013). They are not only responsible for attending to these issues through their CSR strategies but also they are somewhat forced through the globalization of their organization with offices in various host countries which are often in developing countries with many 'needs' (Munro, Arli, & Rundle-Thiele, 2018), enforcing them to be even "more accountable for their impacts on the communities where they operate." (Voltan, Hervieux, & Mills, 2017, p. 347). As multinational corporations already have experience in this, they should be the best commanders to help usher in the new era of globalization. There is now an urgent need for businesses to move from reporting specifically on what they are *doing*, to reporting the *impact* of what they are doing. This is central to proving a company's 'purpose' and turning 'SDG washing' (as mentioned in Chapter 3) into real and honest implementation. Future research must target these areas.

As this book has documented, a deep transformation is needed and some of this is already progressing through selection of CSR Social Initiatives (SIs) and social projects that are aligned with 'purpose' and scaled-up for deeper social and environmental impact, which is real and measurable. This also requires, inclusion, co-creation, and engagement across *all stakeholders* and cross-generational 'preneurs'. Problem solving at this level requires an evolving and new type of CSR, which is sustainable, and incorporates social and corporate entrepreneurialism and intrapreneurialism within a systems approach that creates value that is shared and integrated at a much deeper and transformed level (CTV).

> Deep change is needed in the purposing, goals and practice of business enterprise. Deep change is needed in the ways that we, as humans, relate to nature and natural systems under severe stress from resource overuse and depletion, a quadrupled population during the 20th century, and human impact on climate. And deep change is needed in the ways in which we relate to each other, use our time and build our communities (Waddock & McIntosh, 2017).

CSR 4.0 is a new model and framework for 'purpose' and 'change.' It must be operational throughout the organization, open to constant renewal, be agile to adapt to current circumstances and be part of a deeply transformed value (CTV) system. Integral to this, CSR 4.0 forces organizations to consider the physical, mental health and well-being of their communities – and this is increasingly important in current times across global populations as we establish the 'new normal.' It is also up to us as citizens to do our part, alongside social intrapreneurs within organizations, to push social projects forward, which solve wicked problems at scale, and at the front of corporate strategy and operations.

Inseparable from this, is the profound need for each and every one of us to decide on our 'purpose' and contribute real authenticity and 'change' to create and be operational in a deeply transformed value (CTV) system. This is 'the new responsibility'. This is our 'shared purpose'.

References

Bakan, J. (2004). *The corporation: The pathological pursuit of profit and power*. Toronto: Viking Canada.

Banerjee, S. B. (2014). A critical perspective on corporate social responsibility. *Critical Perspectives on International Business, 10*(1/2), 84–95. doi:10.1108/cpoib-06-2013-0021

Brugmann, J., & Prahalad, C. K. (2007, February). *Cocreating business's new social compact*. Boston, MA: Harvard business review.

Carlson, C. R., & Wilmot, W. W. (2006). *Innovation: The five disciplines for creating what customers want*. New York, NY: Crown Random House.

Elkington, J. (1994). Towards the sustainable corporation: Win-win-win business strategies for sustainable development. *California Management Review, 36*(2), 90–100.

Emerson, J. (2000). *The nature of returns: A social capital markets inquiry into elements of investment and the blended value proposition* (Vol. 1). Boston, MA: Division of Research, Harvard Business School.

Fioramonti, L. (2017). *Wellbeing economy: Success in a world without growth*. Johannesburg: Pan Macmillan SA.

Freeman, R. E. (1984). *Strategic management: A stakeholder approach*. Boston, MA: Pitman.

Hart, S., & Prahalad, C. K. (2002). The Fortune at the Bottom of the Pyramid. *Strategy+ Business, 26*, 54–67.

Jeffrey, S., Rosenberg, S., & McCabe, B. (2018). Corporate social responsibility behaviors and corporate reputation. *Social Responsibility Journal, 14*(5), 2–15. doi: 10.1108/srj-11-2017-0255

Kanter, R. M. (1999). From spare change to real change: The social sector as beta site for business innovation. *Harvard Business Review, 77*(3), 122–132.

Levin. (2020). The 3 pillars of responsible leadership for the 2020s. Retrieved from https://www.weforum.org/agenda/2020/01/responsible-leadership-corporations-stakeholders-ygls/

McIntosh, M. (2015). *Thinking the twenty-first century: Ideas for the new political economy*. Sheffield: Greenleaf Publishing.

Munro, V. (2013). Stakeholder understanding of corporate social responsibility (CSR) in emerging markets with a focus on Middle East, africa (MEA) and asia. *Journal of Global Policy and Governance, 2*(1), 59–77. doi:10.1007/s40320-013-0026-3

Munro, V., Arli, D., & Rundle-Thiele, S. (2018). CSR engagement and values in a pre-emerging and emerging country context. *International Journal of Emerging Markets, 13*(5), 1251–1272. doi:10.1108/IJoEM-04-2018-0163

Porter, M. E., & Kramer, M. R. (2011). The big idea: Creating shared value. *Harvard Business Review, 89*(1–2), 1–17. Retrieved from http://www.nuovavista.com/SharedValuePorterHarvardBusinessReview.PDF

Prafitri, R. (2017). *Creating shared value (CSV) in east java, Indonesia: A critical analysis of CSV impacts on dairy farming communities.* (PhD Thesis), Murdock University, Retrieved from http://researchrepository.murdoch.edu.au/id/eprint/42583

Schwab, K. (2015). The Fourth industrial revolution: What it means and how to respond. *Foreign Affairs.* Retrieved from https://www.foreignaffairs.com/articles/2015-12-12/fourth-industrial-revolution

Schwab, K. (2016). *The Fourth industrial revolution: What it means, how to respond.* Geneva: World Economic Forum. Retrieved from https://www.weforum.org/agenda/2016/01/the-fourth-industrial-revolution-what-it-means-and-how-to-respond/

Schwab. (2019). Davos manifesto 2020: The universal purpose of a company in the Fourth industrial revolution. Retrieved from https://www.weforum.org/agenda/2019/12/davos-manifesto-2020-the-universal-purpose-of-a-company-in-the-fourth-industrial-revolution/

SDG Business Hub. (2020). UN global compact-accenture strategy CEO study on sustainability 2019. Retrieved from https://sdghub.com/project/un-global-compact-accenture-strategy-ceo-study-on-sustainability-2019/

The New York Times. (2008). *Barack Obama's Feb. 5 Speech.* Retrieved from https://www.nytimes.com/2008/02/05/us/politics/05text-obama.html.

UNGC. (2020). Retrieved from https://www.unglobalcompact.org/library/5715.

UNGC-Accenture. (2019). *UNGC-Accenture Strategy CEO Study on Sustainability 2019.* Retrieved from https://www.accenture.com/_acnmedia/PDF-109/Accenture-UNGC-CEO-Study-Infographic.pdf.

Visser, W. (2011). *The age of responsibility: CSR 2.0 and the new DNA of business.* London: Wiley.

Visser, W. (2017). Innovation pathways towards creating integrated value: A conceptual framework. *International Humanistic Management Association, Research Paper Series*, 17–41. doi:10.2139/ssrn.3045898.

Voltan, A., Hervieux, C., & Mills, A. (2017). Examining the win-win proposition of shared value across contexts: Implications for future application. *Business Ethics: A European Review, 26*(4), 347–368. doi:10.1111/beer.12159.

Waddock, S., & McIntosh, M. (2017). *SEE change: Making the transition to a sustainable enterprise economy.* London: Routeledge.

Index

Printed in the United States
By Bookmasters